ACADEMIC WOMEN

ACADEMIC WOMEN

Voicing Narratives of Gendered Experiences

Edited by
Michelle Ronksley-Pavia, Michelle M. Neumann,
Jane F. Manakil and Kelly Pickard-Smith

BLOOMSBURY ACADEMIC
LONDON • NEW YORK • OXFORD • NEW DELHI • SYDNEY

BLOOMSBURY ACADEMIC
Bloomsbury Publishing Plc
50 Bedford Square, London, WC1B 3DP, UK
1385 Broadway, New York, NY 10018, USA
29 Earlsfort Terrace, Dublin 2, Ireland

BLOOMSBURY, BLOOMSBURY ACADEMIC and the Diana logo are trademarks of
Bloomsbury Publishing Plc

First published in Great Britain 2023
Paperback edition published 2024

Series design by Charlotte James
Cover image © Jonathan Knowles/Getty Images

A catalogue record for this book is available from the British Library.

A catalog record for this book is available from the Library of Congress.

ISBN: HB: 978-1-3502-7426-6
PB: 978-1-3502-7427-3
ePDF: 978-1-3502-7428-0
eBook: 978-1-3502-7429-7

Series: Bloomsbury Gender and Education

Typeset by Deanta Global Publishing Services, Chennai, India

We wish to dedicate this book to women working in any field in higher education, and to all who identify as women working in academia, in all corners of the world. And for our families: from Michelle Ronksley-Pavia: Frank, Steven, mum Ann and Aunty Jen; from Michelle M. Neumann: my husband, children, family and friends; from Jane F. Manakil: my parents Francis and Rose and daughter Rose; and, from Kelly Pickard-Smith: thank you all who encouraged us in this endeavour and continued to support us in our chosen careers.

CONTENTS

FIGURES

TABLES

CONTRIBUTORS

Eleonora (Ele) Belfiore has recently been appointed Director of the new Interdisciplinary Centre for Social Inclusion and Cultural Diversity at the University of Aberdeen, UK. The vision for the centre is to work with colleagues across the university to realize the potential of the arts, humanities and social sciences to lead to progressive change in our society. Her research examines the social impact of the arts, its place in cultural policy rhetoric and the notion of the transformative power of the arts that underlines the impact discourse. She is co-founder and co-director of WIASN. She was the lead co-author of the influential monograph *The Social Impact of the Arts: An Intellectual History* (2008) and her more recent publications focus on cultural value and equity issues in arts labour.

Amy Bonsall is the founder of WIASN. She is currently a researcher at the University of Manchester's Science and Engineering Education Research and Innovation Hub, UK, was the 2021 winner of the staff volunteer of the year and winner of the presidential medal for her voluntary work. Amy is one of the Shaw Trust's top twenty most influential disabled influencers of 2021. She is the co-artistic director of Bilimankhwe International Theatre. Her research focuses on theatre production, women in academia and creativity in STEM education. She is the editor of *Talking Bodies Vol. II: Bodily Languages, Selfhood and Transgression* (2020).

Rebekah Bray is an administrative specialist for the College of Arts, Humanities and Social Sciences Dean's Office at Eastern Washington University, USA. She received her MEd in Adult Education in June of 2020. This work originally began as her master's thesis and will be her first-ever publication. She is interested in gender equity in the workplace, specifically in institutions of higher education, and hopes to continue her research with a focus on the experiences of women of colour and those who identify as part of minority groups.

Nathalie Busschaert is Assistant Professor at Tulane University, USA. She obtained her BSc and MSc in chemistry at the Katholieke Universiteit Leuven, Belgium, and her PhD in supramolecular chemistry from the University of Southampton, UK, under the supervision of Professor Philip A. Gale. Nathalie continued research in supramolecular chemistry under the supervision of Andrew D. Hamilton at the University of Oxford, UK, and New York University, USA. She started her independent career at Tulane University, USA, in 2017. The Busschaert group is working on molecules that can selectively bind to lipid headgroups and is exploring various applications of transmembrane transport.

Claudia Caltagirone is Associate Professor of Inorganic Chemistry at the University of Cagliari, Italy, working on the supramolecular chemistry of anion and metal ion recognition and sensing and self-assembled supramolecular architectures. She obtained her PhD in chemistry in 2006 at the University of Cagliari under the supervision of Professor Vito Lippolis and then she moved to the University of Southampton for two years as an academic visitor in the group of Philip Gale. She is a co-founder of WISC and in September 2021 she was in charge of the organization of the first WISC Workshop at the University of Cagliari.

Sarah Casey teaches communication at the University of the Sunshine Coast, Australia. She researches in rural women's studies, communication campaigning, entrepreneurship and feminist activism. She leads the Real Rural Women's Leadership, Real Stories of Country Women and Real Rural Digital Solutions projects which support women living in extreme weather conditions such as long-term drought. Sarah is the secretary of the Australian Women's and Gender Studies Association and the co-editor of the associated journal, *Feminisms, Gender and Advocacy* (with Gail Crimmins). Sarah tweets at @sarahjcasey and at @feministingoz.

Kelly Coate is Pro Vice Chancellor for Education and Students at the University of Sussex, UK, and professor of higher education. She has worked previously at King's College London, UK, University College London, UK, and the National University of Ireland in Galway, Ireland. Her research focuses on aspects of higher education including the curriculum, gender and internationalisation. She is on the editorial boards of the journals *Teaching in Higher Education*, *Journal of Education Policy* and *Higher Education Research and Development*.

Gail Crimmins is Deputy Head (Learning and Teaching), School of Business and Creative Industries, University of the Sunshine Coast, Australia. She is a feminist academic who employs arts-informed and narrative methodologies to uncover and re-present the voices and experience of often 'yet to be voiced' (Arnot & Reay, 2007) women. Gail has published three books and over thirty academic papers.

Emily Draper is a UK Research and Innovation Future Leaders fellow. She received her PhD from the University of Liverpool, UK, in 2015 with Professor Dave Adams. She carried out postdoctoral research at Liverpool and then at the University of Glasgow, UK. She became a Leverhulme Trust Early Career Fellow and a Lord Kelvin Adam Smith Fellow in 2017. She took up a lectureship position at Glasgow in 2018, working on self-assembled organic electronics before taking maternity leave in 2019 and 2021.

Trevor G. Gates is Assistant Professor of Social Work in the College of Humanities, Arts and Social Sciences at Colorado State University-Pueblo, USA. His research interests include global social work practice, allyship, cultural responsiveness and inclusion with lesbian, gay, bisexual, transgender and queer+ communities. Prior to working as an academic, Trevor was a clinical social worker and chemical dependency counsellor in Dallas and Chicago.

Michaele Hardie completed a PhD in chemistry under the supervision of Professor Richard Robson and Bernard Hoskins at the University of Melbourne, Australia (1996). After several postdoctoral appointments, including at the University of Toledo, USA, and Monash University, Australia, she was appointed lecturer in inorganic chemistry at the University of Leeds, UK (2001), where she is now professor of supramolecular chemistry. Her research interests include coordination and metallo-supramolecular chemistry of host-type ligands, coordination polymers and crystal engineering.

Cally Haynes is Lecturer in Organic Chemistry and Chemical Biology at University College London, UK. She studied at the University of Oxford, UK, and completed a PhD and initial postdoctoral work at the University of Southampton, UK, under Professor Phil Gale. In 2013 she left academia and worked in scientific publishing with the Royal Society of Chemistry. She returned to the supramolecular chemistry field in 2015 for postdoctoral work at the University of Cambridge, UK, until 2019 when she moved to London to establish her own group. She is a co-founder and vice chair of WISC, currently coordinating the website and online resources.

Jennifer Hiscock is Reader in Supramolecular Chemistry, chair of WISC and UKRI Future Leaders research fellow within the School of Chemistry and Forensic Science at the University of Kent, UK. She studied for a PhD in the group of Professor Phil Gale at the University of Southampton, UK, and carried out postdoctoral research in the same group until 2015. She moved to the University of Kent, UK, as the Caldin research fellow and was appointed lecturer in chemistry there in 2016. Her current research interests focus on the development of supramolecular self-associating amphiphiles (SSAs) as antimicrobial, anticancer and drug adjuvant agents.

Genine Hook works as Adjunct Lecturer in Sociology at the University of New England, Australia. She completed her PhD from the Faculty of Education at Monash University, Australia, in May 2015. Her research explored the experiences of sole parents at universities in Australia and her thesis was awarded the Vice Chancellor's Commendation for Thesis Excellence in 2015. Genine's first book was published in July 2016, titled *Sole Parent Students and Higher Education: Gender, Policy and Widening Participation*. Her research focuses on gender performativity, higher education, family-based violence, familial norms, feminist pedagogy and social policy.

Rumana Hossain is Associate Professor at the Department of English, Jahangirnagar University, Bangladesh. She recently received her PhD from the University of Leeds, UK. She also has an MA in TESOL specializing in teacher education from the same university. Rumana has been in the field of education and language teaching for the past twenty years and has extensive university-level teaching experience both in the UK and Bangladesh. Her publications and areas of interest cover a wide range, including sociolinguistics, teacher development, social and academic mobility, language teaching and learning, students' sense of belonging and, more recently, neoliberalism and feminism.

Kristin Hutchins is Assistant Professor of Chemistry at Texas Tech University, USA. Kristin studied chemistry at the University of Iowa where she earned her BS and PhD. Kristin obtained her PhD in 2015 while working under the supervision of Leonard MacGillivray. She conducted postdoctoral research at the University of Illinois at Urbana-Champaign with Jeffrey Moore. Kristin began her independent career in 2017; the Hutchins group focuses on using supramolecular chemistry and crystal engineering strategies to control the properties of solid-state organic materials.

Janice Johnson is Assistant Professor in HRM at Coventry University, UK. She is a chartered companion and branch chair of the Chartered Institute of Personnel and Development. Her research interests focus on diversity and inclusion issues, modern racism and critical race theory. She has been a speaker on HRM matters at conferences and Heads of HR forums and a member of the Judging Panel for the Employee Benefits Awards UK.

Katrina (Kate) Jolliffe received her BSc (1993) and PhD (1997) from the University of New South Wales, Australia, with Professor Michael Padden-Row. She held positions at Twente University, the Netherlands, the University of Nottingham, UK, and the Australian National University, Australia, before moving to the University of Sydney, Australia, in 2002, where her current position is Payne-Scott professor. She is a fellow of the Australian Academy of Science. Her research interests focus on the design and synthesis of functional molecules.

Marion Kieffer is an R&D scientist at InnoMedica, a small Swiss pharma company, working on liposomal drug formulations. She made the tough call to leave academia behind after completing a PhD and post-doc in supramolecular chemistry in the UK.

Marianne Kongerslev is Associate Professor of American Literature and Cultural Studies at Aalborg University, Denmark. She earned her PhD in American studies from the University of Southern Denmark in Odense and was visiting scholar at the Appalachian Center at the University of Kentucky in 2019. Her research on Native American literature, US popular culture, feminisms/gender studies and critical race studies has been published in both English and Danish and has appeared in international journals, including the *Polish Journal for American Studies* and *Women, Gender and Research*. She is currently working on a book project titled *Spiteful Fiction*, with funding from the Carlsberg Foundation.

Jennifer Leigh is Senior Lecturer at the Centre for the Study of Higher Education, University of Kent, UK. She edited *Conversations on Embodiment across Higher Education* (2019), co-edited *Ableism in Academia* (2020) and co-authored *Embodied Inquiry: Research Methods* (2021). She is lead author of *WISC: Collectively Crafting the Rhythms of Our Work and Lives in STEM* (2022). Her next book will be *The Boundaries of Qualitative Research: With Art, Education, Therapy and Science* (2023). Her research interests include embodiment, creative research methods, academic identity and ableism. She tweets as @drschniff and @suprachem.

Jinfang (Jackie) Liu is a PhD candidate of human resource development at the University of Minnesota, USA. Before she came to the United States, she was the Chinese language and culture trainer at the British Embassy, Culture and Education section, Beijing, China. Her research focuses on women's leadership and cross-cultural leadership.

Jane F. Manakil is Senior Lecturer and Clinician in the School of Medicine and Dentistry, Griffith University, Australia. Jane is a single parent and a registered dental practitioner. Jane holds a specialty qualification in periodontology and is a fellow of the Higher Education Academy. Manakil has had more than thirty-two years of teaching experience with a research interest in periodontal disease management and scholarly activities. Jane is the editor of three published books, has created digital resources for management of oral diseases and has also published articles on various topics in national and international peer-reviewed journals.

Anna McConnell is a co-founder of WISC and Vice Chair (Organization). She studied chemistry at the University of Canterbury in New Zealand before obtaining a DPhil under the supervision of Professor Paul Beer at the University of Oxford. Following postdoctoral research stays at the California Institute of Technology and the University of Cambridge in the groups of Professor Jacqueline Barton and Professor Jonathan Nitschke, respectively, she became a junior professor at Christian-Albrechts-Universität zu Kiel in Germany in November 2016. The McConnell group's research focuses on stimuli-responsive metal-organic cages, dynamic covalent chemistry and luminescent complexes.

Dena McMartin is Vice-President (Research) at the University of Lethbridge, Alberta, Canada, and is a leading researcher in rural water management. Her research programme focuses on rural water quality and quantity needs in Canada and abroad, the impacts of climate extremes on water availability and rural livelihoods, characterization and remediation of oilsands-process water contamination, and best practices in agriculture for improved water quality and quantity management.

Uvanney Maylor is Professor of Education at the University of Bedfordshire, UK. Her research interests include race, ethnicity, culture, educational equity, inclusion and social justice. She has extensive experience in conducting research in primary and secondary schools and in further and higher education. Her leadership work has sought to examine factors impacting on Black educators' progression in diverse higher education contexts.

Joanna McIntyre is Senior Lecturer in Media Studies and Course Director of the Bachelor of Media and Communication at Swinburne University of Technology, Melbourne, Australia. She has published widely on issues of gender, media and Australian culture, particularly in relation to marginalized communities and their representation. Her most recent edited collection is *Gender and Australian Celebrity Culture* (2021), with Anthea Taylor.

Michelle M. Neumann is Associate Professor in the Faculty of Education, Southern Cross University, Australia. She is a mother of five children and has had over ten years' experience teaching in primary and secondary schools. Her research interests are in early childhood education, early literacy development and digital technology. Neumann has created several educational apps and digital resources for early childhood education and has published a book, several book chapters and research articles in national and international peer-reviewed journals.

Kelly Pickard-Smith is Honorary Research Fellow of the University of Manchester, UK, and the equality, diversity and inclusion manager for the Christie NHS Foundation Trust. She is also a co-founder and co-director of WIASN. Her PhD researched equity and access in education and employment in mathematically demanding courses and careers through creative methods. Her most recent paper, based on her PhD research, was published in the *International Journal of Research & Method in Education* in 2021.

Michelle Ronksley-Pavia is Diversity and Inclusive Education Lecturer in the School of Education and Professional Studies, and researcher with the Griffith Institute for Educational Research, Griffith University, Australia. She is a parent, caregiver and person with disability. Her research focuses on disability, inclusion, diversity and initial teacher education. As an international leading researcher and expert in the field of gifted education and twice-exceptionality (gifted students with disability), Ronksley-Pavia has published widely on a range of important topics including stigma and disability, bullying and disability and contemporary issues in initial teacher education. Ronksley-Pavia is an Australian Delegate to the World Council for Gifted and Talented Children.

Alison Sammel specializes in the teaching, learning and communication of Science, Climate Action and the Sustainable Development Goals. Sammel investigates what it might mean for education to engage with post-Anthropocentric pedagogies. She has a strong history of multidisciplinary research agendas with Canadian colleagues (from engineering and social marketing) about fresh water and climate change. Sammel works closely with her local community to promote and support educators in gaining access to local Indigenous cultural perspectives and respectfully embedding these perspectives in their practice.

Christina Schwabenland is Reader in Organizational Behaviour at the University of Bedfordshire, UK, and the director of the Centre for Leadership Innovation. Her research interests focus on non-profit sector organizing with a more specific focus on gender. She has published two research monographs and articles in *Human Relations, Gender, Work and Organization* and *Public Administration*. Her most recent article is 'Solidarity with Soufra: Dividuality and Joint Action with Palestinian Refugees', published in *Organization* (2021).

Shelly Shaffer is Associate Professor of Literacy Education at Eastern Washington University, USA. Her research interests are Young Adult literature, pedagogy of teaching literature, preservice teaching and practice, content area literacy and equity in education. She has published chapters and articles on using Young Adult literature in secondary classrooms. Her edited book *Contending with Gun Violence in the ELA Classroom* (2019) focused on how to address, discuss and teach about gun violence in English classrooms.

Anna Slater is Royal Society University Research Fellow at the University of Liverpool, UK. She obtained her PhD from the University of Nottingham, UK, in 2011 in the group of Professor Neil Champness. Following postdoctoral positions in porphyrin self-assembly and organic materials, she took up a Royal Society-EPSRC Dorothy Hodgkin Fellowship in 2016. Her current fellowship began in January 2021. Her research interests include molecular design and process control for the formation of bespoke supramolecular architectures, organic materials and macromolecules. She joined WISC as vice chair in 2020. She has two daughters (who are three and six years old) and a hidden disability and tweets as @AnnaGSlater.

Ea Høg Utoft is Postdoctoral Researcher at the Danish Center for Studies in Research and Research Policy at Aarhus University, Denmark. In 2019, Utoft was a visiting fulbright scholar at Northeastern's Department of Anthropology and Sociology, Boston, USA. Her research interests cover gender and diversity in higher education, as well as feminist knowledge production and epistemic injustice. Methodologically, she works mainly with and through ethnography and autoethnography. Utoft's work is published in *Gender, Work & Organization* and her PhD dissertation theorizing the Danish context as a 'postfeminism gender regime' is available online through the Politicas PhD series.

Larissa von Krbek is Emmy Noether Junior Research Group Leader at the Kekulé-Institute for Organic Chemistry and Biochemistry, University of Bonn, Germany. She studied chemistry at Freie Universität Berlin and obtained her Dr. rer. nat. under the supervision of Professor Dr Christoph A. Schalley in 2016. Following a postdoctoral stay in the group of Professor Jonathan Nitschke at the University of Cambridge, she moved to start her independent career in 2020. The Krbek group is working in the areas of supramolecular chemistry, systems chemistry and out-of-equilibrium self-assembly. Larissa is a vice chair of WISC working on communications together with Cally.

Davita Watkins is Associate Professor of Chemistry at the University of Mississippi, USA, where her research interest is in developing supramolecular synthesis methods to make new organic semiconducting materials for applications in optoelectronic devices, as well as studying their structural, optical and electronic properties. Her group also investigates the design of dendrimer molecules for biomedical applications. Her research allows her group to use tools from all areas of science, including analytical, computational and materials chemistry. In addition, they get to enjoy collaborating with a number of theoreticians and other experimentalists.

Lisa Watson is Dean of the Faculty of Business at Athabasca University, Alberta, Canada. As a consumer psychologist Watson's research involves helping people to make decisions to improve their overall well-being. This includes examining personal influences on consumer choices and social marketing research to help people make healthier and more socially and environmentally sustainable choices.

Catherine Wilkinson is Reader in Childhood and Youth Studies and Programme Leader for Education Studies at Liverpool John Moores University, UK. Catherine teaches across the Education Studies and Early Childhood Studies degree programmes. Previously, Catherine worked as a lecturer in children, young people and families in the Faculty of Health and Social Care, Edge Hill University, UK. Catherine has also worked as a postdoctoral research associate in the School of Education at Durham University. She completed her PhD in environmental sciences at University of Liverpool, funded by an ESRC CASE award.

Samantha Wilkinson is Senior Lecturer in Childhood and Youth Studies at Manchester Metropolitan University, UK. Samantha joined Manchester Metropolitan University in 2016, initially working as a lecturer in human geography, before moving to the School of Childhood, Youth and Education Studies in 2018. Samantha completed a PhD in human geography at the University of Manchester, UK. Her doctoral research explored young people's alcohol consumption practices and experiences. Following this, she undertook a research fellow post at the University of Nottingham, where she worked on a project that aimed to broaden our understanding of good home care for people with dementia.

PREFACE

The need for this compilation emerged primarily from the four editors' experiences of working in academia, interacting with gendered institutionalized systems and practices, and recognizing how these were shaping and reshaping our individual and collective experiences and identities as women working in higher education. We pondered if these experiences were shared by other women across institutions around the world. And so began our journey from emerging naiveté to conceptualizing this timely edited volume. At the heart of our motives to create this book was a distinct determination to shine a light on the experiences of academic women (and those who identify as women in academia), to highlight and frame their lived experiences as told through narratives of happenings and occurrences. Importantly, we sought to bring together a woven tapestry revealing women's gendered experiences, from their diverse perspectives, to explore collective and individual experiences of intersectionality occurring in institutions across the globe.

Through this collection of shared and individual experiences, we attempt to manifest and give voice to the many existent inequities still occurring across the world for academic women from all backgrounds. We hope that insights, narratives and experiences shared by contributing authors will provide readers with global insights and understandings of the intersectional nature of women's lived experiences in these institutional gendered spaces – of culture, class and dis/ability, and of the conglomerate of intersectionality experienced by women – cisgender, transgender, non-binary, gender-neutral, agender, gender-fluid and gender-queer individuals. There is no one 'Academic Woman'; thus, we are all 'Academic Women', collectively and individually striving to create better systemic practices, processes and understandings across institutions for each other and for those wanting to enter into academia.

SERIES EDITORS' FOREWORD

Marie-Pierre Moreau, Penny Jane Burke and Nancy Niemi

Contemporary debates concerned with the global urgencies of addressing inequalities point to the topicality and social significance of the field of gender and education. The intersection of gender and education is a buoyant site of scholarly and political mobilization occupied by a multitude of ontological and epistemological positions, theories and methodologies. Key themes shaping the field range from schooling, tertiary education and lifelong learning, digital and social media, educational policies and practice, gendered and sexual violence, gender identities and sexual orientation, the politics of representation and 'truth', the relationship of gender equity to environmental justice, embodiment and difference, and knowledge production. However, this is not an exhaustive list, and gender and education as a field relates to multiple historical, contemporary and intersectional issues of our times.

This research series is concerned with publishing rigorous and original research which critically engages with contemporary debates about gender and education as they unfold in a range of institutional, local, national and transnational contexts, in, across and between the spaces that are often hidden from view through complex geopolitical and inequitable global relations. Indeed, these debates include critical attention to the problematic of spatial and geopolitical relations, which are attached to categorizations in their many troubling forms. Intersectional and international perspectives are a central tenet of the series to broaden, provide depth and extend the field of gender and education in all of its complexities. Engaging with insights from across gender and education studies – including theories of intersectionality that provide a critical lens on gender and its relationship to other identity markers, positionalities and systemic inequalities – the series engages societal debates and theoretical developments within the field. It invites a growing understanding of the intersections between and across different structural and political forces that shed light on gender inequalities.

Linked to its feminist ethos, the series is a home for monographs and edited volumes authored by emerging and established scholars concerned with gender inequalities and social justice as they pertain to intersectional aspects of gender and education in a broad range of social and institutional contexts. This intersectional and international outlook is also a strong feature of the editorial team. The editors are based in the United Kingdom, the United States and Australia, with a strong commitment to generating knowledge from positions of inter/national, institutional and/or positional marginalization and/or difference, and the series benefits from the insights of our outstanding editorial board, including researchers from across the world.

The series is intended for a readership composed of academics and postgraduate research students, as well as feminist practitioners and activists from across the world with an interest in gender and education and, more broadly, social justice. In particular, we hope that it will appeal to academics whose work is broadly located in the field of gender and education and with a subject background in education, sociology, gender studies or in other social science or humanity subjects; to students enrolled on these programmes; and to practitioners based in schools, higher education and non-governmental organizations.

Gender equity in higher education has been an enduring focus of feminist research over many decades now. Despite this, women continue to navigate complex gender inequalities in pedagogical spaces, with numerous strategies in place attempting to level the playing field. Many of these strategies, however, rest on deficit assumptions, including the notion that the problem is that individual women lack confidence. It is therefore timely that this collection examines the intersectional complexities of gender and academic identity and how structural and cultural inequalities shape women's lived experiences of academic spaces differently. This volume sheds light on the many expressions of being an academic woman while also analysing the ongoing gendered dynamics of power, inequality and difference. In analysing the diversity of what it means to be an academic woman, *Academic Women* also makes an important contribution in developing a collective understanding of how gender continues to be shaped by institutional structures and practices, with effects at the personal level of identity and experience across a range of geographical, institutional and local contexts.

FOREWORD

Kelly Coate

Academic Women: Voicing Narratives of Gendered Experiences is a rich and diverse collection of writings that illuminate the lived experiences of women from around the world who are carving out their careers in higher education. This volume is a valuable contribution to the ever-expanding body of literature that offers feminist insights into academic careers. The focus on women's narratives across a range of national contexts and intersectional lenses provides new perspectives on what can sometimes feel like a very familiar 'problem': the slow progress over decades of pushing for women academics to achieve equity in their workplaces.

This volume exemplifies in a vivid manner that collectively the voices of women are stronger and louder. The experience of reading it reminded me (in a very positive way) of some of the early collections of feminist writings from the academy: the years when 'the personal is political' was a common form of expressing why it was so important to make women's lives public. Granted, this collection very much reflects its contemporary context, but it does feel part of a long and distinguished tradition which continues to enable us to better understand how gender inequities play out in universities.

For those readers familiar with this tradition, the experience of encountering these voices as a collective is simultaneously heartening and depressing. Sometimes the experience verges on being devastating, but to list here the snippets of narratives and statistics that most shockingly reveal misogyny, racism and inequalities would detract from the overall sense of optimism that is needed if women are to survive in academia. Optimism in these chapters often stems from the supportive communities and networks that women create. While mentoring, networking and finding other feminist support groups can help women get ahead, it has to be acknowledged that academia remains a hyper-individualistic culture that more often rewards competition rather than collaboration.

In a sense, therefore, the collective resistance to gender inequalities in academia is a meta-narrative here. The journey through the chapters leads to a culmination of sorts of a powerful story of online community activism – a mobilization against patriarchy through the WIASN Facebook group – which is a fitting summation of many of the themes throughout the book. Along the way I gained insights about – inter alia – women in supramolecular chemistry, Chinese PhD students in the United States and Black women's experiences in UK higher education. All of the chapters reflect the contemporary context, through some of the impacts of the pandemic, the increased international mobility of women scholars, and the ways in which online social networks have become sites of resistance and activism. For younger and newer women coming into higher education, the volume will certainly offer stories which resonate.

On a personal level, I felt a sense of connection to the writings here. I have been researching women in higher education from a variety of perspectives for over the past two decades and have worked my way up through an academic career into a senior leadership role. I have written about my own experiences, read the experiences of many others and will continue doing so for as long as possible. We hopefully all gain strength through hearing and sharing our voices, and I hope the readers encountering the stories in these pages do as well.

ACKNOWLEDGEMENTS

We would like to express our deepest gratitude to the many people who have supported, inspired and guided us over the lifespan of this book project from its earliest inceptions to its publication. And to the insightful and thought-provoking contributions of each of our chapter authors – we thank you immensely. Without you all, this book would not have been possible.

In particular, the co-editors of this book would like to immensely thank our inspirational lead editor Michelle Ronksley-Pavia, for her tireless work in managing and organizing our numerous editorial meetings, guiding chapter authors, problem-solving arising challenges, keeping to publishing deadlines, attending to all the finer details and above all being so incredibly well-organized. Her exceptional professionalism and work ethic enabled the whole book to be realized and come to fruition. Michelle Ronksley-Pavia is an awesome inspiration to us all!

While it is not possible to name everyone who provided support in one way or another, a few deserve to be singled out before we begin our collective journey through the narratives of women's experience working in academia. As editorial team we would like to give our warm appreciation to the following mentors for believing in the initial conceptualization of this book and for providing invaluable advice in writing and compiling this unique volume: Leonie Rowan (GIER, Griffith University, AU) and David Geelan (University of Notre Dame, AU, previously Griffith University, AU). Immense thanks go to Leonie Rowan for taking Michelle Ronksley-Pavia's dream of this book seriously, providing encouragement and mentorship and setting an example of being an excellent colleague and friend in the world of academia. And to David, for mentoring Michelle Ronksley-Pavia in the finer points of making the dream a reality and in seeking a publisher.

We owe a debt of gratitude to the Griffith Institute for Educational Research (GIER) for the moral support and editing support procured by Lynanne McKenzie, and to the Institute's Director, Professor Leonie Rowan, and Acting Directors Steven Hodge and Stephen Billet, for ongoing invaluable advice on the finer points of publishing an edited book. And to the in-house GIER copy editor, Elizabeth Stevens, for her attention to detail and skilful copyediting, thank you!

Thanks to the Bloomsbury Gender and Education series editors, Marie-Pierre Moreau (Anglia Ruskin University, UK), Penny Jane Burke (University of Newcastle, AU) and Nancy S. Niemi (University of Maryland Eastern Shore, USA). Thank you to Penny Jane for meeting with us and answering our often-naïve questions so thoughtfully and understandingly!

Thank you to Bloomsbury Academic publishers, especially Alison Baker (Senior Publisher, Education and Linguistics), for meeting with us online despite the ten-hour time difference between the UK and Australia! Thank you for supporting us and answering our multitude of queries throughout the manuscript stages. And a huge thank you to Anna Elliss (Education Editorial Assistant) at Bloomsbury Publishing for being so kind and compassionate throughout the whole publication process in responding to our many questions!

Thanks also to the initial book proposal reviewers, chapter reviewers and final manuscript reviewers: your feedback and advice helped to shape this work to what it has become. Again, our warmest gratitude goes out to the chapter authors who worked so generously with us to craft their work for publication in this edited volume. We would also like to thank the many authors who submitted chapters, but then for a multitude of reasons could not see them come to fruition in this edited volume.

Our acknowledgments would not be complete without thanking the Foreword author Professor Kelly Coate, for her invaluable support of our book. We are also particularly grateful for the support of our families, friends and colleagues, without whom this book would never have made it off the ground!

.

Introduction

Gendered Narrative Experiences of Women in Academia

Michelle Ronksley-Pavia, Michelle M. Neumann,
Jane F. Manakil and Kelly Pickard-Smith

Introduction

The introduction to the book unpacks and defines concepts and perceptions of gendered women's experiences in academia (framing around the work of Kaufman 2018, and others: Burke 2021; Cordova and Knecht 2019; Mirza 2014; Vaiou 2018). Here we outline how each individual chapter contributes to the book *en masse*. Setting the scene for the book, we briefly discuss the historical discourse of gendered micro and macro architecture and evolution in academia, in this way providing an initial framing for conceptualizing women's experiences from an intersectional lens in and through academia.

This edited volume provides captivating understandings of individual and collective gendered experiences; suggesting, in essence, that globally we share similar obstacles, yet there are differences in how oppression and inequity impact different and diverse groups of women. Individually and collectively, we explore the gendering of women's experiences in academia through the lens of intersectionality and narratives of experience. This is a cogent theme throughout the book, which reflects on women's experiences as always raced, classed, nuanced and complex. Each of the chapters in this book is written by academics from diverse backgrounds who collectively explore current issues facing their academic communities across the globe.

Gendered narrative experiences of women in academia

The chapters in this book, *Academic Women: Voicing Narratives of Gendered Experiences*, provide an essential read on the subject of women working, studying and experiencing academia from the many varied positions across the world. We are optimistic that the contributions from true scholars in the field of women in academia can further support all women experiencing life in the patriarchal academy. The insights and experiences shared by contributing authors provide readers with a global overview of the nature of women's lived experiences in these gendered spaces – of culture, class, dis/ability and the conglomerate of intersectionality experienced by women – cisgender, transgender, non-binary, gender-neutral, agender, gender-fluid and gender-queer individuals.

This book is designed to develop collective understanding about how gender is shaped by different structures, institutionalized systems and practices in academia and, further, how these (re)shape experiences and identity of women on an individual level. Each chapter in this book provides important insights into individual and collective contemporary women's experiences in academia from international perspectives, including gender equity, and barriers to success and achievement. Bringing together these intersectional perspectives enables women to engage in scholarly discourses around gendered experiences in academia. The voices of these authors emphasize the ongoing issues impacting women in academia with an international lens, and feature women's experiences in academia as being in some respects similar, but in other respects quite different. The chapter authors explore how women attend to critical issues as they arise to bring together narrative collections of understandings of macro and micro discourses and systemic practices of experience for women academics; from those who are at the beginning of their careers through to well-experienced and established academics.

The conceptualization of this book began some time ago in the mind of our lead editor, Michelle Ronksley-Pavia; it was only finally verbalized when the first three editors were brought together as 'chosen' participants in a university-wide programme called *Women in Leadership*. Michelle Ronksley-Pavia and Michelle M. Neumann already knew each other, sharing not only the same first name but at that time, the same university department – the School of Education and Professional Studies at Griffith University (Australia) – with offices directly across the corridor from each other. Meeting Jane F. Manakil, from the School of Medicine and Dentistry at the same university during the *Women in Leadership* program led to articulation of Michelle Ronksley-Pavia's idea of voicing academic women's experiences in some kind of written form.

Later, the three of us met Kelly Pickard-Smith, whom Michelle Ronksley-Pavia already knew through Kelly's administration of the Facebook group WIASN (Women in Academia Support Network). Through this group, women working in academia had also articulated narratives of their experiences. There was clearly a need, not only for women to voice their experiences but also for other women to become aware of these experiences: to realize they had some shared narratives, irrespective of starting points, backgrounds and places of work.

Instigating the formation of this book, we very soon realized that even collectively we knew little of the theoretical underpinnings of this familiar world we had long been part of but had not even remotely begun to understand. Working with the Bloomsbury Gender and Education series editors, Marie-Pierre Moreau, Penny Jane Burke and Nancy S. Niemi, we were supported in developing our proposal and evolving our understanding of the theoretical and empirical works preceding and framing our contribution to the vast work of feminist scholars with and about women working, living and being in academia. We did not specifically set out to systematically explore axes of identity (oppression) through intersectionality, but this clearly became one of the unexpected foci of contributing authors in this space. In the process of developing this book it is evident how the chapter authors, in drawing on current research literature of gendered experiences of academic and personal experience, find similarities across our collective experiences, that are not only local but also global, requiring collective approaches to addressing intersectional oppression of women in the academy.

Each chapter is a nuanced exploration of contemporary narratives in the field, whether from the chapter authors' own research or a synthesis of projects, literature reviews or autoethnographic lived experiences, from and by women in academia. This edited volume brings together a collection of lived experiences on a range of contemporary concerns relating to women academics, to explore how women attend to issues bringing together collectives of problem solving and building resistance for women academics; from those who are at the beginning of their careers to those already well experienced. This book can be used as a reference on occasion or as a guide to the many and varied experiences of academic women across the world.

Organization of the book

This comprehensive volume can act as a reference point for all women and their colleagues working in universities and colleges across the world, and we hope it makes a valuable and significant contribution to published work in the field. This book is comprised of distinct yet connected chapters, each taking a unique and often personalized narrative view of the chapter authors' lived experiences of working and being in academia.

The first chapter, 'Concepts and perceptions of gendered women's experiences in academia' (Ronksley-Pavia et al.), provides the reader with an overview of concepts and perceptions of some historical and contemporary issues in gendered experiences of women who work in academia. The entire chapters in the book have been conceptualized and written on the historical discourses around feminism, patriarchy and gendered experiences for women in the academy; this is not the intent of this first chapter. Readers are invited to engage with this first chapter as a framing of the conceptualization of this unique book espousing specific and varied live-experience narratives from the diversities of women working in these spaces. In Chapter 1, Ronksley-Pavia et al. recognize and acknowledge that gender is more than a biological attribute; it encompasses the effects of socialization and social ordering, leaving gender as an unfixed identity. The authors approach this chapter as an empowered and collective group of women with their own experiences and expertise through their individual and collective experiences working in the academy, realizing that not only do they have a vested interest in women's experiences in academia but also the authors embodied many of those experiences, specifically the stories or narratives of their own lived experiences. Gendered experiences are clearly impacting the lives of academic women at all stages of their careers. Achieving gender equity is a societal issue, and addressing gendered barriers in academia should assist in providing a more equitable workplace for women.

In Chapter 2, 'The caring coven: Sensing in- and out-of-placeness in masculinist, neoliberal academia' (Høg Utoft and Kongerslev), the authors explore, through five autoethnographic vignettes, the lived experience of two cisgender women working across two universities and two different academic fields in Denmark. Inspired by Sara Ahmed's *Living a Feminist Life* (2017), the authors analyse narratives illustrating personal stories of 'epistemic injustice', that is, instances of gender-specific silencing, exclusion and oppression of certain, marginalized knowledges that may be indicative of larger structural problematics. Bringing in- and out-of-placeness to the fore alongside dynamics of epistemic justice, the chapter explores the complex mechanisms through which such sensations of (un)belonging emerge. Although women in academia are often portrayed as 'feminist killjoys' and though the authors try to embody this figure as individuals against a system, they frequently come up against walls and often end up walled off. Using the witches' coven as a 'hopeful signifier' of care and collectivity, Høg Utoft and Kongerslev discuss how humour as resistance, in the context of feminist, caring communities, can provide spaces in which to breathe and rest for women in academia. Thus, by invoking the rebellious witch figure as an agent of collectivity and (sarcastic) rebellion, the authors offer a provocation to work towards epistemic justice and a more caring academe.

The third chapter of the book, 'Collective feminist resistance and agitation from within Australian universities – Slaying the dragon' (Crimmins et al.), explores how sexism circulates and thrives in and through contemporary narratives, discourses and systems of thought, especially in academia. The authors explore sexism as a shape shifter, forming and reforming, wreaking havoc in its wake. One manifestation of sexism is gender-based violence (GBV) which, while instigated mostly at the individual level, is founded on ideological gender-related macro-social factors such as traditional gender role beliefs and negative attitudes towards gender equality. As academics, collectively Crimmins et al. seek to expose and derail sexism through their teaching, research and engagement activities. In Chapter 3, the authors offer a narrative of how five academics working across several institutions and four disciplines use activism within (and beyond) academia in an attempt to slay 'the seven-headed dragon of sexism' (van den Brink and Benschop 2012). Because slaying this dragon requires resilience and persistent, overlapping feminist strategies, the authors suggest that academics must work collectively to raise the consciousness of students and colleagues to activate for change and future world solidarities.

In Chapter 4, 'Experience of Bangladeshi women academics in a neoliberal world – Return from study abroad' (Hossain), the author investigates the lived experience of the reintegration of Bangladeshi women academics. These experiences of reintegration show that these academic women feel a glass ceiling over them. The author recognises the 'visibly existent otherwise non-existent' social justice and gender parity serve enough to imprison the progression of these women academics. Furthermore, Hossain discusses that Bangladesh, a developing country, aims to increase the presence of women working in academia and that Bangladesh as a nation has made considerable progress in the advancement of women. The current trend in academia seems to place men and women on the same grounds, when clearly this is not the case for some academic women working in Bangladeshi academia.

Chapter 5, 'Exploring Black women academics' experiences in English universities using critical race theory' (Johnson, Schwabenland and Maylor), sees the authors discuss how Black women remain the most marginalized and socially disadvantaged group working in academic posts within universities in England. Furthermore, the authors argue that the ethnic composition of English universities reflects a history of racial inequality and, although widening participation policies have had a significant effect on reducing the under-representation of Black and minority ethnic students, they have had much less effect on reducing inequalities among Black staff (ECU 2015). Johnson et al. share their findings from a larger study of seventeen Black women academics working in English universities. Their study employed critical race theory to provide an insight into the multilayered ways in which the frequency and depth of racism are experienced and routinely perpetuated in English universities.

Chapter 6, 'Bias against women academics in student evaluations of teaching: Tarring and feathering in academia' (Ronksley-Pavia), unpacks the discriminatory and gender-biased nature of the widely used higher education student evaluations of teaching. Ronksley-Pavia acknowledges the global prejudice against women that the United Nations (2020) report calls 'a deeply ingrained bias'. In universities across the globe, instructor gender has been demonstrated as playing a key influential role in shaping student ratings. As such, women are particularly vulnerable to the impact of gender-biased teacher evaluations. The author discusses the inherent bias of these evaluations against women and further intersectionalities of race, class, age, ability and disability, which form a conglomerate of biases and prejudice which perpetuate barriers to workplace gender equality that directly impact women. Ronksley-Pavia juxtaposes amalgamated lived-experience narratives of women teaching in academia to situate the narrated 'realities' of gendered experiences in relation to relevant literature. The author proposes that prejudiced teacher evaluations are akin to some students 'tarring and feathering' female academics, yet institutions continue to perpetuate misogynistic student evaluation practices despite seemingly being progressive in implementing institutional policies purportedly addressing bias against women.

In Chapter 7, 'Challenges for Chinese women PhD students in the United States of America – The new foot-binding cloth' (Liu), the author considers the lived experiences of international Chinese women doctoral students. As one of the most educated groups of Chinese women, international Chinese women doctoral students in the United States of America (ICWDSUS) will influence the gender values of their communities. Influenced by the intersection of two strong patriarchal cultures in China and the United States, ICWDSUS suffer doubly from discrimination. Without understanding the challenges for their career development, it is hard for ICWDSUS to prepare for their success, whether in China or in the United States. This chapter specifically examines some of the challenges for ICWDSUS from both cultures. The results reveal areas for ICWDSUS, educators and higher education authorities to consider women's career development interventions for ICWDSUS.

In Chapter 8, 'Gender inequality in the higher education workplace: Demanding a seat at an antiquated table' (Bray and Shaffer), the authors explore prior research and their latest study addressing the pressing need for opportunities that can lead to women occupying positions of power in the higher education workforce. Bray and Shaffer add to current research in the field by sharing the findings of their mixed-methods study aimed at discovering the experiences of women working at university. While the need for women in higher education leadership positions remains high, there are seemingly unlimited barriers standing in the way of them occupying these spaces. This study uncovered strategies used by participants for advancement, promotion and sustainability in the workplace. While the majority of women surveyed did not feel as though they had been the victim of gender discrimination, Bray and Shaffer's study reported findings about a lack of progressive ideologies, male-focused leadership, stereotypes about women who spoke up and the need for further education regarding sexual harassment and gender bias.

In Chapter 9, 'A joint autoethnographic account of two young women in academia: On overcoming imposter syndrome' (C. Wilkinson and S. Wilkinson), the authors explain the well-documented concept of imposter syndrome by exploring a range of research studying the incidence and impact of the phenomenon then focusing on imposter syndrome as related to doctoral students and teaching evaluations. Wilkinson and Wilkinson report on what is likely the first study to use a joint autoethnographic approach to explore the lived experiences of imposter syndrome, specifically of 'unbecoming' imposters, for two young women in academia in the United Kingdom. Adopting an intersectional lens (age and gender), the authors include excerpts from personal research diaries reflecting on their lived experiences of overcoming feelings of being imposters. Through narrative, the authors have developed a collective understanding of how both gender and age are shaped by, and shape structures, systems and practices in academia. Making key contributions to the field using an intersectional lens, this chapter enables further understanding of the complexities of how the authors, as young women, are positioned, and position themselves, within academia. C. Wilkinson and S. Wilkinson argue that, as well as offering a more nuanced approach than the exploration of their gendered identities alone, intersectionality offers a way of explaining the complexity of their lived experiences. Within the chapter the authors promote the under-utilized method of joint autoethnography and argue for its usefulness as a multivocal and reflexive methodological approach.

In Chapter 10, 'Women in supramolecular chemistry narratives of resilience and community building in a gender-constrained field' (Leigh et al.), the authors bring together findings from Women in Supramolecular Chemistry (WISC) – an international network focusing on creating intersectional kinship, supporting women working in the field – and a collaborative autoethnography where women reflect on the embodied and emotional experiences of academic work in a field dominated by men. Acknowledging that the voices and embodied narratives of women and other marginalized genders (e.g., non-binary and trans) are largely absent in STEM (science, technology, engineering and mathematics), the authors recognize that within many STEM disciplines, the gender gap is wider than in other non-scientific fields. Leigh et al. share how a group of women collectively found a sense of feminism, through a willingness to trust, to innovate and to step out of their disciplinary norms and play with qualitative research and new ideas. As such, the authors are uniquely positioned to share the invisible, embodied, emotional experiences of women and other marginalized genders in supramolecular chemistry.

In Chapter 11, 'Feminist online communities: The story of the Women in Academia Support Network (WIASN) – A tale of resistance and online activism' (Pickard-Smith, Belfiore and Bonsall), the authors offer a theoretically framed but very personal account of the development of the WIASN – a global online, trans-inclusive community of academic women and non-binary members. This chapter is primarily about storytelling: it tells a story of women storying. Storying entails building on the very personal, vulnerable and shared realities of surviving in academia to sustain the activism and resistance that allow the group to envisage and 'story' new possibilities for the academy and new models of academic work. Through the experiences of the authors as WIASN group administrators, this chapter recounts a narrative of women striving to see themselves and to be seen as academics worthy of taking up space, working to make the academy a caring and supportive space and creating new modes of academic service that boost and nourish rather than drain. The authors propose to show how collectively we can narrate a better version of academia and, in the process, build it.

In Chapter 12, 'Three female academics discuss gender issues and sustainability: A water engineer, a consumer psychologist and a science educator walk into a bar ...' (Sammel, Watson and McMartin), the authors share their experiences through an informal, playful dynamic that occurred between the three senior colleagues as they came together to have a conversation in a virtual pub. The colleagues from different disciplines reflect on ecological unsustainability in academia and implications for their climate action-based teaching and research. From different parts of the world, these academic women shared experiences of working in patriarchal, neoliberal institutions.

In the concluding Chapter 13, 'Cogent themes from women's gendered experiences of working in academia', Ronksley-Pavia et al. draw together recurrent themes from across the chapters to discuss understandings and implications from the sharing of women's narratives of gendered experiences in and through academia. It is essential to understand that these experiences are always raced, classed, gendered, abled and so forth, because of intersectional identities and experiences that take place in and across a varied assortment of global academic environments. Through the experience narratives shared in this book, chapter authors have provided nuanced understandings of how gendered experiences are shaped by different academic structures, systems and practices in their institutions and through different life-world global contexts. In this final chapter, the authors question why the onus seems to come back almost always to women in the academy being somehow responsible for devising answers to the issues raised about gender inequity, when meaningful responses require systemic changes that speak to (and from) the kinds of individual and collective experience narratives espoused in this edited volume.

References

Ahmed, S. (2017), *Living a Feminist Life*, Durham, NC: Duke University Press.

Burke, P. J. (2021), 'Gendered, Neoliberalism, and Corporatized Higher Education', in N. S. Niemi and M. B. Weaver-Hightower (eds), *The Wiley Handbook of Gender Equity in Higher Education*, 1st edn, 69–90, Hoboken, NJ: Wiley & Sons Inc.

Cordova, A. J. and L. M. Knecht (2019), 'Liminal Knowledge: Positioning Intersectionality in Academia', *Cultural Studies – Critical Methodologies*, 19 (3): 203–13.

ECU (2015), *Equality in Higher Education – Staff Equality Data Report for HEIs: Statistical Report Research Report*. London: Equality Challenge Unit [Online]. Available online: http://www.ecu.ac.uk/publications/equality-higher-education-statistical-report-2015/ (accessed 31 August 2021).

Kaufman, A. (2018), 'The Athena Effect: Strong Womxn or Straw Womxn?' WWU Honors Program Senior Projects. 97. Available online: https://cedar.wwu.edu/wwu_honors/97 (accessed 1 November 2021).

Mirza, H. S. (2014), 'Decolonizing Higher Education: Black Feminism and the Intersectionality of Race and Gender', *Journal of Feminist Scholarship*, 7 (Fall): 1–12. Available online: https://digitalcommons.uri.edu/jfs/vol7/iss7/3 (accessed 30 October 2021).

United Nations (2020), 'Tackling Social Norms: A Game Changer for Gender Inequalities'. Available online: http://hdr.undp.org/sites/default/files/hd_perspectives_gsni.pdf (accessed 25 January 2022).

Vaiou, D. (2018), 'Intersectionality: Old and New Endeavors?' *Gender, Place and Culture*, 25 (4): 578–84. Available online: https://doi.org/10.1080/0966369X.2018.1460330 (accessed 30 October 2021).

van den Brink, M. and Y. Benschop (2012), 'Slaying the Seven-headed Dragon: The Quest for Gender Change in Academia', *Gender, Work & Organization*, 19 (1): 71–92. Available online: https://doi.org/10.1111/j.1468-0432.2011.00566.xVan (accessed 1 November 2021).

Chapter 1

Concepts and Perceptions of Gendered Women's Experiences in Academia

Michelle Ronksley-Pavia, Michelle M. Neumann,
Jane F. Manakil and Kelly Pickard-Smith

Introduction

The use of *women* or *woman* in this chapter includes all representations of female gender identities. Furthermore, we recognize and acknowledge that gender is more than a biological attribute; it encompasses the effects of socialization and social ordering, leaving gender as an *unfixed identity* (Marshall 1994; Ren and Caudle 2020). The notions of femininity and masculinity are shaped by culture, values and social institutions (Acker 1990; Connell 2002; West and Zimmerman 1987). We approach this chapter as an empowered and collective group of women with our own experiences and expertise through our work in the academy. We realized that not only do we have a vested interest in women's experiences in academia, but we embodied many of those experiences, specifically through the narratives of our own lived experiences. In this conceptualization, our understanding of and relation with narratives of academic women's experiences is informed by the work of Clandinin (2013), who frames narratives through processes of inquiry, knowledge that is 'personal, practical, shaped by, and expressed in practice' (9). Stories, or narratives have existed for millennia, even before what we understood as spoken language; cave-dwellers drew, painted and etched their stories onto hard-rock surfaces. As Clandinin and Rosiek (2007) articulate:

> Human beings have lived out and told stories about that living for as long as we could talk. And then we have talked about the stories we tell for as long. These lived and told stories and the talk about the stories are one of the ways that we fill our world with meaning and enlist one another's assistance in building lives and communities. (35)

In the process of developing this book it is evident through drawing on current research literature, that our experiences are not only occurring locally but also have similarities to the experiences of other academic women across the globe. Together, authors in this edited volume have evidenced that gendered intersectional experiences are clearly impacting the lives of academic women at all stages of their careers.

Narratives and their intricate connection with lived experiences form the glue between intersectionality as a framework for sharing, discussing, problematizing and unpacking our individual and collective narratives as women in academia. Intersectionality is said to address the crossroads of identities, how we all have multiple intersecting identities—woman, sexuality, gender, roles and responsibilities, roles assigned and prescribed by ourselves and others, disability, race, class and conflicting identities. Essentially, the intersectional nature of our multiple individual, group and collective identities and 'the intersectional nature of identities together, shape the lived experiences of individuals because of interlocking systems of oppression and marginalization often associated with those identities' (Mitchell and Sawyer 2014: 195). Our reflections begin by introducing some current and historical feminist literature and theorizations of women's work in academia.

Concepts and perceptions of gendered women's experiences in academia

To begin outlining narrative identities of women, it is important to discuss narrative and lived experience in terms of some statistics and literature about how women have been (and continue to be) represented in the academy. These data provide an overview of patterns of inequality and inequity.

Although women (and girls) make up half of the world's population, they are under-represented in many areas of academia compared to males. According to the IESALC Report (UNESCO 2021), women continue to constitute the majority of graduates with bachelor's and master's degrees (53 per cent in 2014). Globally, women's educational attainment tripled between 1995 and 2018 (UNESCO 2021). The exceptions to this were Central and Southern Asia, where there was uniformity. The IESALC Report noted that in sub-Saharan Africa men were overrepresented, with fewer female students enrolled when compared to males (UNESCO 2021). Yet worldwide only 46 per cent of doctoral degrees are awarded to women and only 30 per cent of the world's university researchers are women, with women representing just 43 per cent of teachers in higher education (UNESCO 2021). The UNESCO (2021) report recommends that across the globe, institutions of higher education need to increase the number of women in leadership positions. In the United States only 38 per cent of women in academia hold a permanent position (Catalyst 2020; National Center for Education Statistics 2016), and in Europe only 24 per cent of women are represented in high-level academic positions (European Commission 2019).

Women's diverse experiences in the academy are undeniably intersectional. The theory of intersectionality acts to represent marginalized or oppressed groups of people in society (Gopaldas 2013). This has emerged from Black feminist theory, ableism and disablism to provide lenses to attempt to understand how diverse aspects such as gender, class and ethnicity intersect and interrelate, to potentially highlight how inequalities are not distinct homogenous categories (Collins 2000). Intersectionality can influence human identity and promote privilege or oppression (Crenshaw 1991). For example, in the United States women comprise 32 per cent of professors but of these 27 per cent are white, 3 per cent Asian/ Pacific Islander and 2 per cent are Black (Hussar et al. 2020). These statistics clearly demonstrate inequalities in academia. Furthermore, academic structures and policies such as teaching-intensive demands and high focus on measuring 'success' as productivity outcomes (e.g. number of publications, impact, citations), act to propagate gendered and intersecting inequalities (Burke 2021). Inadequate provision of resources, time and space for academics further exacerbates gender discrimination in institutions (Burke, Crozier and Misiasek 2017), and this is clearly reflected through the kaleidoscope of gendered experiences of academic women.

Women academics

Compared to their male counterparts, women academics tend to have greater teaching and service loads, caregiver responsibilities and experience more stress, anxiety and guilt (e.g. parental) than male academics (Damaske et al. 2014; Morley 2005; Probert 2005). Alarmingly, the academic gender gap is widening, often due to women's work duties at home, which can negatively impact on their work-life balance and subsequently health and well-being (Fleetwood 2007; Yildirim and Eslen-Ziya 2021). Compound this with the increasing demands of the COVID-19 pandemic on women's workloads (e.g. childcare and trying to work from home), women remain disproportionately impacted, with working from home potentially 'signaling an unrecognized backslide to traditional gender inequalities of the 1950s' (Aldossari and Chaudhry 2020: 827). The impacts of the COVID-19 pandemic on academics have been felt across the world, with many experiencing a state of complete exhaustion, also known as burnout (Gewin 2021). Women have felt the impacts of the pandemic at higher rates than their male counterparts, with statistics suggesting that about 75 per cent of female academics had deteriorating work-life balances in 2020, compared to just under 66 per cent of male academics (Gewin 2021).

Despite many higher education institutions across the world having equity and diversity policies, including those purporting gender equity, institutional practices still embed patriarchal tendencies, which further favour neoliberalized characteristics that shape higher education into corporatized institutions (Burke 2021), stifling opportunities for women who (want to) work in academia. Having policy is not the same as enacting that policy. Enacting policy means not just giving lip service to making change everyone's business, but explicitly implementing change that specifically addresses embedded misogynistic practices in academia. These systemic practices often stem from broader institutional procedures, processes and structures built on a long history of exclusion of women. There is no doubt that the nature of academic work is challenging as workloads intensify and become increasingly untenable, where higher education institutional structures and leadership are complicit in perpetuating this experience for many academics. Yet, the experiences of academic women continue to be silenced or remain silent. Greater demands for financial sustainability, accountability, efficiency and quality are draining academics (Thomas 2013; Tytherleigh et al. 2005), many of whom are bending over backwards to meet competing demands and breaking their backs in the process. However, academics possess innate attributes – such as a drive to discover new knowledge – that fuels their determination and resilience. The 'traditional' work of academics and higher education institutions is being eroded as academics are overburdened by increased teaching demands and increased competition for meagre resources.

The goalposts of academia are constantly shifting to meet the corporatized structures that now make up many higher education institutions, with the result that the needs of academics are often swept aside. Policy, operational changes, increasing class sizes and the marketization of higher education, along with reductions in government research and educational funding, are of growing concern for academics around the world (Kinman and Jones 2008). Even more so for women academics, especially those working in traditionally male-dominated fields, such as science. Only one woman of colour has ever won a Nobel Prize for Science, and fewer than 3 per cent of winners of the prestigious prize are women (Wetzel 2021). But of course, women are not just under-represented in the fields of science in the Nobel Prize Awards, the other fields of Literature and Peace have seen far fewer women recognized by these prestigious awards. Since the Awards began in 1901, 876 men have won an award, compared to just 58 women (Statista 2020) (or 59 if you count Marie Currie twice!). The largest gender gap appears in Economics (2 women, 84 men) and Physics (4 women, 216 men) (Nobel Foundation 2021). Interestingly, a study into the gender gap in prestigious international research awards found that these gender disparities played out across the world; of the 3,445 awards given between 2001 and 2020 women represented just 19 per cent of award recipients (rising from 6 per cent between 2001 and 2005) (Meho 2021). There is a recognized lack of gender equity among recipients of these types of academic awards and prizes. Intriguingly, questions have arisen given this lack of representation of women in prestigious awards, about the role that titles and the names of awards (and historical awarding of such prizes) may play in whether women receive such recognition (Krause and Gehmlich 2022). The results from Krause and Gehmlich's research suggest that there may indeed be a link between the (male) name of an award and who receives it, concluding that where an award is not named after a (male) person, the gender balance of awardees is more equitable, including more women. In essence, women may be more likely to be a recipient of an award that is not named after a man (Gibney 2022)!

Women's positions in contemporary higher education

Higher education systems have ongoing disparities in gender composition in the hierarchical nature of levelled positions (e.g. lecturer, senior lecturer, associate professor, professor), with women being under-represented in senior positions. For example, only 13 per cent of higher education institutions across twenty-seven EU countries were led by women in 2009 (Morley 2014). Across Australian universities (Universities Australia 2016) only 25 per cent of vice chancellors were women and only 34 per cent of heads of schools or faculties were women.

To illustrate the gender imbalance further, a recent study by Liu et al. (2021) explored gender inequity across academic levels in Australia, New Zealand, the United States, Canada and Europe in the field of veterinary science. Liu et al. (2021) found that although women occupied up to 48 per cent of academic positions, female academics were more likely to hold lower rank positions. In other words, the gender composition was skewed towards more men being above associate professor level. The authors concluded that more work is needed to eliminate gender inequity in academia.

As a result of some government and institutional monitoring of gender representation in academia over the past three decades, there has been some progress in improving gender balance (OECD 2019). However, despite initiatives such as equity strategies recruitment programmes and networking platforms (e.g. Women's Information Network of Europe), there remains international evidence that the higher education sector is facing continual challenges with respect to addressing gender imbalances, particularly in certain fields (e.g. STEM) (OECD 2019).

Work and Careers Australian University survey (WCAU) gathered data from employees (professional, academic, casual) of Australian Public Universities. Within this sample of 23,869 survey respondents, there were 9,032 academic staff, of which 51 per cent were women and 49 per cent were men (Strachan et al. 2016); women are represented at slightly higher numbers. However, the findings from this survey highlight that more women had academic roles at the lower academic levels, with fewer women in higher-level positions compared to men (Strachan et al. 2016). Furthermore, across the disciplines, men predominated in positions at associate professor and professor levels, with the greatest difference at professor level (women 7 per cent, men 19 per cent) (Strachan et al. 2016), highlighting the continued existence of gender imbalance across higher levels in academia.

The gender pay gap in academia is a constant issue, for example in the UK there is a 12 per cent gender wage disparity evidenced between men and women (UCU 2015). Some improvements across the OECD are being made with women in academic workforces increasing their average share by five percentage points from 2005 to 2016, which holds some promise (OECD 2019). However, more work is required by governments, institutions and academia to close gender gaps.

Women and leadership in the academy

Women's leadership opportunities are scarce in higher education settings, and this can be particularly evident in different countries, and different cultural environments (Bhatti and Ali 2020). Due to traditional social norms, power is often associated with 'bread winners' who are usually male partners as they still tend to have higher incomes and, thus, claim their perceived right to power and career choice priority (Cha 2010). These issues are further compounded by sociocultural factors such as class, age, spiritual, cultural and societal expectations, and beliefs about how women should 'be' (Farooq et al. 2020).

Similarly, across the globe research has shown that the under-representation of women in leadership roles in higher education is an ongoing issue, with some research pointing to less than 30 per cent of women in higher education having senior leadership positions (Cook 2012; Gallant 2014). This trend reinforces masculine hegemony and patriarchal structures where women are perceived as 'less than' their male counterparts. Stereotyped perceptions and misogynistic views of who an academic should be are evident in statements tossed around, such as 'Women are not better leaders', 'Women don't deserve senior leadership positions as they lack leadership qualities', 'She cannot handle pressures and gets scared very soon' and 'Women are not good leaders, they are emotional' (Bhatti and Ali 2020: 23). So-called feminine qualities such as tolerance, flexibility, modesty and accommodation are dismissed as female 'weaknesses', rather than being seen as potential strengths in diverse workforces. Leadership and authoritarian attributes that favour masculine characteristics still work against women's rights to fair and equitable access to career progression in academia (Burke 2021).

Hegemonic masculinity takes hold as a cultural 'norm', as evidenced in institutionalized misogynistic practices related to areas of academia (e.g., promotion and career advancement opportunities), which subconsciously venerate the 'power of men' and constrain women from reaching their 'full potential' (Connell and Messerschmidt 2005). This effect in turn reduces some women's self-esteem, self-confidence and self-efficacy, reinforcing feelings of not being 'good enough' for university leadership roles (Desai, Chugh and Brief 2014; Madden 2011), perpetuating the pathologizing of 'imposter syndrome' for women. Imposter syndrome is often put forward as affecting women who are high achievers and is often framed as predominantly impacting women, who are said to find it hard to accept their achievements (Tulshyan and Burey 2021). To make matters worse, women academics are further impacted because of other gendered experiences they encounter in their workplaces. When men make unacceptable 'jokes' or make misogynistic assertions about women, the onus is frequently on women to report bullying and harassment, which can be an arduous process that can have ongoing negative impacts on their career. While most institutions have policies, processes and procedures in place for reporting such unacceptable behaviours, women bear the brunt of this reporting and of reconciling and living with such incidents; the reporting and subsequent investigation process is often arduous and further marginalizes female survivors. However, if women embrace so-called stereotypical masculine traits, women are frequently labelled as aggressive when being assertive, and 'bossy' or 'opinionated' when speaking out. In addition, criticisms and judgements by higher-level male academics are particularly troubling for women working in Asian countries (Morley and Crosouard 2016; Sinha 2016). Such gendered experiences force female academics to work harder than their male counterparts. This can lead to increased risk of work-life imbalance, health disorders, demoralization and loss of identity, as women may begin to question their choice of an academic career (Roomi and Parott 2008).

Women are frequently approached to do more work than men, with males tending to refuse job requests more quickly than women (Kinahan, Dunne and Cahill 2020). Academic women are more frequently asked to take on student pastoral care roles and to complete more administrative tasks, along with cleaning and tidying tasks, than their male counterparts (Kinahan, Dunne and Cahill 2020). Furthermore, these stereotyped demands have no direct benefit to promotion or career progression but use up valuable time that women could be spending on academic pursuits. Fairer workload allocation models for women may help alleviate such gendered experiences (Kinahan, Dunne and Cahill 2020).

Gendered language

Ongoing idealized views of an academic community of knowledge are more rhetoric than reality, obscuring traditional 'collegiate' organizational principles that have largely excluded women (Harley 2003). Historically, academia based on concepts and knowledge produced by a patriarchal society in which (white) men are privileged above others tends to focus on the traditional supremacy of males in highly stratified academic cultures. Embedded in classed, gendered and colonialist structures, male-dominated academic language and terms were born from times where males were the only students allowed to learn in the hallowed halls of leading institutions. In the past, students were predominantly young men from wealthy upper-class families, families who could afford to send their male offspring to a prestigious higher education institution. These were definitely not places where women or where working-class individuals could attend as students. The continuation of gendered nomenclature for university qualifications, status and leadership positions carries (and in some instances) continues the perpetuation of patriarchally entrenched institutional foundations. Ponder some leadership roles or positions at most institutions – *research fellow*, *fellow of* (insert name of some prestigious body/institution) – often denoting exclusive membership of some group or organization. Yet, if as women we do not use our titles as *fellows*, we are not showing our full academic standing/qualifications, the all-important *evidence* of *impact* and *growth* as an academic. In particular, gendered language, especially around academic qualifications (e.g. bachelor's and master's degrees, research *fellow*), used across institutions needs to change and reflect the contributions and qualifications of women. Most universities across the world still use the masculine term 'bachelor' for university degrees. A more gender-neutral term could be used for academic achievements. Removing gendered terminology altogether as has been required in other workplaces (e.g. policeman – police officer, chairman – chairperson/chairwoman), and may potentially address this problem of gendered language. Do women have to remain satisfied and comfortable with titles that reflect the ongoing patriarchal, colonial and classist remnants of their origins in male-dominated academia?

Home and caring

Research evidence suggests that women are universally at an increased risk of being discriminated against in academic workplaces (O'Connell and McKinnon 2021). This can be attributed to elements such as power structure imbalances, social pressures and stereotypes to 'have it all' and be able to 'do it all' (Fitzsimmons, Callan and Paulsen 2014) – whatever 'it' is meant to be! Women with families are frequently further disadvantaged when seeking promotions or leadership positions, often feeling compelled to prioritize family or conversely feeling guilty for not prioritizing their child-caring and family responsibilities over their career (Haile, Emmanuel and Dzathor 2016; Ward and Wolf-Wendel 2012). Furthermore, marital responsibilities and child and family obligations often inhibit women from advancing in their careers (Hochschild and Machung 2012; Manzoor 2015). There are increasing numbers of single parent/mothers, for example, in Australia one in eight families are single mother families (Sebastian and Ziv 2019).

It is difficult for women to avoid personal trade-offs and costs between academic careers and family (O'Connell and McKinnon 2021). Women still carry the bulk of household responsibilities, with the burden of managing a household falling predominantly on women, an additional role (Ren and Caudle 2020) with additional cognitive demands (e.g. remembering special occasions and preparing for those). Family responsibilities such as childcare, eldercare and housework also act as hurdles to career advancement in academia (Ren and Caudle 2020). Women often face complex family, personal and professional tensions around issues relating to mobility and family/caregiving responsibilities that frequently and disproportionally fall on to women, which further restrict career opportunities. Extensive research continues to demonstrate that academic women across the globe are still sacrificing promising career opportunities due to caregiving and family responsibilities, with women academics making more personal sacrifices than men (Beddoes and Pawley 2013; Fox, Fonseca and Bao 2011; Huppatz, Sang and Napier 2019; Morrison, Rudd and Nerad 2011; Thompson and Dey 1998). Expectations and perceptions of being able to 'do it all' can discourage women from reaching out for support because they may believe that they need to be viewed by their colleagues as 'perfect', due to unrealistic gendered expectations frequently felt, and/or placed on women academics (O'Connell and McKinnon 2021). Discovering innovative and sustainable ways to empower women to succeed in academia are essential to our not only surviving but thriving.

Feeling supported to bring babies and children to work may create a cultural shift, especially if partners are proactive in taking on childcare responsibilities, which will also assist to reduce the outside workload pressures on academic women (O'Connell and McKinnon 2021; Ren and Caudle 2020). In the university workplace there should also be adequate parenting leave, facilities and spaces available for women to feel comfortable engaging in child-caring activities at work (e.g. breastfeeding). Providing these practical supports may go some way to supporting academic women in navigating some of the challenges they face as both mothers and academics (O'Connell and McKinnon 2021).

Conclusion

Gendered experiences continue to impact on the lives of academic women across the world as evidenced from some of the statistical overviews we have shared throughout this chapter, where women continue to be under-represented in prestigious academic awards and in senior leadership positions. Achieving gender equity is a societal issue, as is addressing gendered barriers in the academy to provide more equitable workplaces for women. It is time to remove gendered language from academia to address entrenched classed, gendered and colonialist structures that remain as ongoing symbols of historically (white) male-dominated institutions. This will only be accomplished by collective approaches where everyone proactively works towards ending the perpetuation of gendered practices that add to the complex layers of challenges for academic women.

References

Acker, J. (1990), 'Hierarchies, Jobs and Bodies: A Theory of Gendered Organizations', *Gender & Society*, 4 (2): 139–58.

Aldossari, M. and S. Chaudry (2020), 'Women and Burnout in the Context of a Pandemic', *Gender, Work & Organization*, 28: 826–34.

Beddoes, K. and A. L. Pawley (2013), '"Different People have Different Priorities": Work–family Balance, Gender, and the Discourse of Choice', *Studies in Higher Education*, 38: 1–13.

Bhatti, A. and R. Ali (2020), 'Gender, Culture and Leadership: Learning from the Experiences of Women Academics in Pakistani Universities', *Journal of Education & Social Sciences*, 8: 16–32.

Burke, P. J. (2021), 'Gender, Neoliberalism, and Corporatized Higher Education', in N. S. Niemi and M. B. Weaver-Hightower (eds), *The Wiley Handbook of Gender Equity in Higher Education*, 1st edn, 65–90, Hoboken, NJ: Wiley & Sons Inc.

Burke, P. J., G. Crozier and L. I. Misiaszek (2017), *Changing Pedagogical Spaces in Higher Education: Diversity, Inequalities and Misrecognition*, London: Routledge.

Catalyst (2020), 'Quick Take: Women in Academia (20 October)'. Available online: www.catalyst.org/knowledge/women-academia (accessed 25 January 2022).

Cha, Y. (2010), 'Reinforcing Separate Spheres: The Effect of Spousal Overwork on Men's and Women's Employment in Dual-earner Households', *American Sociological Review*, 75: 303–29.

Clandinin, D. J. (2013), *Engaging in Narrative Inquiry*, Walnut Creek, CA: Left Coast Press Inc.

Clandinin, D. J. and J. Rosiek (2007), 'Mapping a Landscape of Narrative Inquiry: Borderland Spaces and Tensions', in D. J. Clandinin (ed.), *Handbook of Narrative Inquiry: Mapping a Methodology*, 35–76, Thousand Oaks, CA: Sage Publications.

Collins, P. H. (2000), *Black Feminist Thought: Knowledge, Consciousness the Politics of Empowerment*, 10th anniversary edn, New York: Routledge.

Connell, R. W. (2002), *Gender*, Cambridge: Polity Press.

Connell, R. W. and J. W. Messerschmidt (2005), 'Hegemonic Masculinity: Rethinking the Concept', *Gender & Society*, 19 (6): 829–59.

Cook, S. G. (2012). 'Women Presidents: Now 26.4% but Still Underrepresented', *Women in Higher Education*, 21 (5): 1–3.

Crenshaw, K. (1991), 'Mapping the Margins: Intersectionality, Identity Politics, and Violence Against Women of Color', *Stanford Law Review*, 43 (6): 1241–99.

Damaske, S., E. H. Ecklun, A. E. Lincoln, and V. J. White (2014), 'Male Scientists' Competing Devotions to Work and Family: Changing Norms in a Male-dominated Profession', *Work and Occupations*, 41: 477–507.

Desai, S. D., D. Chugh and A. P. Brief (2014), 'The Implications of Marriage Structure for Men's Workplace Attitudes, Beliefs, and Behaviors Toward Women', *Administrative Science Quarterly*, 59 (2): 330–65.

European Commission (2019), *SHE Figures 2018, European Commission, Luxembourg*. Available online: https://ec.europa.eu/info/publications/she-figures-2018_en (accessed 1 October 2021).

Farooq, M., N. M. Ahmad, A. Q. Mushtaq, R. M. Ahmad, F. H. Ali and A. B. Mujahid (2020), 'Role of Women at Top Management in Public Sector Universities of Islamabad, Pakistan', *Journal of the Research Society of Pakistan*, 57 (1): 181–94.

Fitzsimmons, T. W., V. J. Callan and N. Paulsen (2014), 'Gender Disparity in the C-suite: Do Male and Female CEOs Differ in How They Reached the Top?', *The Leadership Quarterly*, 25 (2): 245–66.

Fleetwood, S. (2007), 'Why Work-life Balance Now?', *The International Journal of Human Resource Management*, 18 (3): 387–400.

Fox, M. F., C. Fonseca and J. Bao (2011), 'Work and Family Conflict in Academic Science: Patterns and Predictors Among Women and Men in Research Universities', *Social Studies of Science*, 5: 715–35.

Gallant, A. (2014), 'Symbolic Interactions and the Development of Women Leaders in Higher Education', *Gender, Work & Organization*, 21 (3): 203–16.

Gibney, E. (2022), 'Women Are More Likely to Win Awards that Are Not Named After Men', *Nature* (online), 1 June 2022. Available online: https://www.nature.com/articles/d41586-022-01506-4 (accessed 5 June 2022).

Gewin, V. (2021), 'Pandemic Burnout is Rampant in Academia', *Nature*, 591: 489–91. Available online: https://www.nature.com/articles/d41586-021-00663-2 (accessed 30 November 2021).

Gopaldas, A. (2013), 'Intersectionality 101', *Journal of Public Policy & Marketing*, 32: 90–4.

Haile, S., T. Emmanuel and A. Dzathor (2016), 'Barriers and Challenges Confronting Women for Leadership and Management Positions: Review and Analysis', *International Journal of Business & Public Administration*, 13 (1): 36–51.

Harley, S. (2003), 'Research Selectivity and Female Academics in UK Universities: From Gentleman's Club to Barrack Yard to Smart Macho?', *Gender and Education*, 14 (4): 378–92.

Hochschild, A. and A. Machung (2012), *The Second Shift: Working Families and the Revolution at Home*, New York: Penguin.

Huppatz, K., K. Sang and J. Napier (2019), 'If You Put Pressure on Yourself to Produce Then That's Your Responsibility: Mothers' Experiences of Maternity Leave and Flexible Work in the Neoliberal University', *Gender, Work and Organization*, 26: 772–88.

Hussar, B., J. S. Zhang, K. Hein, A. Wang, J. Roberts, M. Cui, F. B. Smith, A. Mann, A. Barmer and R. Dilig (2020), *The Condition of Education 2020*, Washington, DC: National Center for Education Statistics.

Kinahan, M., J. Dunne and J. Cahill (2020), 'In Pursuit of Career Advancement in Academia: Do Gendered Pathways Exist?', in E. Drew and S. Canavan (eds), *The Gender-Sensitive University*, 1st edn, 41–51, New York: Routledge.

Kinman, G. and F. Jones (2008), 'A Life Beyond Work? Job Demands, Work-Life Balance, and Well-being in UK Academics', *Journal of Human Behavior in the Social Environment*, 17: 41–60.

Krause, S. and K. Gehmlich (2022), 'Does the Persistent Lack of Female Recipients of Academic Awards have to Surprise Us if Few Scientific Prizes and Medals Are Named after Women?', *EGU General Assembly 2022*, Vienna, Austria, 23–27 May 2022, EGU22-2562. Available online: https://doi.org/10.5194/egusphere-egu22-2562 (accessed 5 June 2022).

Liu, X., R. Dunlop, R. Allavena and C. Palmieri (2021), 'Women Representation and Gender Equality in Different Academic Levels in Veterinary Science', *Veterinary Sciences*, 8: 159.

Madden, M. (2011), 'Gender Stereotypes of Leaders: Do They Influence Leadership in Higher Education?', *Wagadu: A Journal of Transnational Women's & Gender Studies*, 9: 55–88.

Manzoor, S. (2015), 'The Impact of Indigenous Culture on Female Leadership in Pakistan', *International Journal of Organizational Leadership*, 4: 414–29.

Marshall, B. (1994), *Engendering Modernity: Feminism, Social Theory and Social Change*, Cambridge: Polity Press.

Meho, L. I. (2021), 'The Gender Gap in Highly Prestigious International Research Awards, 2021-2020', *Quantitative Science Studies*, 2 (3): 976–89.

Mitchell, D. and D. C. Sawyer (2014), 'Prefatory: Informing Higher Education Policy and Practice Through Intersectionality', *Journal of Progressive Policy & Practice*, 2 (3): 195–8.

Morley, L. (2005), 'Gender Equity in Commonwealth Higher Education', *Women's Studies International Forum*, 28: 209–21.

Morley, L. (2014), 'Lost Leaders: Women in the Global Academy', *Higher Education Research & Development*, 33/1: 114–28.

Morley, L. and B. Crossouard (2016), 'Women's Leadership in the Asian Century: Does Expansion Mean Inclusion?', *Studies in Higher Education*, 41 (5): 801–14.

Morrison, E., E. Rudd and M. Nerad (2011), 'Onto, Up, Off the Academic Faculty Ladder: The Gendered Effects of Family on Career Transitions for a Cohort of Social Science PhDs', *The Review of Higher Education*, 34: 525–53.

National Center for Education Statistics, IPEDS Data Center (2016), 'Full-time Instructional Staff by Faculty and Tenure Status, Academic Rank, Race/Ethnicity and Gender (Degree Granting Institutions)', *Fall Staff 2015 Survey*. Available online: https://nces.ed.gov/ (accessed 1 October 2021).

Nobel Foundation (2021), 'Women who Changed the World: Nobel Prize Awarded to Women'. Available online: https://www.nobelprize.org/prizes/lists/nobel-prize-awarded -women/ (accessed 5 June 2022).

Sebastian, A. and I. Ziv (2019), 'One in Eight: Australian Single Mothers' Lives Revealed', *Report of a National Survey Undertaken in 2018 by the Council of Single Mothers and their Children*. Available online: https://www.csmc.org.au/wp-content/uploads/2019/12/One-in-Eight-Families_CSMC-National-Survey-Dec-2019.pdf

O'Connell, C. and M. McKinnon (2021), 'Perceptions of Barriers to Career Progression for Academic Women in STEM', *Societies*, 11: 27. Available online: https://doi.org/10.3390/soc11020027 (accessed 30 November 2021).

OECD (2019), 'Benchmarking Higher Education System Performance', Higher Education, OECD Publishing, Paris. Available online: https://www.oecd-ilibrary.org/sites/b150d324-en/index.html?itemId=/content/component/b150d324-en" https://www.oecd-ilibrary.org/sites/b150d324-en/index.html?itemId=/content/component/b150d324-en

Probert, B. (2005), '"I Just Couldn't Fit It In": Gender and Unequal Outcomes in Academic Careers', *Gender, Work & Organization*, 12: 50–72.

Ren, X. and D. J. Caudle (2020), 'Balancing Academia and Family Life: The Gendered Strains and Struggles Between the UK and China Compared', *Gender in Management: An International Journal*, 35: 141–65.

Roomi, M. A. and G. Parrott (2008), 'Barriers to Progression of Women Entrepreneurs in Pakistan', *Journal of Entrepreneurship*, 17: 59–72.

Sinha, C. (2016), 'Adjustment of Married Women in Relation to Age and Job Status', *International Journal of Scientific and Research Publications*, 6 (1): 42–5.

Statista (2020), 'The Nobel Prize Gender Gap: Nobel Prize Winners Between 1901 and 2020 by Category and Gender'. Available online: https://cdn.statcdn.com/Infographic/images/normal/2805.jpeg

Strachan, G., D. Peetz, G. Whitehouse, J. Bailey, K. Broadbent, R. May, C. Troup and M. Nesic (2016), 'Women, Careers and Universities: Where to from Here?' Centre for Work, Organisation and Wellbeing, Brisbane: Griffith University. Available online https://staff.uq.edu.au/files/245/women-careers-university.pdf (accessed 5 June 2022).

Thomas, E. (2013), *The Funding Environment for Universities: An Assessment*, London: Universities UK. Available online: www.universitiesuk.ac.uk/highereducation/Documents/2013/FundingEnvironmentForUniversities.pdf (accessed 1 October 2021).

Thompson, C. J. and E. L. Dey (1998), 'Pushed to the Margins: Sources of Stress for African American College and University Faculty', *The Journal of Higher Education*, 69: 324–45.

Tulshyan, R. and J. Burey (2021), 'Stop Telling Women they have Imposter Syndrome', *Harvard Business Review*, 11 February 2021. Available online: https://hbr.org/2021/02/stop-telling-women-they-have-imposter-syndrome#:~:text=Imposter%20syndrome%20is%20loosely%20defined,difficult%20to%20accept%20their%20accomplishments (accessed 5 June 2022).

Tytherleigh, M. Y., C. Webb, C. L. Cooper and C. Ricketts (2005), 'Occupational Stress in UK Higher Education Institutions: A Comparative Study of all Staff Categories', *Higher Education Research and Development*, 24: 41–61.

UCU (2015), 'The Gender Pay Gap in Higher Education', University and College Union, London. Available online: https://www.ucu.org.uk/media/8620/The-gender-pay-gap-in-higher-education-201516---full-report-May-17/pdf/ucu_2015-16genderpaygapreort_full_may17.pdf (accessed 5 June 2022).

United Nations Educational, Scientific and Cultural Organization (2021), 'Women in Higher Education: Has the Female Advantage Put an End to Gender Inequalities?',

IESALC Report. Available online: https://unesdoc.unesco.org/ark:/48223/pf0000377182 (accessed 1 December 2021).

Universities Australia (2016), 'Women Count: Australian Universities 2016', Universities Australia, Sydney. Available online: https://www.universitiesaustralia.edu.au/uni -participation-quality/Equity-and-Participation/Women-in-universities/Universities -Australia-Executive-Women-Group#.W_ZOv28rLIV (accessed 5 June 2022).

Ward, K. and L. Wolf-Wendel (2012), *Academic Motherhood: How Faculty Manage Work and Family*, New Brunswick, NJ: Rutgers University Press.

West, C. and D. H. Zimmerman (1987), 'Doing Gender', *Gender & Society*, 1 (2): 125–51.

Wetzel, C. (2021), 'No Nobel Prizes in Science Went to Women This Year, Widening the Awards' Gender Gap', *Smithsonian Magazine*, 8 October 2021. Available online: https:// www.smithsonianmag.com/smart-news/the-nobel-gender-gap-widens-as-no-women -awarded-science-prizes-180978835/ (accessed 5 June 2022).

Yildirim, T. M. and H. Eslen-Ziya (2021), 'The Differential Impact of COVID-19 on the Work Conditions of Women and Men Academics during the Lockdown', *Gender Work Organ*, 28: 243–9. Available online: https://doi.org/10.1111/gwao.12529 (accessed 20 December 2021).

Chapter 2

The Caring Coven

Sensing in- and Out-of-Placeness in Masculinist, Neoliberal Academia

Ea Høg Utoft and Marianne Kongerslev

Sensing in- and out-of-placeness

In *Living a Feminist Life* (2017), Sara Ahmed states, 'the histories that bring us to feminism are the histories that leave us fragile. Feminism might pick up (or more hopefully pick us up) from the experiences that leave us vulnerable and exposed. Feminism: how we survive the consequences of what we come up against by offering new ways of understanding what we come up against' (22). This chapter details a few moments of our lives which have cemented our feminist identities as scholars in masculinist, neoliberal academia. Our playful claim is that, for better or for worse, feminists are the witches of contemporary Danish academia. To echo Zwissler (2018), 'in the contemporary Western context, feminism and witchcraft are fused both by their proponents and detractors' (11), suggesting the ambivalent and ambiguous figuration invoked by our phrase 'the Caring Coven'. As a hopeful but fluid signifier, the caring coven helps us make sense of our experiences of belonging and unbelonging in different fields, departments and universities.

Our experiences do not exist in a vacuum. Women and other minoritized folks have long documented and theorized their experiences of academic life as a means of critiquing institutional discrimination and inequity. A central, often implicit, theme runs through this literature, namely, what it means to find communities in which minoritized persons feel a sense of in-placeness in academia with its embedded histories of gendered and racialized injustice (Grasswick 2017). In this context, being 'out of place' is the norm for women – especially women of colour (Wright, Thompson and Channer 2007). In the literature, such communities have for example been labelled 'feminist spaces' (Deschner, Dorion and Salvatori 2020), 'everyday utopias' (de Los Reyes and Mulinari 2020) or 'third worlds' (Lund and Tienari 2019).

Our ambition is to bring sensations of in- and out-of-placeness to the fore of this chapter by exploring the mechanisms through which they emerge. We present five autoethnographic, narrative vignettes (Humphreys 2005), which represent a personal, intuitive knowledge, enabling us to produce 'insightful and emotionally-rich readings of organisational life' (Sambrook and Herrmann 2018: 224). Taking a narrative approach to autoethnography shifts our attention from 'the told' to 'the telling' (Riessman 2003: 8). Stressing function over form, analysing narratives opens a window on the culture of a group of tellers (Sparkes 2005) – here, women scholars in the masculinist, neoliberal academy. In the vignettes, we aim for resonance by giving readers a sense of being there in the scenes with us. While the vignettes are personal for us, they are not about us per se, which is also why we refrain from naming them as the experience of this or that author. Instead, a general resonance includes the reader in 'the generative process of the text' (Franzosi 1998: 546) and turns our narratives into small episodes of resistance for everyone against a culture in which women are not perceived to belong (Ahmed 2017; Pullen 2018).

We are inspired by the concept of epistemic injustice, both as originally conceptualized by Fricker (2007) and as subsequently adapted by others (e.g. Dotson 2011; Grasswick 2017; McKinnon 2017). We focus primarily on the subtype *testimonial injustice* and secondly on *hermeneutical injustice* as a kind of background noise, a pervasive injustice in forms of understanding and in conveying understanding that especially racialized and gender-minoritized folks experience. Testimonial injustice relates to ways in which listeners in an exchange – due to bias – perceive a speaker as untrustworthy, whereas hermeneutical injustice occurs when there is a lack of equal contribution to modes of understanding, leading to marginalization of certain knowers. In the vignettes, we illustrate this theoretical framework by offering embodied examples. For example, we show how epistemic injustice manifests: when one protagonist (Vignette II) attempts to introduce a gendered analysis in a specific context, this knowledge is rejected by colleagues. Like any social interaction, 'biases and stereotypes can influence epistemic interactions' (Grasswick 2017: 315), and in the following we do not distinguish between academic exchanges as epistemic or social; they are both. Political attacks against – and the institutional lack of recognition of – for example, feminist research, queer and critical race studies (Grasswick 2017; Pereira 2017) may be unfolded through epistemic injustice. Specifically, we are interested in the ways in which structural epistemic injustice shapes marginalized groups' experiences of in- and out-of-placeness in the academy by delegitimizing not only their scientific knowledge claims (such as terminology deemed illegitimate, doubting scientific quality, or undervaluing contributions to research) but also their lived experiences. What becomes clear is that the two are inextricably linked, because – as hermeneutical injustice suggests – marginalized groups utilize the knowledge produced by unrecognized disciplines to make sense of their lives. Such dynamics of injustice further produce *participatory injustice* (Grasswick 2017), namely, barriers for minorities to participate in scientific knowledge production.

Such forms of injustice also affect our lives as scholars working in Denmark. Danish academia is an intensely white, Eurocentric space and we write from this space as well as in reaction to it. Our vignettes are written from the positionality of two white Danish ciswomen, one queer and one straight, but they also involve women we know, including women of colour. Our intention is not to exclude their voices from these stories nor to subsume them under our own. Their voices matter and must be heard, but their stories are not ours to tell. Furthermore, we are aware that many white feminist spaces hardly feel welcoming to women of colour. Therefore, anchoring our chapter in the premise that solidarity and care may be fostered, not despite but through our differences (Plotnikof and Utoft 2021), we invoke the coven and its central figure, the witch, as a symbol of refusal, resistance and community. As long as epistemic injustice continues to make women scholars 'space invaders' (Ahmed 2017) in the masculinist, neoliberal academy, this chapter's proposed concept of the caring coven may be the space we need to vent, cry, recharge, cackle and transform the magic of feminist care (Chatzidakis et al. 2020) into movements against oppressive, exclusionary institutions.

Part one – Out of place

Vignette I: I recoil

I still feel awkward in my new department. I've only been a PhD student here for a few months. I'm having coffee with three other female PhDs, who – like me – all study something related to gender. I only know two of them superficially. I moved to this city to start the PhD and hope that these women may be a new feminist community for me? I am mistaken. I mention to them that I really appreciate being part of this little meeting, as I often feel that I can speak more freely without men present. An uncomfortable silence ensues. I see the others glancing at each other. 'Don't you think, you just need to get to know everyone a bit better?' one of them asks. What can I say except 'Perhaps' and shrug apologetically? We each briefly introduce our research topics. With a sinking sensation in my stomach, I realize that these women are not 'gender researchers' in the way that I perceive myself. We do not speak the same language at all and I feel like an idiot for having no clue what using gender 'as a variable' means. We talk for a while, but the conversation is forced. It becomes crystal clear to me that these women are unlikely to turn out to be the community that I hoped for when one of them exclaims, 'I hate it when people assume that I'm a feminist just because I do research on gender!' I recoil and shrink into myself while we finish our coffees.

Vignette II: Knuckling under

We're gathered online for a seminar on blended learning. The conversation turns to strategies for improving teacher-student relations and the presenter states that, to create a sense of community and a flatter power structure so the students feel more comfortable speaking up in class, teachers should 'talk themselves down' to seem more approachable. In the Zoom chat, I type a question about the gendered aspects of this. Yet again, I'm the one who must point out gender stuff and, as the comment is ignored, I feel annoyed but also anxious. Did they not see it? Did they choose to ignore it? Was I really being unreasonable? After more than an hour, the course leaders follow up and I expand on the gendered ramifications of trying to be more buddy-like with students. This may work well for men who will seem more caring, but for femme-presenting teachers, there is a risk of being perceived as unprofessional as we're always already expected to care. Throughout the exchange, I am shaking. I have been here before. I have been laughed at, ignored, scoffed at and brushed aside as overly sensitive. 'Why does everything have to be gendered?' The question is an old one that echoes in my mind, haunting and alienating. A female colleague chimes in, in a familiar tone, that she doesn't understand my concern because she has never gotten sexist comments or been perceived as less professional. I am shaking worse now but manage to say, in probably too spiteful a tone, 'Good for you . . .'. Rattled and exhausted, I don't register what I say afterwards. I zone out, making a mental note to be less annoying, to take up less space, to knuckle under. I can't wait for the seminar to be over.

A sense of feeling out of place runs through both vignettes. Physically, feminist scholars are usually either organized within a dedicated gender studies department or centre or scattered across the university within their respective environments (Heijstra and Pétursdóttir 2021). The latter applies in both vignettes. Being isolated as the only department 'gender person' (Henderson 2019), or one of only a few, has several implications. In the first vignette, the narrator was confronted with the *male*stream approaches of her new department: quantitative, positivist research. Coming from the humanities and the qualitative-interpretivist tradition, the narrator experienced an insurmountable gap between her own understandings of 'what (real, proper) research is' versus that of her new, potential peers, triggering feelings of imposter syndrome. In the second vignette, the protagonist engages feminist knowledge claims, namely, the 'gendered ramifications of being buddy-like with students', but her point is initially ignored and later gaslit. As feminist research transgresses the hegemonic objectivity ideal and in this way challenges dominant research paradigms, it is often considered unscientific (Grasswick 2017). Furthermore, many feminist scholars understand their work not only as knowledge production but also as critical intervention in the academy itself (Heijstra and Pétursdóttir 2021; Pereira 2017). This places feminist researchers in a precarious and paradoxical position: one of simultaneous belonging and not belonging, as seen in Vignette I, where we see the narrator's need to find a sense of social belonging within her new department but, as one of her colleagues in the conversation strongly disavows feminism, she realizes that she will not.

Similarly, a professional-academic belonging appears unlikely, as evident from the second vignette especially. As 'killjoys', feminist scholars disrupt and challenge the status quo of their workplaces by calling out gendered and racial injustice (Ahmed 2017). Macoun and Miller contend that departmental seminars and meetings often become performances of academic authority through 'disconnected monologues' rather than genuine dialogue (2014: 291). This tendency may be even more pronounced in online meeting formats, which in and of themselves seem to hamper dialogue (Saatchi et al. 2019). This means that to voice a divergent opinion becomes even harder. To minimize the disruption caused by her point, the protagonist in the second vignette writes her question in the Zoom chat but is later asked to elaborate. Macoun and Miller note that to defend and explain a position is 'lonely and stressful' and that 'fear and anger do not enhance mental acuity' (2014: 29), which we sense in the protagonist's embodied reaction: her increasing shaking. According to Ahmed (2020), trying to address an institutional problem often means inhabiting the institution 'all the more' (n. p.); that is, killjoys stand out in the crowd as unwelcome troublemakers. The protagonist of the second vignette knows exactly how her colleagues make that sentiment known: by brushing her complaint aside. When people's complaints are buried, 'those who complain can end up feeling that they too have been buried' (Ahmed 2020: n. p.).

This self-censoring also illustrates a subcategory of epistemic injustice which deals with what Dotson calls 'testimonial smothering', a form of 'coerced silencing' (2011: 224). When the content of a testimony – broadly understood – is unsafe or risky, when the audience has failed to demonstrate their competence and/or willingness to hear testimonies because of 'pernicious ignorance' (2011: 244), speakers can be coerced into truncating their testimonies. By doing this, only part of a complaint is uttered, leaving the audience lacking in information and the speaker without justice. In both vignettes, the narrators truncate their testimonies so as to not further engage in what they perceive as risky and unsafe conversations, with interlocutors who are unwilling to hear them. In the first vignette, coming up against epistemic walls rooted in different scientific traditions causes the silencing, and in the second vignette, pernicious ignorance is the cause. Although these are only *instances* of silencing, many instances can in time become part of a larger structural *practice*, perpetuated and enforced by similar instances. The result is a physical sinking and shrinking (Vignette I) and an ever-resurfacing (but unrealistic) determination to conform and to 'knuckle under' (Vignette II).

Thus, epistemic injustice also extends to individuals' lived experiences. In the first vignette, the narrator feels able to speak more freely in women-only company – presumed by her to be feminist company. This is questioned through the suggestion that familiarity ensures openness and equality in conversations with men. The colleague's 'unnecessarily sceptical question' is a microinvalidation (Dotson 2011: 247), a form of gendered and/or racialized insult that (intentionally or not) puts the recipient in a subservient, epistemically unjust position. In this case, the narrator's experiences are invalidated because the other woman occupies a different epistemic position and therefore engages in both hermeneutically and testimonially unjust practices. Whether she intends this microinvalidation to silence or not, this is the effect. Underlying her comment is also a surprise or wonder why someone would not aspire to be 'one of the guys' at the department. In the second vignette, the fact that the female colleague has not experienced sexism herself precludes the possibility that others may have. The gaslighting is palpable: While the actions and words of the colleagues may not be ill-intended, they are condescending as they suggest that, for them, 'you probably misunderstood everything' appears highly probable. The responses of our colleagues in these vignettes are characterized by a 'postfeminist sensibility' (Gill 2017), through which people's interactions become presumed decoupled from gendered power dynamics ('Don't you think, you just have to get to know everyone a bit better?'), creating a sort of 'gender fatigue' (Kelan 2009) ('Why does everything have to be gendered?'), and any need for feminist knowledge, politics or activism is fiercely repudiated (McRobbie 2004) ('I hate it when people assume that I'm a feminist just because I do research on gender!'). The situations illustrate that women are not per definition the allies of women (McKinnon 2017), that solidarity is fostered by 'withness' not 'sameness' (Lund and Tienari 2019; Plotnikof and Utoft 2021), and that internalized misogyny and sexist discourses severely affect the ways in which women understand institutional and systemic processes in their interactions with the academic world.

A final theme runs through the two vignettes, namely, that as a lone 'gender person' (Henderson 2019) in an academic environment, you are – what we may term – 'presumed masculinist' (inspired by Ahmed's 'presumed heterosexual' 2017). In other words, you are presumed to subscribe to mainstream research approaches as well as hegemonic cultural beliefs, such as postfeminism's myth that gender equality is achieved (Gill 2017). Both vignettes, in this way, involve 'an unbecoming' masculinist (Ahmed 2017) or a 'coming out' as feminist, when the protagonists voice feminist life experiences and knowledge claims. In other words, 'passing' as something (straight, white, masculinist, etc.) only comes up when one does not pass. You are presumed *in*, until – depending on whom we encounter – we are discovered as *not in* (Ahmed 2017: 119). In a context where being *not in* is the norm, spaces in which we are unconditionally *in* become all the more important.

Part two – In place

Vignette III: Embodying the feminist killjoy

In a messy circle in a large airy room, an attempt at avoiding hierarchy, we sit squirming resentfully. On both sides of me a female colleague. Everyone is tense and I sense hostility and boredom? I'm bored. Or, I guess, distracted by other thoughts. I don't want to be here. This room is not safe. My old anxieties are re-emerging and I'm trying to embody the 'feminist killjoy' that the pin I stuck to my shirt this morning proclaims me to be. I am not. I am prepared and yet I am not ready. The purpose of the circle is to air out differences that have arisen among the teacher group. I don't want to be part of this. I am a junior scholar and I have no clout or power. I feel powerless. When my colleague on the right starts crying, I panic. I know I have to speak next and I know my eyes will tear up and overflow too. And then they do. Not because I'm sad. I'm angry and frustrated and unsettled. This is not a circle of care.

This will result in more hostility, and nothing will be resolved. I want to flee. There are feminist colleagues in the room and I try to focus on them. I look to my left and my fellow feminist killjoy looks me straight in the eye and raises her chin ever so slightly. I envision myself channelling her stoic, silent gaze, making it my own, fortifying me. This is what care can be. My tears cease and I speak.

Vignette IV: Together we can cope

The four of us are sitting in the meeting room; relaxed, relieved, laughing. The invited speaker just presented her equally devastating and fascinating research about the victims of femicide at our monthly feminist research network meeting. A few hours before, while preparing, the speaker came crying into my office. 'Some days their stories just really get to me,' she said. 'Of course,' I replied. Her presentation moved me deeply. Most other listeners have gone now. Teacups and breadcrumbs from the sandwiches served are scattered across the table, but I feel like none of us are in a hurry to clear out and go back to our respective departments. I sense that the others, like me, are stalling to savour the freedom of that space for just a moment longer. I can breathe here. We can talk about the horrors of femicide; the injustice of victim blaming. And together we can cope with the heartbreak through gallows humour, which to outsiders would seem utterly inappropriate. 'Well,' someone says and picks up a cup to indicate finality. 'Just a minute longer,' I plead in my mind, while also painfully aware of all the writing I planned to do today. Ha! Unlikely. Still, I feel a sort of lightness in my body. Today's meeting will recharge and refuel me. Our network meetings always do. Our small community gives me the strength I need once I exit that door, knowing – although I may feel so at times at work – I am not alone.

Individual resilience that falls short of empowerment is a key theme of these vignettes. In the first one, the protagonist's feelings of alienation in a strange, discomfiting and hostile environment – increased by the situation: collegial mediation – illustrates the out-of-placeness of certain bodies in certain spaces. Although every*body* in that space might be on edge, this feeling is often heightened by the already-existing misfit status of some bodies in academia (Wright, Thompson and Channer 2007). In Vignette IV, the narrator laments the absence of a more pervasive collectivity for feminists in academia, resulting in a feeling of almost desperate sisterhood and in near self-segregation from the world outside of the meeting. The spaces in which we feel *in place* occur spontaneously as we open them up for each other and ourselves, but they are temporary. We must always leave and always have to move in a sometimes-hostile environment and academic system. 'I sense that the others, like me, are stalling to savour the freedom of that space for just a moment longer. I can breathe here.' The vignette's tone is longing, yearning for a place to be without constraints on emotionality and on feminist research, mundane obstacles to our thriving (Heijstra and Pétursdóttir 2021). To carve out these spaces for ourselves and others is a tiresome, ordinary task, and we are called upon to be feminists at work (Ahmed 2017), to work on defying the norms and the system that excludes so many and constrains so many more.

Furthermore, in both vignettes, actors cry, an act perceived as unsuitable for academic settings (Hacker 2018). Crying here is transgressive, but in both vignettes, the weepers are met by understanding, not condemnation. As Hacker points out in 'Crying on Campus' (2018), crying and getting teary-eyed are functions of a bodily, 'distinctively human act' (283), but she also elaborates, stating that 'crying acts as a gendering border that reinforces common patriarchal perceptions of hierarchical essentialist differences between the sexes' (282). This crying, however, is not merely a sign of stereotypical feminine weakness and emotionality. Rather, Hacker calls this 'distress crying' and argues that 'the most common emotional trigger for crying is the feeling of powerlessness or helplessness, often in combination with sadness, anger, fear, or disappointment, and [. . .] women cry in conflict circumstances much more than men' (2018: 285). In Vignette III, the two women's crying results from the distress of being asked to perform emotionally in a stressful setting. When the first woman cries, the narrator knows she will too. She does not want to. She wants to be tough: 'I'm trying to embody the "feminist killjoy" that the badge I stuck to my shirt this morning proclaims me to be. I am not.' At least this is her own initial reading of her emotional response.

The reaction of the protagonist in Vignette III may be read differently, however. It might work to establish a bond, a sisterhood of weepers. If 'crying is, in many cases, a social performance – a symbolic interaction embedded in cultural and institutional contexts' (2018: 284), this kind of crying can perform collectivity. The protagonist in this vignette cried out of empathy for her colleague, on the one hand, and from stress, on the other hand. Her crying constituted a transgression in masculinist academia, but her feminist colleague signals acceptance and fortitude through the simple act of not looking away. The fellow feminist becomes a witness. Witnessing someone struggling and not ignoring it, but truly seeing – the 'stoic, silent gaze' or a simple, reassuring 'Of course' – become acts of collectivity and care. Although in Vignette III the protagonist succumbs to tears initially, she seemingly bounces back, not only by her own powers of resilience but by the fortifying support of a feminist ally.

Similarly, in Vignette IV, the women discussing femicide open up a space for the act of crying and showing emotions to become acceptable, both in the relation between women, who are scholars, and in relation to our research (Kara 2013). These acts of crying together illustrate what Hacker calls 'sisterhood crying' (284), which functions both as collectivity-building and as resistance. Authoritative, academic distance to one's subject matter is often taken as an ideal in positivist-centred scientific fields (Kara 2013; Pullen 2018) but, importantly, femicide (defined as a form of murder committed because of the victim's perceived gender identity or gender-divergence) is not just an academic pursuit. It is part of a larger felt experience of people who are read or identify as femme, whose lives are made precarious by misogynist violence and pervasive sexist discourses. Thus, crying not only shows empathy and care for colleagues but also reaches beyond the instance to open up a space for a different kind of caring academia.

In sum, both Vignettes III and IV express a desire for room to breathe and emote, spaces in which feminist academics can find strength and sisterhood, for lack of a better phrase. This is not to be understood as a necessarily gendered community – although it is often read as such through masculinist discourses – but a community of caring scholars building mutual support and a specific kind of friendship (Deschner, Dorion and Salvatori 2020; Macoun and Miller 2014). 'Our small community gives me the strength I need once I exit that door, knowing – although I may feel so at times at work – I am not alone,' as one protagonist declares. Giving and receiving fortitude and pauses in which to breathe is care (Chatzidakis et al. 2020; Lund and Tienari 2019; Plotnikof and Utoft 2021). In Vignette III, in addition to the supportive witnessing of the stoic colleague, the colleague who cries invites others to join her by opening up an emotional space otherwise foreclosed in that hostile meeting. Similarly, in Vignette IV, the women discussing femicide make showing and sharing emotions acceptable in that space. Echoing Ahmed, who succinctly proposes a kind of working definition of this kind of care as 'Feminism: how we pick each other up' (2017: 1), the protagonist of Vignette IV claims that 'together we can cope'.

Vignette V: The caring coven

> In my office behind closed doors, we are sitting in a semicircle, rudely disrupted by the shape of the room. The four of us are laughing, but we cannot remember what made us laugh. We are also discussing a serious problem, the issue of sexual power imbalances between male teachers and female students and the rumours of a relationship. We are discussing sexual violence. We are discussing the precarity we are all feeling working in a deeply neoliberal institution. But we are laughing. Someone has made a sarcastic quip or a mock-sexist joke. Someone brings up that time a male colleague passed three of us in the hallway and made a joke about the spot being where all the feminists hang out. He folded his body into a mock-cowering stance while laughing. We were standing by the door to the copy room. We laugh at the fact that he seemed spooked. As if we were magical creatures whose powers increase when we are legion. Someone says, 'Well, we're basically witches, right?' and someone responds, 'Yeah, this is a coven gathering' and we laugh. Later, chatting online, we collectively invent the term 'the caring coven' to describe our little feminist collective. Someone sets the standard emoji of our chat to the yellow humanoid crying-laughing, tears shooting from its eyes, head thrown back, mouth open, cackling.

Moving beyond mere coping into active resistance and feminist joy, we end with the image of the cackling emoji on purpose: to highlight the ways in which feminist collectivity brings not just patriarchy-approved forms of empowerment but also joy. Feminist collectivity breaks down walls; it brings to the fore care and laughter

(Kaeppel, Grenier and Björngard-Basayne 2020; Plotnikof and Utoft 2021). Although the vignette leads with an image of seclusion (the closed office door), its dominating affective expression centres on connection through laughter and feminist humour (Fahs 2019). The role of sarcasm in the situation remembered is key. Among its many functions, sarcasm is often perceived as more offensive than non-sarcastic comments (Dews, Kaplan and Winner 1995), a feature that becomes prominent in this vignette. This sarcasm may function as a 'weak critique' (Kimport 2013: 64). It is aggressive and rooted in anger (Traister 2018) and often fails to effectively dismantle the hegemony of masculinist academic institutions. In this example, sarcasm is used similarly: to critique and mock, as well as to safely 'challenge white male authority sideways' (Traister 2018: 102). More importantly, this is sarcasm intended to create a sense of belonging behind protective walls, rather than to break down existing ones.

Like the experiences illustrated in the first two vignettes, Vignette V recounts a feminist critique of 'stranger danger' (Ahmed 2017: 143). The male colleague's reaction to newly hired women colleagues, in a space traditionally and continuously employing mostly male lecturers, is significant. His reaction signals his failure to acknowledge three women as belonging, as valid inhabitants of that space. The additional quip labelling the women *feminists* illustrates that to be a woman in academia is to be read as feminist, although Vignettes I and II show that this is not always the case. Several women talking in a group, in academia, is somehow dangerous, threatening. His spontaneous reaction was apprehension. While perhaps a minor incident, it is a form of microaggression too often experienced by minoritized people (Dotson 2011; Wells 2013). Most importantly, by discursively and affectively constructing the women as dangerous, the male colleague – in his role as gatekeeper – *disinvites* them from the institutional setting. They are made 'space invaders' (Ahmed 2017: 9) through a process of estrangement that implies being identified as not 'being entitled to be here; as someone who endangers who is here' (117).

In response to his reaction, the vignette's protagonists construct a counter-narrative by sarcastically inventing themselves as the quintessential object of fear for patriarchy: a witches' coven (Federici 2014). Conjuring the witch figure connects contemporary women with centuries of systemic misogyny and gender-based violence (Federici 2014; Zwissler 2018). They are us; we are them. We know their fear; we know their pain. Like the label 'feminist' today, cast as a slur, in the Middle Ages '"witch" [stood] for a woman not properly subservient to patriarchy' (Zwissler 2018: 14). Therefore, symbolic of secrecy (even conspiracy), power and sexuality, among other elements deemed dangerous when associated with women, the coven has the potential to destabilize the status quo – if only for a moment or as imagined destabilization. Mirroring the social zeitgeist (Weaver 2021; Zwissler 2018), in academia, feminists are the witches of our times. By appropriating this narrative, the women in the vignette strike back. They embody the killjoy witches they are perceived to be: 'As if we were magical creatures whose powers increase when we are legion.' However, the transformation of the group of women into magical creatures is not purely wishful fantasy, and their powers do in fact increase when united. Our ideal of the caring coven will become increasingly realizable as women and other minoritized folks, over time, achieve critical mass in academic spaces. The coven should be seen as a form of 'hopeful signifier', in Ahmed's words. As she states:

> To build feminist dwellings, we need to dismantle what has already been assembled; we need to ask what it is we are against, what it is we are for, knowing full well that this *we* is not a foundation but what we are working toward. By working out what we are for, we are working out that *we*, that hopeful signifier of a feminist collectivity. (2017: 2, her italics)

Thus, establishing feminist dwellings in academia, such as the caring coven, entails and requires an act of resistance and, importantly, an orientation towards a different, hopeful future. Laughing at the absurdity of this situation functions as a reclamation of space. Laughing together as a collective in a space claimed by one as *her* office, where she has invited the others to rest, builds additional space for breathing, sharing, laughing and caring.

The coven revisited

Our metaphor of the caring coven is an attempt at solidarity, a tool for starting a movement towards achieving epistemic justice, not only challenging the unjust structures and knowledge hierarchies of academia but also increasing understanding of different lives and scholarly experiences. Although welcoming communities like our coven are often makeshift and transitory vis-à-vis the permanency of the masculinist, neoliberal university, they are nevertheless prefigured spaces of support, friendship, safety, care and places to vent; a 'prefiguration' (Deschner, Dorion and Salvatori 2020) that precedes their formalization in 'the real world'. However, we have to wonder whether any degree of formalization would subvert the sense of belonging that caring spaces offer for feminist, women scholars. Without out-of-placeness, would we ever feel in place in that profound and almost desperate way? The institutions' putting up of walls (Ahmed 2017) may be one way in which feminist scholars sense out-of-placeness, but putting up walls, like closing a door, may also be a way in which feelings of being in place emerge. Similarly, out-of-placeness may bring us to tears, but crying is not only linked with sensations of out-of-placeness. Not much implies safety and care like spaces in which tears are welcomed, in a sisterhood of weepers. And refusing to laugh with the colleague at his sexist joke in the corridor, but instead cackling spitefully at what it represents in the safety of the witches' coven, is not the kind of laughter that 'slapstick' humour produces; it is resistance to that which required us to close that door in the first place. While there may be a risk that such feminist collectivity turns into separatism, for as long as women remain minoritized and marginalized in academia, self-isolating in caring covens may be the only form of self-preservation.

Our hope is that with these vignettes, we have illustrated the complexity of our experiences in Danish academia as space invading, rebellious witches. We laugh, but it is laughter mixed with tears. We cackle, but it is cackling mixed with fear. We care, but it is caring despite the uncaringness of the institution (Plotnikof and Utoft 2021). The institution is still walled off and walled in. However, within these walls, we are starting to breathe and to create space for others to breathe with us. But we need more spaces of care. We need that care to spread beyond the shelter of the coven. Otherwise, we risk becoming careless and uncaring too. Imbuing the academy with a politics of interdependence and care, to echo the interdisciplinary group of scholars known as the Care Collective, requires feminist collaboration and community. Establishing dwellings in which to breathe entails sensing collective belonging, because 'above all, to put care centre stage means recognizing and embracing our interdependencies' (Chatzidakis, Hakim, Littler, Rottenberg and Segal 2020: 5). 'A feminist movement is built from many moments of beginning again,' as Ahmed states in her introduction to *Living a Feminist Life* (2017: 6). The caring coven is one such moment.

References

Ahmed, S. (2017), *Living a Feminist Life*, Durham, NC: Duke University Press.

Ahmed, S. (2020), 'Complaint Collectives', *Feminist Killjoys Blog*. Available online: https://feministkilljoys.com/2020/07/31/complaint-collectives/ (accessed 9 October 2021).

Chatzidakis, A., J. Hakim, J. Littler, C. Rottenberg and L. Segal (2020), *The Care Manifesto: The Politics of Interdependence*, London: Verso Books.

de Los Reyes, P. and D. Mulinari (2020), 'Hegemonic Feminism Revisited: On the Promises of Intersectionality in Times of the Precarisation of Life', *NORA-Nordic Journal of Feminist and Gender Research*, 28 (3): 183–96.

Deschner, C. J., L. Dorion and L. Salvatori (2020), 'Prefiguring a Feminist Academia: A Multi-vocal Autoethnography on the Creation of a Feminist Space in a Neoliberal University', *Society and Business Review*, 15 (4): 325–47.

Dews, S., J. Kaplan and E. Winner (1995), 'Why Not Say It Directly? The Social Functions of Irony', *Discourse Processes*, 19 (3): 347–67.

Dotson, K. (2011), 'Tracking Epistemic Violence, Tracking Practices of Silencing', *Hypatia*, 26 (2): 236–57.

Fahs, B. (2019), 'Reinvigorating the Traditions of Second-Wave Radical Feminism: Humor and Satire as Political Work', *Women's Reproductive Health*, 6 (3): 157–60.

Federici, S. (2014), *Caliban and the Witch: Women, the Body and Primitive Accumulation*, Brooklyn, NY: Autonomedia.

Franzosi, R. (1998), 'Narrative Analysis—Or Why (and How) Sociologists Should be Interested in Narrative', *Annual Review of Sociology*, 24 (1): 517–54.

Fricker, M. (2007), *Epistemic Injustice: Power and the Ethics of Knowing*, Oxford: Oxford University Press.

Gill, R. (2017), 'The Affective, Cultural and Psychic Life of Postfeminism: A Postfeminist Sensibility 10 Years on', *European Journal of Cultural Studies*, 20 (6): 606–26.

Grasswick, H. (2017), 'Epistemic Injustice in Science', in I. J. Kidd, J. Medina and G. Pohlhaus (eds), *The Routledge Handbook of Epistemic Injustice*, 313–23, London: Routledge.

Hacker, D. (2018), 'Crying on Campus', in Y. Taylor and K. Lahad (eds), *Feeling Academic in the Neoliberal University*, 281–300, Cham: Palgrave Macmillan.

Heijstra, T. M. and G. M. Pétursdóttir (2021), 'Sisterly Advice for Feminists in Academia When Playing the Game and Working the Cracks', *Gender and Education*, 34 (3): 247–61.

Henderson, E. F. (2019), 'On Being the "gender person" in an Academic Department: Constructions, Configurations and Implications', *Journal of Gender Studies*, 28 (6): 730–42.

Humphreys, M. (2005), 'Getting Personal: Reflexivity and Autoethnographic Vignettes', *Qualitative Inquiry*, 11 (6): 840–60.

Kaeppel, K., R. S. Grenier and E. Björngard-Basayne (2020), 'The F Word: The Role of Women's Friendships in Navigating the Gendered Workplace of Academia', *Human Resource Development Review*, 19 (4): 362–83.

Kara, H. (2013), 'It's Hard to Tell how Research Feels: Using Fiction to Enhance Academic Research and Writing', *Qualitative Research in Organizations and Management: An International Journal*, 8 (1): 70–84.

Kelan, E. K. (2009), 'Gender Fatigue: The Ideological Dilemma of Gender Neutrality and Discrimination in Organizations', *Canadian Journal of Administrative Sciences*, 26 (3): 197–210.

Kimport, K. (2013), *Queering Marriage: Challenging Family Formation in the United States*, Ithaca, NY: Rutgers University Press.

Lund, R. and J. Tienari (2019), 'Passion, Care, and Eros in the Gendered Neoliberal University', *Organization*, 26 (1): 98–121.

Macoun, A. and D. Miller (2014), 'Surviving (Thriving) in Academia: Feminist Support Networks and Women ECRs', *Journal of Gender Studies*, 23 (3): 287–301.

McKinnon, R. (2017), 'Allies Behaving Badly: Gaslighting as Epistemic Injustice', in I. J. Kidd, J. Medina and G. Pohlhaus (eds), *The Routledge Handbook of Epistemic Injustice*, 167–74, London: Routledge.

McRobbie, A. (2004), 'Post-feminism and Popular Culture', *Feminist Media Studies*, 4 (3): 255–64.

Pereira, M. d. M. (2017), *Power, Knowledge and Feminist Scholarship: An Ethnography of Academia*, London: Routledge.

Plotnikof, M. and E. H. Utoft (2021), 'The "New Normal" of Academia in Pandemic Times: Resisting Toxicity Through Care', *Gender, Work & Organization*, 29, 1259–1271.

Pullen, A. (2018), 'Writing as Labiaplasty', *Organization*, 25 (1): 123–30.

Riessman, C. (2003), 'Performing Identities in Illness Narrative: Masculinity and Multiple Sclerosis', *Qualitative Research*, 3 (1): 5–33.

Saatçi, B., R. Rädle, S. Rintel, K. O'Hara and C. N. Klokmose (2019), 'Hybrid Meetings in the Modern Workplace: Stories of Success and Failure', in H. Nakanishi, H. Egi, I. A. Chounta, H. Takada, S. Ichimura and U. Hoppe (eds), *Collaboration Technologies and Social Computing. CRIWG+CollabTech 2019. Lecture Notes in Computer Science*, 11677: 45–61, Cham: Springer.

Sambrook, S. and A. F. Herrmann (2018), 'Organisational Autoethnography: Possibilities, Politics and Pitfalls', *Journal of Organizational Ethnography*, 7 (3): 222–34.

Sparkes, A. C. (2005), 'Narrative Analysis: Exploring the Whats and Hows of Personal Stories', in I. Holloway (ed.), *Qualitative Research in Health Care*, 1st edn, 191–208, Berkshire: Open University Press.

Traister, R. (2018), *Good and Mad: The Revolutionary Power of Women's Anger*, New York: Simon & Schuster.

Weaver, M. (2021), '"Witch'" Tweets Reflect Society's Fear of Older Women, says Mary Beard', *The Guardian*, 9 February. Available online: https://www.theguardian.com /books/2021/feb/09/mary-beard-witch-tweets-reflect-society-fear-older-women (accessed 27 September 2021).

Wells, C. (2013), 'Microaggressions in the Context of Academic Communities', *Seattle Journal for Social Justice*, 12 (2): 319–48.

Wright, C., S. Thompson and Y. Channer (2007), 'Out of Place: Black Women Academics in British Universities', *Women's History Review*, 16 (2): 145–62.

Zwissler, L. (2018), '"I am That Very Witch': On The Witch, Feminism, and Not Surviving Patriarchy', *Journal of Religion & Film*, 22 (3): Article 6.

Chapter 3

Collective Feminist Resistance and Agitation from within Australian Universities

Slaying the Dragon

Gail Crimmins, Sarah Casey, Joanna McIntyre,
Genine Hook and Trevor G. Gates

Introduction

To confront the sexism that we encounter as academics and to explore our collective strategies of resistance, we begin this chapter by identifying international contexts in which we work to frame the interconnected manifestations of sexism and offer a rationale for our activist work. We then invoke the feminist strategy of sharing personal narratives so as to demonstrate the varying aspects and impacts of sexism that compel our actions. As Frank (2010) suggests: 'Stories have the capacity to deal with human troubles, but also the capacity to make TROUBLE' (28, original emphasis). Stories can animate our imagination, provoke action and can, in effect, plot different possible futures in our lives and those of others. As academics, the 'different possible futures' we imagine are animated in and through our teaching, research and engagement. We share these in narrative description of the personal though interconnected approaches we undertake to slay 'the seven-headed dragon of sexism' (van den Brink and Benschop 2012). The seven-headed dragon analogy is used to illustrate the difficulty in eradicating sexism, a phenomenon that is many faced and multifaceted. Sexism is considered by van den Brink and Benschop (2012) to be both dangerous and difficult to slay, and its 'seven-headedness' suggests the need for more than one slayer simultaneously targeting its many heads. Slaying the seven-headed dragon (van den Brink and Benschop 2012) requires sustained, collaborative and coordinated efforts.

Similarly, Ahmed (2015) reminds us that the consistent presence of sexism contributes to its continuation; we need to be vigilant in identifying its manifestations and vigilante in seeking to eradicate it. We five academics share stories of how we expose sexism as an activist strategy to challenge both its manifestations and underlying precepts through disparate yet complementary strategies in our work. As van den Brink and Benschop (2012: 72) observe, 'academia is not a monolithic entity' and gender practices operate differently in different academic fields. These varying contexts and their differing effects on gender inequality are exactly why we bring together and address here a range of experiences and strategies – the differing swords – we employ to slay the many changing faces of sexism.

What is activism?

Martin, Hanson and Fontaine (2007) define activism as a precursor to political action that transforms a community, develops a formal organization or extends in scale to reach social networks beyond the initial embeddedness of the instigating activist. An activist strategy or act exists as one part of a longer narrative, as 'many activists are struggling towards goals that lie some distance into the future . . . real and lasting political change cannot be achieved unless the culture – people's values, beliefs and opinions – is changed along with it' (Maddison and Scalmer 2006: 84). Flood, Martin and Dreher (2013) identify that academia can be a site for activism in a number of ways, including as a means for conducting research which involves or is intended to lead to social change, as a site for progressive strategies of teaching and learning, and as advising and supporting activist students. We add to this by suggesting that engaging in social change via university policy formation is also activist work within the academy. We will discuss how we activate three main strategies: activist pedagogy, activist research and activist policy formation, in the following case study of narratives.

Contexts in which we work

Before we examine particularities of our experiences in academia, it is necessary to acknowledge certain broader social contexts that affect us all as we live and work in the higher education sector in the 'global West' during the current digital era. To do so, we start by considering one of the most dangerous heads of the vicious beast of sexism – gender-based violence (GBV).

In 2014, Elliot Rodger uploaded several overtly misogynistic YouTube videos, rants that were fuelled by his feelings of sexual rejection. Shortly after he went on a stabbing and shooting spree near the University of California, killing six people. Four years later, in 2018, Alek Minassian uploaded a Facebook post that read: 'All hail the Supreme Gentleman Elliot Rodger!' Ten minutes later he drove a van into a pavement of pedestrians in Toronto, Canada, killing eleven people and injuring fifteen. Rodger and Minassian were not lone wolves engaging in random acts of terrorism. They were part of the 'incel' movement, a digitally connected global community of men who blame women for their 'involuntary celibacy'.

In June 2018, 22-year-old woman Eurydice Dixon was raped and murdered on a football field on her way home in Melbourne, Australia. The following day the picture of a 25-metre by 5-metre ejaculating penis was painted on the ground where Dixon's body was discovered. Andrew Nolch, who pleaded guilty to the act of vandalism, described his act as an attack on feminism. Furthermore, Nolch's lawyer, Glenn Thexton, told the court that Nolch's views were held by many others in society (Thomson 2018). Nolch walked free from court, required only to undertake community service.

In June 2020, US man Cole Carini was injured by the home-made bomb he had created to use against 'hot cheerleaders' (NZ Herald 2020). Police identified that the 23-year-old's deadly plot to target cheerleaders was inspired by 'incel' mass shooter Rodger (NZ Herald 2020).

The incel movement is part of, and fuels, the 'manosphere', which is a 'loose confederacy' of misogynistic online interest groups affiliated with men's rights activism (MRA) (Ging 2017: 638). The manosphere manifests via an informal but enthusiastic network of blogs, forums and websites where commentators (most often men) focus on issues relating to men's rights, a masculine and oppositional counterpart to feminism. Exemplifying the popularity of these groups, before it was shut down in November 2017 one incel group's blogsite had accumulated 40,000 members (Tait 2018). When sites such as this are shut down, the manosphere continues to exist through a multitude of other sites and codes.

While these manifestations of sexism may seem remarkable, sexism materialized as GBV is a phenomenon that impacts a significant percentage of women, girls, transgender and non-binary people. It is estimated that 35 per cent of women worldwide have experienced either physical and/or sexual intimate partner violence or sexual violence by a non-partner at some point in their lives (World Health Organization 2013). The higher education context, though not impervious to such manifestations of sexism, does provide an opportunity to address the belief systems that are the foundations to gendered violence.

Higher education context

Alertness to sexism and misogyny is also critical in university contexts specifically, which, as van den Brink and Benschop (2012: 89) observe, are often 'traditional masculine academic environments'. Notably, Cantor et al. (2015) sampled 27 higher education institutions (HEIs) and 150,000 students in the United States and found that 23 per cent of women experienced sexual contact involving physical harm or incapacitation, and 62 per cent experienced sexual harassment. Across Europe, Feltes et al. (2012) found that 35 per cent of women experienced sexual violence during their time at university and 61 per cent experienced harassment. The Australian Human Rights Commission (2017) survey of 30,000 students across all 39 Australian universities found that 36 per cent of women students were sexually harassed and 10 per cent were sexually assaulted during the previous year. In the United Kingdom, the Hidden Marks survey (National Union of Students 2018) identified that 14 per cent of women students experienced serious physical or sexual assault and 68 per cent of women experienced verbal harassment during their time at university. These discriminations are clearly gendered phenomena. Yet, while the vast majority of victims are women who are victimized by men, which reflects deep-seated sexism, transgender and non-binary people are also at a high risk of being victim to gender-based/sexual violence. According to the

2015 US Transgender Survey (National Center for Transgender Equality 2015), nearly one in ten (9 per cent) respondents were physically attacked in 2015 because they are transgender, while nearly half (47 per cent) were sexually assaulted at some point in their lifetime.

GBV, misogyny-driven homicides and highly masculinist ideas that incite such actions are reflective of gendered and sexist beliefs and discourses. According to Ruether (1993), sexism is a form of oppression based on gender privilege of men over women. It is primarily perpetrated by men and those who benefit most from it, and is perpetuated through discourses, communicated both explicitly and covertly, that men should determine the social and economic roles and status of all genders, including how women's bodies should be presented and utilized.

It has been argued that to reduce all manifestations of sexism, including GBV, educators need to address macro-social factors to promote societal attitudes towards equality and change traditional gender role socialization (Zapata-Calvente et al. 2019). Correspondingly, Rodin and Steinberg (2003) argue that universities play a unique role in society as the makers of new knowledge and the nurturers of new interpretations: 'those of us in universities have a special responsibility for exercising personal as well as institutional and social leadership' (n.p.). That is, *we the university* must activate for positive change and future world solidarities.

We acknowledge our privilege or 'freedom to' facilitate a future unlike the present (Grosz 2010) and accept that to help create a future unlike the present, we need to expose the problem and offer alternative world views. Yet, in naming the problem of sexism we are positioned as the problem (Ahmed 2015). To (somewhat) protect each other and ourselves from the impacts of being named the problem, we develop an 'Undercommoning Collective'. 'Undercommonings' are comprised of people who join together to forge solidarities to protect individuals from the tensions and contradictions of the contemporary academy, and who attempt to transform universities into 'visions, actions and experiments for a radically different world' (Webb 2018: 7). Thus, we work together to engage in feminist and critical pedagogy to expose sexism in a bid to support gender equity and slay the seven-headed dragon of sexism.

Narratives

Genine Hook

I draw my privilege as an early-career academic beginning a rare permanent ongoing lecturing position teaching sociology within the school of social sciences at a regionally based university in Australia. Building a collectivist sense of solidarity with my feminist colleagues enabled me to exist within this new conservative and precarious higher education context. My feminist pedagogy seeks to disrupt the idea that individuals can engineer their own success: that success is an attitude, a personal responsibility. This pedagogy shapes both the content and method of my teaching. As a sociologist my university teaching holds clear focus on structural and individual constructs of gender norms and layers of disadvantage. My feminist pedagogy counters the 'objective' notion of academic knowledge by drawing on my own experiences and research to shape classroom discussions, raising awareness and debates in relation to gendered norms which becomes a critical entry point of challenging and combatting sexism. Following Ahmed (2017), my academic activism explores 'how in becoming feminists we are doing intellectual as well as emotional work' (7).

My feminist pedagogy emerges in the classroom through the connection between intellectual and emotional work by shaping student discussion which challenge the hetero-coupled logics of the 'ideal' or normative family. As a sole parent and academic, I draw on theories of gender to challenge the structures of 'the family' and to offer personal examples of queer lives, beyond hetero-norms. This contesting of heteropatriarchal expectations and norms of 'the family' seeks to queer the familial stronghold of hetero-coupled families and is an effective way of introducing theory to students. By traversing through gendered binaries of mothering and fathering, sole parent experiences open up a potential for re-thinking kinship, thereby contributing to feminist activist politics and the invisibility of the carer 'within broader concerns relating to the complexity of "caring"' [ES1] (Taylor 2010: 635). Drawing on the experiences of sole parents provides an example of the everyday (re)production of gender norms and the value of care within our community.

It is often women in academia who highlight care work, and I argue that there are risks with incorporating narratives of self and personal stories within academic spaces. One of the risks is student backlash because to challenge familial norms is often to challenge the firmly held expectations and privilege of conservative students who can resent this. Our feminist collective resistance is one way to manage the personal and professional impacts of student backlash, with solidarity, debriefing together and sharing strategies to support each other to combat student anger, which is one manifestation of the seven-headed dragon of sexism. Another risk of highlighting care in both academic teaching and research is being situated as 'not serious' about research, which has clear implications for sustained success in the academy.

Despite these and other risks, my feminist pedagogy draws directly on lived experience and the 'personal is political' of women's stories in the academy and in families. I draw on my own sole parenting and much celebrated divorce to challenge the repetitions of familial norms, knowing that this allows other forms of kinship and families to come into view. In this way I seek to challenge students to queer the idea of 'the family' and the rhetoric of kinship and alternative ways of being family. Following Halberstam (2011), my queer critique of family is 'one method for imagining, not some fantasy of an elsewhere, but existing alternatives to hegemonic systems' (89). To include the stories of sole parents as a queer critique of 'the family' is a useful way to introduce the structural framework of families and to contrast this with the individual experiences within the broader expectations and mechanisms of the normative family. It is the capacity for students to see the inherent connection between structure and the individual as the basis for sociology and for contesting sexism and norms that disadvantage women. As a woman and early-career academic, I am often nervous to draw on my own personal experiences of sole parenting, but narratives of queer lives and 'queer families can help us question our assumptions about gender and sexuality norms' (Newman 2018: 5). This pedagogy also enables the skills of students to build these arguments for themselves and to rehearse critiques of how gender operates in the everyday, which is the foundation of exposing and challenging sexism.

Trevor G. Gates

Most of my academic training and experience has been in the United States, where I worked as a social worker and academic specializing in lesbian, gay, bisexual, transgender and queer+ (LGBTQ+) issues. In my teaching, I also draw upon my lived experience as a gay white male. In a higher education setting and, indeed, in most of my life, I share my identities as the intersection of both marginalization and privilege. As a male-identified person with white skin, I am sometimes invited into the 'boys' club' of higher education because I am perceived to be one of them. At other times, once the 'boys' club' decides that I am not one of them because I am married to another man and identify as part of the LGBTQ+ community, my ideas are sometimes discounted or discredited. I slay the dragon by being visible and being myself even when there are consequences to being myself. In some instances, I am no longer invited to meetings, or conversely I am invited to every single discussion about a wide range of gender and LGBTQ+ issues, as though I am the expert on all of these issues. I become the poster child for all LGBTQ+ people even though there is rich cultural diversity in LGBTQ+ communities (Craig et al. 2017). I draw upon all of these experiences in the classroom space as an academic activist.

My academic activism as an adult educator and social worker broadly uses relational, humanist-feminist and anti-oppressive approaches, informed by principles of active citizenship, social change and professional engagement with historically marginalized communities (Merriam, Caffarella and Baumgartner 2007). In social work education, an anti-oppressive practice framework – a framework that calls into question the oppressive power imbalances in society that shape an individual's interaction with others (Dominelli 2002; Hines 2012) – can be helpful. Anti-oppressive practice also examines practitioners' contributions to the disempowerment of racial, ethnic, cultural, gender and sexual minorities. An anti-oppressive framework requires that the practitioner develop reflexivity, or critical awareness of how their power and privilege can affect their assumptions, values and actions (Cavener and Vincent 2020; D'Cruz, Gillingham and Melendez 2007). However, reflexivity about our power and privilege is uncomfortable and requires courage (Fernando and Bennett 2019). As a social work educator, my practice is informed by a core belief about the inherent dignity and worth of people. Social change occurs in the classroom space when we directly encounter one another as fellow citizens, learners and colleagues (Gates 2020; Ross 2020; Ross et al. 2017).

Encountering one another as fellow citizens, learners and colleagues only occurs when we acknowledge and openly confront privilege. By privilege, I mean the unearned authority of dominant groups to engage in attitudes, behaviours and beliefs that maintain the dominant group's position (Bennett and Gates 2019; Liu 2017). Whiteness and maleness are understood to afford certain people and groups the ability to dominate and influence various domains of society, including adult and higher education (Garner 2017). My goal in the classroom is to openly acknowledge and confront my privilege as a white male so that learners, especially my male learners, can begin to question and confront their privilege. I slay the seven-headed dragon by challenging students and colleagues to think about the intersection of sexism with racism, homophobia and other forms of privilege. In this process, I also believe that it is essential for me to openly declare and be willing to discuss my marginality as a gay man. Many of my learners also occupy this complex space, and I believe that I should not be asking them to be open, authentic and trusting unless I can offer them the same.

Gail Crimmins

I recognize the privilege of an ongoing appointment. For over five years I was employed on short-term and sessional contracts, one of the 61,000 academics employed on casual or short fixed-term contracts in Australian universities (May et al. 2011). As a woman casual academic, I was one of the silent majority (minority) of academics in Australian universities who do not feel we have a legitimized space or place in the academy (Crimmins 2016b). During that time, and since, I have/had a choice: a choice between being academically and affectively compliant and non-complaining or living a feminist life (Ahmed 2015). Accepting a feminist life, I research and re-present the lived experience of women academics.

I initially undertook a narrative inquiry into the lived experience of women casual academics and theatricalized and created films out of the women's narratives to maximize an audience's affective engagement with the stories/women. I presented the performance at inter/national conferences so that the women's stories could be heard as counterpoint to the quantitative data largely created 'about' casual academics by non-casual academics (Crimmins 2018). Indeed, hitherto, most research about the casualization of academia had been undertaken by those in ongoing/permanent tenure and had predominantly focused on the causes and consequences of the increase of casualization in higher education (Crimmins 2016a). The embodied narratives I developed instead demonstrate that most women casual academics rage, weep and question their marginalization, and so I deliberatively employ aesthetic discursive strategies to disrupt traditions of adversarial and masculine ways of communicating.

In the role of Union Committee member, I advocate for gender equity in the university's union 'enterprise bargaining' (EB) process (in Australia the pay and conditions of staff are negotiated at the local or 'enterprise' level) within which I work (Crimmins 2021). Although the introduction of EB in 1991 is said to mitigate the development of a national gender equity framework for universities, trade unions operating through inequality regimes rarely prioritized gender equity even when they did lead national negotiations (Ledwith 2012). In response,

Cooper (2012) argues that bargaining teams should reflect increasingly feminized constituencies. Briskin (2014) suggests that feminist negotiators and negotiations are required for women's concerns to be prioritized. I therefore engage feminist pedagogies by facilitating union members to share their experience of gender inequity in universities and to propose EB policy that would directly address their experience. In doing so, we democratize the process of EB discussion and decision-making. As a result, the university's EB agreement now includes research grants and mentorship for academics returning to work as well as for (highly biased) student evaluations not to be considered as the central measure of excellence in learning and teaching within academic appraisals or promotion applications and the like.

I finally research and write collaboratively with a group of women academics called The Women Who Write (Black, Crimmins and Jones 2017; Crimmins et al. 2018). We write as a group not only to counter the individualist and individualizing culture of contemporary academia but also to take refuge and to feel safe/r in numbers. Finally, this chapter is borne out of another supportive alliance of which I am part: the Gender Agendas collective. We, the co-authors of this work, know that 'the corporate-imperial university consolidates its position while dissenting voices are quashed or forced out' (Webb 2018: 97) but we resist the pressure to conform by forming allegiances to discuss and share our affective dissonance. As Hemmings (2012) argues, we can use our affective dissonance between what we think the academy should be and how it is to form affective solidarity and the willingness to engage in collective feminist activism. We are united in our stance, though we use different strategies to slay the seven-headed dragon.

Joanna McIntyre

As a lecturer in media studies, I integrate feminisms, queer theory and masculinities studies into the media-focused curriculum I create and teach. I work to avoid a transactional model of education and instead implement tenets of critical pedagogy (Freire 1972), which expounds conditions that can facilitate 'transformative social justice learning' (Alberto Torres 2007). Taking a Freirean approach, Carlos Alberto Torres (2007) defines 'transformative social justice learning ... as a social, political, and pedagogical practice' that occurs 'when people reach a deeper, richer, and more textured and nuanced understanding of themselves and their world' (243–4). As a cis woman, I have met with resistance and even overt hostility from (usually men) students when I introduce issues of gender inequality and encourage self-reflexive dialogue about gender politics in lectures and tutorials. It has been my experiences of such resistance and hostility, however, that have made me keenly aware of the pressing need for critical pedagogy, as well as of its transformative potential.

Paulo Freire (1972) expounded that critical pedagogy requires people to be met wherever it is they live, and as each educational context differs, critical pedagogies must therefore be adjusted as necessary so that education can be truly liberatory (Coté, De Peuter and Day 2007). In the context of Australian universities in the second decade of the twenty-first century, I remain conscious that I work with many students who are caught in the rise of 'popular misogyny' (Banet-Weiser 2018: 2), which is dialectically opposed to feminisms. Furthermore, through engaging with students, it sometimes becomes clear that they are linked in with the digitally networked misogyny of the manosphere, including incel groups (Ging 2017: 638). Nevertheless, critical pedagogy and feminisms are old friends (see hooks 1994) and, in the face of these divisive and damaging cultural forces, I use both so as to – as Henry A. Giroux (2000) reminds us, it is imperative – establish pedagogical conditions in which students can develop a sense of perspective and hope in order to recognize that the way things are is not the way they have always been or must necessarily be in the future. My understanding of feminisms and critical pedagogies has helped me to establish dialogue (in the Freirean sense) with students and to critique my own positioning amid socio-historical power relations.

Although the rhetoric of critical pedagogies has more recently been questioned in relation to its practical applicability (see Buckingham 1998), Giroux (2000) insists that we must maintain hope in order to construct educational practices that are informed by critique and the possibility of change. In this spirit of hopefulness, I wish to share one particularly striking illustration of the continuing liberatory potential of such pedagogy in contemporary times, which I witnessed firsthand. Not long after I began as a lecturer, a white, cis man in his late teens who held strong MRA ideologies joined my classes. By his own admission, he was passionate about his MRA stance. However, over his time at university he re-evaluated his beliefs and became conscious of the histories and impacts of social inequalities; by the time he completed his undergraduate degree, he identified as a feminist and submitted an honours thesis that analysed a media text using various feminist standpoints and histories. He has since expressed to me numerous times that his change in perspective only came about because of his educational experiences and opportunities in my classes. I tell this story to contribute to educational discourse which provides a utopian moment of hope and possibility. Although 'there is no one-size-fits-all approach' to slaying the many heads of the dragon that is sexism (van den Brink and Benschop 2012: 89), in the privileged space of universities, the implementation of critical pedagogies and transformative social justice learning can be wielded as a particularly sharp sword.

Sarah Casey

After years of precarity, I now work in a full-time ongoing role at a regional university. Academics often inhabit privileged spaces. It is, after all, as Mayock and Radylescu (2010) remind us, 'The Academy, with its capital "A" . . . both a real place and a metaphorical space that sends explicit and implicit signals about the traditions of white male privilege and of hierarchy' (1). It is imperative for me as a feminist academic not only to acknowledge my privilege but also to attempt to disrupt normalizing discourses about gender and power. Challenging entrenched societal attitudes is imperative to slaying the seven-headed dragon of sexism. As noted in the introduction to this chapter, GBV does not occur in isolation. Although not the only factor in violence prevention, addressing societal attitudes is a crucial component in fighting the epidemic of GBV. Research indicates that 'the strongest predictors of attitudes supportive of violence against women are people having a low level of support for gender equality and a low level of understanding of the behaviours constituting violence against women (relative to other respondents)' (Webster et al. 2018: 2).

I challenge attitudes to fight the dragon through my pedagogical practices and in curricular choices, for example, by challenging dominant ideologies and provoking critical thought about media representation and through the ways I refuse to be silent, sometimes even when uncomfortable silence is the only way to speak out.

I embed feminist thought into the classroom. As an activist educator for social change, I see education as transformative. I am reminded of a family member's words when I was sixteen, urging me to escape the rural town in a post-Bjelke-Peterson Queensland: 'Get a degree and get out of here. Always have your own money. Don't rely on anyone', and of how my grandmother – pregnant from eighteen to forty-five – fought for her eight children to be educated and to leave entrenched poverty behind. I have seen and received the benefits of that fight: it changed lives of the generations that came after, and for me, central to my activism is 'hope'. I feel I have a responsibility as a privileged white cis feminist activist academic to *keep going*. hooks (1994) elaborates on a 'pedagogy of hope', contending that entering a classroom with hope is vital as an empowerment strategy to keep going with the working for justice. hooks calls upon educators to expose students to critical thinking for building community, as 'hope emerges from those places of struggle' (hooks 1994: xiv). When the tiredness from the demands of the 'zombie university' (Brabazon 2016) consumes me, I retreat and recharge in groups such as Gender Agendas and organizations such as the Australian Women's and Gender Studies Association.

Women-identified workers are situated in what Pocock (2005) calls 'work/care regimes' (32) in which labour markets and economies rely on both the underpaid and unpaid work of women. Burnout from these pressures and precarity of neoliberal university life due to consistently being under surveillance by students and managers, the inundation of digital traffic and cultural expectations about rapid response time, is a reality that we regularly face. Further complicating this is that students' ratings of teaching contain gender biases, and that 'students perceive, evaluate, and treat female instructors quite differently than they do male instructors' (MacNell, Driscoll and Hunt 2015: 291). Reflecting upon some of these inequalities in the corporate university, I draw strength for activism from the works of those who have come before and those currently writing and activating in the contemporary academy. Solidarity found in groups like Gender Agendas is critical for feminist academics for, as Ahmed (2010) reminds us, 'the feminist is usually the one who is viewed as "causing the argument," who is disturbing the fragility of the peace' (65). In this sense, speaking on and about feminism, naming oneself as a feminist will always be seen as a disturbance by someone. And as Lipton and Mackinlay (2017) note, even in gender studies, the classroom as a space for talking feminist is not without trepidation. Nonetheless, I have encouraged activism to students who have joined online feminist groups, attended feminist events with me and spoken on panels about their experiences as feminists, and I have taught students how to create and manage online feminist activist campaigns. These experiences give me hope to continue to slay the seven-headed dragon of sexism as 'despair is the greatest threat. When despair prevails, we cannot create life-sustaining communities of resistance' (hooks 1994: 29).

Conclusion

As Smith and Ulus (2019) argue, neoliberal universities create 'hostile atmospheres unsupportive of vulnerability and uncertainty' (1); we are pitted against others/each other in this environment to 'compete'. We must remember, in the words of Tara Brabazon (2016), that 'within these zombie universities, those of us who are not the undead, who have not been transformed into drooling walkers looking for brains to eat, have a choice' (9). Our choice is group solidarity and hypervigilance against individualism and sexism. We understand that we must work collectively to raise the consciousness of students and colleagues to activate for change and future world solidarities. As identified, slaying the dragon of gender inequality and discrimination (van den Brink and Benschop 2012) requires sustained, collaborative and coordinated efforts – ones that are as multifaceted as the beast itself. We thus engage in collective and affective activism and pedagogical interventions as we unite through varied and differing strategies to slay the seven-headed dragon of sexism, one head at a time.

References

Ahmed, S. (2010), *The Promise of Happiness*, Durham, NC: Duke University Press.

Ahmed, S. (2015), 'Sexism – A Problem With a Name', *New Formations: A Journal of Culture/Theory/Politics*, 86: 5–13.

Ahmed, S. (2017), *Living a Feminist Life*, London: Duke University Press.

Alberto Torres, C. (2007), 'Transformative Social Justice Learning: The Legacy of Paulo Freire', in M. Coté, G. De Peuter and R. J. F. Day (eds), *Utopian Pedagogy: Radical Experiments Against Neoliberal Globalization*, 242–7, Toronto: University of Toronto Press.

Australian Human Rights Commission (2017), *Change the Course: National Report on Sexual Assault and Sexual Harassment at Australian Universities*, Sydney: Australian Human Rights Commission. Available online: https://www.humanrights .gov.au/sites/default/files/document/publication/AHRC_2017_ChangeTheCourse _UniversityReport.pdf (accessed 7 July 2018).

Banet-Weiser, S. (2018), *Empowered: Popular Feminism and Popular Misogyny*, Durham, NC: Duke University Press.

Bennett, B. and T. G. Gates (2019), 'Teaching Cultural Humility for Social Workers Serving LGBTQI Aboriginal Communities in Australia', *Social Work Education*, 38 (5): 604–17. Available online: https://doi.org/10.1080/02615479.2019.1588872 (accessed 20 March 2020).

Black, A. L., G. Crimmins and J. K. Jones (2017), 'Reducing the Drag: Creating v Formations through Slow Scholarship and Story', in S. Riddle (ed.), *Producing Pleasure within the Contemporary University*. Series: *Bold Visions in Educational Research*, 59, 137–55. Rotterdam: Sense Publishers.

Brabazon, T. (2016), 'Don't Fear the Reaper? The Zombie University and Eating Braaaains', *Kome: An International Journal of Pure Communication Inquiry*, 4 (2): 1–16.

Briskin, L. (2014), 'Strategies to Support Equality Bargaining Inside Unions: Representational Democracy and Representational Justice', *Journal of Industrial Relations*, 56 (2): 208–27.

Buckingham, D., ed. (1998), *Teaching Popular Culture: Beyond Radical Pedagogy*, New York: Routledge.

Cantor, D., B. Fisher, S. Chibnall, R. Townsend, H. Lee, C. Bruce and G. Thomas (2015), *Report on the AAU Campus Climate Survey on Sexual Assault and Sexual Misconduct*. Available online: https://www.aau.edu/sites/default/files/%40%20Files/Climate %20Survey/AAU_Campus_Climate_Survey_12_14_15.pdf (accessed 7 July 2019).

Cavener, J. and S. Vincent (2020), 'Enhancing Knowledge and Practice of "Personal Reflexivity" among Social Work Students: A Pedagogical Strategy Informed by Archer's Theory', *Social Work Education*. Advance online publication. Available online: https:// doi.org/10.1080/02615479.2020.1764522 (accessed 20 March 2020).

Cooper, R. (2012), 'The Gender Gap in Union Leadership in Australia: A Qualitative Study', *Journal of Industrial Relations*, 54: 131–46.

Coté, M., G. De Peuter and R. J. F. Day (2007), 'Introduction: What is Utopian Pedagogy?', in M. Coté, G. De Peuter and R. J. F. Day (eds), *Utopian Pedagogy: Radical Experiments Against Neoliberal Globalization*, 3–20, Toronto: University of Toronto Press.

Craig, S. L., G. Iacono, M. S. Paceley, M. P. Dentato and K. E. Boyle (2017), 'Intersecting Sexual, Gender, and Professional Identities among Social Work Students: The Importance of Identity Integration', *Journal of Social Work Education*, 53 (3): 466–79. Available online: https://doi.org/10.1080/10437797.2016.1272516 (accessed 20 March 2020).

Crimmins, G. (2016a), 'A Reflection on a Humanistic Approach to Narrative Inquiry Into the Lived Experience of Women Casual Academics', *Reflective Practice*, 17 (4): 483–94. Available online: https://doi.org/10.1080/14623943.2016.1175342 (accessed 20 March 2020).

Crimmins, G. (2016b), 'The Spaces and Places That Women Casual Academics (Often Fail to) Inhabit', *Higher Education Research and Development*, 35 (1): 45–57.

Crimmins, G. (2018), *Theatricalising Narrative Research on Women Casual Academics. Palgrave Studies in Gender and Education*, Basingstoke: Palgrave.

Crimmins, G. (2021), 'Engaging Feminist Pedagogies to Support Equality Bargaining in Academia', *Gender and Education*, Ahead-of-print: 1–16. doi: 10.1080/09540253.2021.1902486

Crimmins, G., A. L. Black, J. K. Jones, S. Loch and J. Impiccini (2018), 'Collaborative Writing "betwixt and between" Sits Jaggedly against Traditional Regimes of Authorship', *TEXT*, 22 (1). Available online: https://doi.org/10.52086/001c.25110 (accessed 20 March 2020).

D'Cruz, H., P. Gillingham and S. Melendez (2007), 'Reflexivity, Its Meanings and Relevance for Social Work: A Critical Review of the Literature', *British Journal of Social Work*, 37 (1): 73–90. Available online: https://doi.org/10.1093/bjsw/bcl001 (accessed 20 March 2020).

Dominelli, L. (2002), *Anti-oppressive Social Work Theory and Practice*, New York: Palgrave Macmillan.

Feltes, T., A. Balloni, J. Czapska, E. Bodelon and P. Stenning (2012), *Gender-based Violence, Stalking and Fear of Crime*, Final Report to European Commission, Directorate General Justice, Freedom and Security (Project JLS/2007/ISEC/415). Available online: https://vmits0151.vm.ruhr-uni-bochum.de/gendercrime.eu/pdf/gendercrime_final_report_smaller_version.pdf (accessed 14 July 2018).

Fernando, T. and B. Bennett (2019), 'Creating a Culturally Safe Space When Teaching Aboriginal Content in Social Work: A Scoping Review', *Australian Social Work*, 72 (1): 47–61. Available online: https://doi.org/0.1080/0312407X.2018.1518467 (accessed 20 December 2021).

Flood, M. G., B. Martin and T. Dreher (2013), 'Combining Academia and Activism: Common Obstacles and Useful Tools', *Australian Universities Review*, 55 (1): 17–26.

Frank, A. W. (2010), 'In defence of Narrative Exceptionalism', *Sociology of Health & Illness*, 32 (4): 665–7.

Freire, P. (1972), *The Pedagogy of the Oppressed*, Harmondsworth: Penguin.

Garner, S. (2017), 'Surfing the Third Wave of Whiteness Studies: Reflections on Twine and Gallagher', *Ethnic and Racial Studies*, 40 (9): 1582–97. Available online: https://doi.org/10.1080/01419870.2017.1300301 (accessed 20 March 2020).

Gates, T. G. (2020), 'Teaching Democracy in the Social Work and Human Service Classroom', in C. Morley, P. Ablett, C. Noble and S. Cowden (eds), *The Routledge Handbook of Critical Pedagogies for Social Work*, 131–42, London: Routledge.

Ging, D. (2017), 'Alphas, Betas, and Incels: Theorizing the Masculinities of the Manosphere', *Men and Masculinities*, 22 (4): 638–57. Available online: https://doi.org/10.1177/1097184X17706401 (accessed 20 March 2020).

Giroux, H. A. (2000), 'Cultural Politics and the Crisis of the University', *Culture Machine* 2. Available online: https://culturemachine.net/the-university-culture-machine/cultural-politics-and-the-crisis-of-the-university/ (accessed 20 March 2020).

Grosz, E. (2010), 'Feminism, Materialism, and Freedom', in D. Coole and S. Frost (eds), *New Materialisms: Ontology, Agency, and Politics*, 139–57. Durham, NC: Duke University Press.

Halberstam, J. (2011), *The Queer Art of Failure*, Durham, NC: Duke University Press.

Hemmings, C. (2012), 'Affective Solidarity: Feminist Reflexivity and Political Transformation', *Feminist Theory*, 13 (2): 147–61.

Hines, J. M. (2012), 'Using an Anti-oppressive Framework in Social Work Practice With Lesbians', *Journal of Gay and Lesbian Social Services*, 24 (1): 23–39. Available online: https://doi.org/10.1080/10538720.2011.611103 (accessed 20 April 2020).

hooks, b. (1994), *Teaching Community: A Pedagogy of Hope*, New York: Routledge.

Ledwith, S. (2012), 'Gender Politics in Trade Unions. The Representation of Women Between Exclusion and Inclusion', *Transfer: European Review of Labour and Research*, 18: 185–99. Available online: https://doi.org/10.1177/1024258912439145 (accessed 20 April 2020).

Lipton, B. and E. Mackinlay (2017), *We Only Talk Feminist Here: Feminist Academics, Voice and Agency in the Neoliberal University*, Cham: Palgrave Macmillan.

Liu, W. M. (2017), 'White Male Power and Privilege', *Journal of Counselling Psychology*, 64 (4): 349–58. Available online: https://doi.org/10.1037/cou0000227 (accessed 20 April 2020).

MacNell, L., A. Driscoll and A. N. Hunt (2015), 'What's in a Name: Exposing Gender Bias in Student Ratings of Teaching', *Innovative Higher Education*, 40: 291–303.

Available online: https://doi.org/10.1007/s10755-014-9313-4 (accessed 20 March 2020).

Maddison, S. and S. Scalmer (2006), *Activist Wisdom: Practical Knowledge and Creative Tension in Social Movements*, Sydney: UNSW Press.

Martin, D. G., S. Hanson and D. Fontaine (2007), 'What Counts as Activism?: The Role of Individuals in Creating Change', *WSQ: Women's Studies Quarterly*, 35 (3 & 4): 78–94.

May, R., G. Strachan, K. Broadbent and D. Peetz (2011), 'The Casual Approach to University Teaching; Time for a Re-think?', in K. Krause, M. Buckridge, C. Grimmer and S. Purbrick-Illek (eds), *Research and Development in Higher Education: Reshaping Higher Education 34*, 188–97, Gold Coast: Research and Development Society of Australasia, Inc.

Mayock E. C. and D. Radylescu, eds (2010), *Feminist Activism in Academia: Essays on Personal, Political and Professional Change*, Jefferson: McFarland & Company.

Merriam, S., R. Caffarella and L. Baumgartner (2007), *Learning in Adulthood: A Comprehensive Guide*, 3rd edn, San Francisco: Jossey-Bass.

National Center for Transgender Equality (2015), *2015 U.S. Transgender Survey Report*. Available online: http://www.ustranssurvey.org/reports (accessed 20 April 2020).

National Union of Students (2018), *Power in the Academy: Staff sexual misconduct in UK higher education*, London: National Union of Students.

Newman, C. (2018), 'Queer Families: Valuing Stories of Adversity, Diversity and Belonging', *Culture, Health & Sexuality*, 21 (3): 352–9.

NZ Herald (2020), 'Incel Cole Carini Blows his Hands off with Homemade Bomb Trying to Kill "Hot Cheerleaders"'. Available online: https://www.nzherald.co.nz/world/incel-cole-carini-blows-his-hands-off-with-homemade-bomb-trying-to-kill-hot-cheerleaders/D553B2I4YDVUECK5VHIRQC7ZNY/ (accessed 20 December 2021).

Pocock, B. (2005), 'Work/Care Regimes: Institutions, Culture and Behaviour and the Australian Case', *Gender, Work & Organization*, 12 (1): 32–49.

Rodin, J. and S. Steinberg (2003), *Public Discourse in America: Conversation and Community in the Twenty-First Century*, Philadelphia, PA: University of Pennsylvania Press.

Ross, D. (2020), *The Revolutionary Social Worker: The Love Ethic Model*, Brisbane: Revolutionaries.

Ross, D., A. Lathouras, J. Riddell, A. Buchanan and V. Puccio (2017), 'Exploring the Value of Immersive Technologies and Authentic Scenarios to Engage Students in Anti-oppressive Praxis', *Advances in Social Work and Welfare Education*, 19 (2): 77–93.

Ruether, R. R. (1993), *Sexism and God-Talk: Toward a Feminist Theology*, Boston, MA: Beacon Press.

Smith, C. and E. Ulus (2019), 'Who Cares for Academics? We Need to Talk About Emotional Well-being Including What we Avoid and Intellectualize Through Macro-discourses', *Organization*, 27 (6): 840–57.

Tait, A. (2018), 'We Must Try to Understand how Unwanted Virginity Leads Self-hating Incels to Murder', *New Statesman America*. Available online: https://www.newstatesman.com/2018/05/we-must-try-understand-how-unwanted-virginity-leads-self-hating-incels-murder (accessed 20 April 2020).

Taylor, Y. (2010), 'Stories to Tell? Reflexive (Dis)engagements and (De)legitimized Selves', *Qualitative Inquiry*, 16 (8): 633–41.

Thomson, J. (2018), 'Misogyny and the Ethics of Digilantism: The Case of Andrew Nolch', *ABC Religion and Ethics*. https://www.abc.net.au/religion/misogyny-and-the-ethics-of-digilantism-the-case-of-andrew-nolch/10214348 (last viewed 30 August 2022).

van den Brink, M. and Y. Benschop (2012), 'Slaying the Seven-headed Dragon: The Quest for Gender Change in Academia', *Gender, Work & Organization*, 19 (1): 71–92. Available online: https://doi.org/10.1111/j.1468-0432.2011.00566.xVan (accessed 20 April 2020).

Webb, D. (2018), 'Bolt-Holes and Breathing Spaces in the System: On Forms of Academic Resistance (or, can the University be a Site of Utopian Possibility?)', *Review of Education, Pedagogy, and Cultural Studies*, 40 (2): 96–118.

Webster, K., K. Diemer, N. Honey, S. Mannix, J. Mickle, J. Morgan, A. Parkes, V. Politoff, A. Powell, J. Stubbs and A. Ward (2018), *Australians' Attitudes to Violence Against Women and Gender Equality. Findings from the 2017 National Community Attitudes towards Violence against Women Survey (NCAS)* (Research report, 03/2018). Sydney: ANROWS.

World Health Organization (2013), *Global and Regional Estimates of Violence Against Women: Prevalence and Health Effects of Intimate Partner Violence and Non-partner Sexual Violence*. World Health Organization, Department of Reproductive Health and Research, London School of Hygiene and Tropical Medicine, South African Medical Research Council. Available online: https://apps.who.int/iris/bitstream/handle /10665/85239/9789241564625_eng.pdf;jsessionid=530A6CD8CFC0FB05E5CE928 CE5F00C45?sequence=1 (accessed 20 April 2020).

Zapata-Calvente, A. L., J. L. Megías, M. Moya and D. Schoebi (2019), 'Gender-related Ideological and Structural Macrosocial Factors Associated with Intimate Partner Violence Against European Women', *Psychology of Women Quarterly*, 43 (3): 317–34. https://doi.org/10.1177/0361684319839367

Chapter 4

Experience of Bangladeshi Women Academics in a Neoliberal World

Return from Study Abroad

Rumana Hossain

Introduction and context

Bangladesh, a developing country, has made considerable progress in the advancement of women (Asian Development Bank 2010). Academic women, being highly intelligent and knowledgeable, are said to contribute greatly to the educational progression of a country as they play a plethora of roles inside and outside academia. This study captures the lived experiences of academic women who have won over the challenges to study overseas for an MA/PhD degree and are back in their professional lives to tell their stories of reintegration. What could have been a time of celebration of their achievements has turned out to be a struggle against the odds and constant compromises. The conservative culture, religious prejudices and predefined gender roles put these women at a disadvantage compared to women in developed countries (Morley and Crossouard 2014). Moreover, the prevailing neoliberal ideology has posed further difficulty and worsened their path to progression.

The conceptualization of religion in Bangladesh, a Muslim majority country, is problematic since its practices are adopted and modified in relation to patriarchal control and subordination of the female population (Hossain and Kusakabe 2005 as cited in Anwar 2015). The societal structure tends to idealize Bengali women as cherished and protected daughters, wives and mothers, whereas men are entrusted with safeguarding family honour through their control over female members (Kalam 2014). Roles assigned to males in society tend to be hierarchical in status and authority, which further marginalizes the position of women and stands as a barrier to empowerment. Domestic work, which comes with a branding of lower status, further lowers the value of women's work. In contrast, men enjoy the power advantage in family life, making important decisions and mitigating conflicts, while wives are left to decide on more domestic affairs like purchasing groceries, cooking and bearing children (Eagly 1987: 23).

Table 4.1 Details of Participating Women Academics

#	Name	Marital status	Discipline	MA/PhD	Years abroad	Years returned	Country studied	Interview on/at Year 2015
1	Haniya	Married with children	Social Sciences	MA + PhD	3	2	India + Aus	14/2 @ 4.00 pm
2	Nusaiba	Married with children	Social Sciences	MA	1	6	UK	2/2 @ 12.00 pm
3	Munia	Married with children	Arts	PhD	4	2	UK	06/2 @ 6.30 pm
4	Rashna	Married with children	STEM	PhD	6.5	4	USA	31/1 @ 10.00 am
5	Maria	Single	Business	MA	1.5	7	UK	08/2 @ 3.00 pm
6	Saba	Married with children	STEM	PhD	4.5	2	Aus	30/1 @ 11.30 am
7	Namira	Single	Arts	MA	1.5	5	USA	03/2 @ 11.45 pm
8	Sophia	Married with children	Arts	Dip + MA + PhD	6	2	Aus + UK + Aus	10/2 @ 2.30 pm
9	Neema	Married with children	STEM	PhD	4	2	UK	04/2 @ 11.45 am
10	Sabena	Single	Arts	MA	1	6	Aus	09/2 @ 2.00 pm
11	Sama	Married with children	Social Sciences	MA	2	5	USA	09/2 @ 10.30 am
12	Maisha	Married	Social Sciences	MA, MPhil + Incomp	1	8	UK	11/2 @ 11.30 am

In a society like this, education – especially higher education for women – was meant for the privileged section of society. In post-independence, Bangladesh's primary aim for female education was to train students into 'enlightened motherhood' (Chanana 1994). However, this policy was later reoriented as 'Education for All' (EFA) and the 'Female Stipend Programme' (FSP) in 1982, two arguably successful programmes (Ahmed and Hyndman-Rizk 2018). Thus, women taking up higher education and joining academia largely depended on the sociocultural belief system in which they grew up. This idea has been reinforced by Morley and Crossouard (2014) where family remains a prime factor in women's advancement in Asian countries. In the same line consideration of higher education abroad, or of building a career in academia, becomes a constraint for Bangladeshi women because of caregiving responsibilities. However, Ahad and Gunter (2017) add that a woman must have determination, strength of character and courage alongside the support of friends and family to move forward. The excerpts from the stories of the following academic women participants (see Table 4.1) illustrate these themes.

Guiding literature

To unpack the meaning of the women participants' experiences, I explore some significant work on women in academia, alongside the concepts of social role theory, the glass ceiling concept and neoliberal feminism. There has been a lack of substantive scholarship on the topic of women in academia in the region, except for larger comparative studies like Jayaweera (1997a, b) and Morley and Crossouard (2014). Morley and Crossouard (2014) report on the predefined social role of women in Asian countries, where women are expected to carry out the dual responsibilities of working outside *and* maintaining family life. The dominant gender roles, backed by religious orthodoxy, which states that women should not be in authoritative positions over men, place significant constraints on women's choices of career. This has also been reported in Kiaye and Singh's (2013) study of South African women and Ahmad, Fakhr and Ahmed's (2011) study of Pakistani women. Morley and Crossouard (2014) in their study on Asian international female students studying in the United States and New Zealand further report that those with family experience more difficulties on re-entry.

Brabant, Palmer and Gramling (1990), and Aiston and Jung (2015) reported similar findings that the women participants studying in the United States changed their values and feelings regarding interpersonal relationships and sexuality and became more liberal during their tenure abroad. Because of this, these women experienced problems readjusting to their families' more conservative values and lifestyles on return. Studies like Brown and Brown (2009) and Jung, Lee and Morales (2013) also report that women who develop a new gender role abroad find returning home to be more challenging, as their new identity becomes incompatible with the traditional gender role expectations of their society (i.e. returning from an individualist to a collectivist culture). In some recent PhD studies (e.g. Alandejani 2013; Almuarik 2019) based on the Saudi Arabian context (which holds very separate expectations of men and women), the major challenge for female participants was to meet social norms, specifically gender expectations, of their home country upon return. This same finding is echoed in Jung, Lee and Morales's (2013: 166) study of female Korean counselling professionals, that the hiring process in the country was discriminatory, and their struggle was further aggravated by the 'readjustment to the more traditional gender role expectation from the Korean society, which includes demanding responsibilities for childcare and maintaining households'. They further reported that this re-entry struggle applied to all professional women across cultures and societies, thus applying to the Bangladeshi women academics in this study.

In this connection, Eagly (1987) explains that members of certain social groups acquire common values and beliefs because of the pressure of socialization they are exposed to during their childhood. As a result, the roles of men and women in society have been segregated and are subject to different expectations. Labelling women as homemakers and men as breadwinners has created a clear distinction between the private and public spheres of life: women will work inside the house, and men will be responsible for connecting the outside world to internal family life. This type of social prejudice, which places an inappropriate share of domestic activities on women and leaving the outside work for men, is found in most traditional societies around the world, including Bangladesh.

In South Asian countries like India, Pakistan and Bangladesh, political leaders tend to exploit religion for political purposes and play with people's religious sentiments. As the conservative culture leads to labelling of feminists as rebels of religion, women's rights and equality issues continuously pass-through processes of progression and regression and fail to gain stability or momentum (Yasmeen 1991). In the same way, the dominant gender norm – that women should not be in authoritative positions over men – places significant constraints on women's choice of career, pointing to the fact that socioeconomic backgrounds and sociocultural belief systems have a huge impact on women in higher education (Morley and Crossouard 2014). In this connection, Ahad and Gunter (2017) find that as Bangladeshi universities, both public and private, are heavily influenced by politics, a woman not only has to be a scholar but also has to prove herself by navigating these politics, posing further difficulty for them. For example, there are only two women vice chancellors at the university level in Bangladesh, one at a women's private university, and the other in a public university ('JU Gets First Female VC' 2014). Even though the head of state – Sheikh Hasina – and the leader of the main opposition party – Begum Khaleda Zia – are women, Yasmeen (1991: 110) explains, 'prompted by a desire to retain power, these women operate within the parameters defined by society and resist questioning the traditional role models.' This conformist attitude of leaders ends up reinforcing the traditional image of women in society.

Another barrier to women is known as the glass ceiling, a term introduced in the 1970s and often referred to as the invisible barriers that women encounter in their career progression (Bombuwela and De Alwis 2013; Sharma and Sehrawat

2014). This concept has also been addressed by David and Woodward (1998: 15), as 'blocking their [women's] aspirations, allowing them to see where they might go, but stopping them from arriving there'. These barriers might be walls of traditions and cultural stereotypes, which prevent women from reaching their desired or deserved positions. Smith, Caputi and Crittenden (2012) state that women's glass ceiling beliefs have a negative impact on their subjective career success (e.g. job satisfaction, psychological well-being and happiness). However, Powell and Butterfield (2015), in their study on the glass ceiling twenty years ago, reported that the nature of glass ceilings has remained essentially stable over a twenty-year period because implications for organizational effectiveness have been widely ignored.

Now, academia is a place in the upper echelons of society, which is based on meritocracy, and it is not possible to exclude women from entering an area which is based on academic ability and achievement. David and Woodward (1998) point to the respondents of the book *Negotiating the Glass Ceiling* and report on sixteen eminent women participants working in higher education across the world who were raised in traditional families. These women grew up with the idea that a smooth transition from childhood to womanhood, leading to marriage and motherhood, was the accepted path for women, so the glass ceiling does not come as a surprise. As similar social constructs exist in Bangladesh, women grow up with the idea that no matter what they become, eventually they are to get married and raise their family. Having access to teaching roles or academia might be viewed as the most convenient profession as it is a respectable job that permits some degree of flexibility. However, to sustain the position, self-determination and courage remain requirements, alongside the support of friends and family (Ahad and Gunter 2017).

Lastly, a pervading neoliberal ethos seems to have an overarching impact on women's experience in higher education. The third wave of feminism that tended to exclude unsuccessful weaker women to encompass only aspirational women blended well with the existing neoliberal ideology. Fraser (2013: 220) suggests that 'second-wave feminism, by forfeiting the demand for economic redistribution, ended up serving as a key enabler for "the new spirit of neoliberalism"'. Feminism in the third wave thus encountered 'neoliberal initiatives of deregulation, privatization, and marketization as a social force' and found itself 'discursively co-opted' (Prügl 2015: 617). However, neoliberal feminism emerged from the false belief that women are equal to men in every way and that they are free to choose any course of action just as men do (Sebastian 2015). Brown (2003) earlier reported similar findings as Baker (2010: 187), who adds '[t]he influential and pervasive ideology of neoliberalism intensifies the fascination with an individuated self-hood' that creates a belief that being an autonomous, self-reflexive individual, with self-interest and a sound rationale will be adequate to conceive the existing social and economic world'.

Neoliberal feminism thus metamorphosed all ideas into personal and individualized terms and shook hands with the values that 'portraying people as atomised individuals allows social problems to be framed as individual failures'

(Brabazon 2021: para 13). This concept of individualism and working together towards one's own improvement is also reported in studies on professional women, for example Meyers (2013), Valian (2005) and Rose (1990). Interestingly, the majority of modern and educated women find this agenda to be reasonable and logical (Rottenberg 2014a). Ahmed (2017), in her significant feminist work on coloured women in academia, suggests that women are constantly subject to patriarchal domination politically, economically, socially and psychologically. Women are generally aware of the prevailing hierarchical status of their male partners/colleagues, and they do seem to respect the imposed social discourse. Even these so-called *empowered* women often start viewing their gender *as a restriction of possibility* as they start navigating the restrictions imposed by society.

This discussion on the condition of academic women in Bangladeshi society leads to these research questions:

1. What common experiences did academic women have on return from study abroad?
2. In what ways were academic women challenged and did they manage to build on their resilience?

Methodology

The underexplored phenomenon of return experiences of women academics deserves 'a complex, detailed understanding' (Creswell 2013: 48) that can only be established by talking to the returnees directly, going to their homes or workplaces and providing them with open spaces to tell their stories without any expectations for the findings. For this study, semi-structured interviews were conducted with twelve female returnee academics working in a wide range of disciplines, from various public and private institutions in Bangladesh, within two to seven years of return from study abroad (the belief that it takes a while for the initial euphoria of homecoming to wear off and the reality of the home environment to set in).

Purposive sampling methods and snowball strategies, as well as convenience strategy (Miles and Huberman 1994), were undertaken to recruit participants who were broadly chosen from the capital city of Dhaka. One facilitating factor in this research was that the interviewer-researcher and the interviewees shared common backgrounds in terms of social identity (occupation, nationality and study abroad experience). This work was also based upon an insider's perspective, attesting further authenticity of the elicited data. Moreover, the researcher being mid-study and devoid of return experience 'bracketed' her from the experienced returnee participants (Marshall and Rossman 2006; Moustakas 1994).

A practice interview was conducted initially that enabled the testing of the research applicability to determine any arising difficulties and to make any required modifications to the research plan and interview schedule (Yin 2009). Ethical approval to conduct the study and protect the rights of the participants was obtained following the code of ethical practice for research, followed by informed consent from the respondents before conducting the interviews (Patton 2002). The participants were reassured that their personal information and the recordings of the interviews would be kept secure and be used for research purposes only and that their identities would remain *incognito,* as pseudonyms would be assigned to protect their identity and privacy (Braun and Clarke 2013; Creswell 2013). As semi-structured interviews are verifiable tools for allowing participants to share their thoughts and opinions related to the research topic (Yin 2009), they allowed the flexibility to follow emerging topics and directions elaborated by the interviewees (Mears 2009). The interviewees were given the scope to decide whether they wished to talk about reintegration on a professional or personal level. The follow-up questions/prompts in the interview schedule were used only when the participants had not touched on the points themselves.

In line with Creswell's (2013) recommendations, the face-to-face interviews took place in safe and mutually agreed-upon locations, either at the participant's workplace or home. All the interviews were carried out in Bengali, the participants' mother tongue, and were recorded and transcribed right after the interview, translating relevant sections of the transcripts. An inductive approach, a process of coding the data 'without trying to let it fit into a pre-existing coding frame' (Braun and Clarke 2006: 83), was adopted and thematic analysis done. The researcher tried to be as reflexive and transparent as possible in reporting and representing the interview data (Mann 2010) to avoid over-reliance on recurring themes and losing some very significant themes which did not appear repeatedly in the interviews (Pavlenko 2007). In putting together all the themes and evidence, the data sets were interpreted by 'abstracting out beyond the codes and themes to the larger meaning of the data' to make sense of it (Creswell 2013: 187). While doing this I became as reflexive and transparent as possible in reporting and representing the interview data (Mann 2010). My interpretation thus became a combination of my personal views and social constructs such as neoliberalism, neoliberal feminism and social role theory.

Findings and discussion

The interviews uncovered some fascinating details of Bangladeshi women academics' return experiences. When asked to narrate their experience on return, the majority of female participants (eleven out of twelve participants) chose to speak about their family reintegration first and then their professional reintegration. They were torn between what to prioritize – career or family – either prior to going or on return from study abroad. Despite being the so-called 'empowered' women in academia, the feelings shared by the participants suggest that they view their gender 'as a restriction of possibility' (Ahmed 2017: 7). The experience of the women academics clearly shows that they are subject to patriarchal domination politically, economically, socially and psychologically.

Effect of prevalent discourses on female academics' return experience

> My children had a life in Sydney, we did have some quality time despite my studies. They went to the beaches, went cycling, swimming and also enjoyed weekend shopping. Now their life has become limited to homework, class tests, more and more studies. With all these they have lots of frustration. As a mother I have to deal with those frustrations. It was tough. After two years they have sort of settled down but still my daughter cries every now and then for Australia. (Sophia)

During the interview, the female respondents started with discussing their families and the struggle associated with their choice to study abroad. Participants Nusaiba, Sama, Saba and Munia expressed their guilt because they either had to separate from their children/family or, despite having their children with them, could not give them sufficient time due to their study pressure. For most of the returnees with children, social security turned out to be a big issue. Children's expectations about their education and social life were greatly raised by their time abroad. Consequently, they were the ones who were forced to make serious compromises to come to terms with their new social environments. Parents, like participants Sophia, Hania and Nima, who were more or less aware of the situation at home, went through real hardships trying to make this transition as smooth as possible for their children. However, what these parents failed to realize is that children were much more involved in their decision to go abroad than they initially thought.

Effect of existing social stigma

> The scenario changed as soon as I came back to Dhaka. You cannot move without a car. You need to come back home by 6.00 pm. If I am late by 15 minutes mom calls up and asks for reasons. Who am I going out with? When? Who's coming? I went back to my childhood days. (Namira)

Of the twelve female participant academics, the unmarried four who went abroad to pursue their MA degrees had to get married immediately on return because of parental pressure arising out of the fear of social stigma. The existing social discourse of getting a daughter married before she becomes highly educated and starts thinking of herself as a liberated woman, raising her voice on equality and progression, pushed Namira, Sara and Maria to get married soon after their return. When Namira went to the United States to pursue her MA studies, she received full support from her mother. She won the Outstanding MA Thesis of the Year award and could have started her PhD immediately. But she was homesick and returned this time as a self-dependent person managing things on her own. By the time she returned she found her mother fully influenced by existing social stigma:

'you are becoming too educated. You have started thinking too highly of yourself' and so on. Adding fuel to the fire, other female relatives joined in:

> Your daughter has already started working in a university and has also done an MA from abroad. Why don't you get her married now? If not now, then when the hell would you get her married?

Namira tried dating her fiancé for a while but her mom wanted to marry her off right away. This time the social stigma of an unmarried girl moving around with her fiancé in a conservative society made her mother force her into marriage within a month. At the time of conducting the interview she was in the horns of a dilemma:

> When I got married my husband worked in Singapore. I took a year's leave to stay with him in Singapore. I also studied and taught there. But I do not know where we are heading next. He wants to go to UK. I want to go to USA. We have to settle midway. But this is where I am now.

Sabina, another participant, did her MA in the UK before she got married but is now thinking of Malaysia as an alternative destination for her PhD studies because her husband does not want to move far from their home country. All these female academics are liberated, as in educated and economically independent academic women, who have eventually conformed to 'man-made' implicit societal norms, sometimes in the form of societal pressure or their partner's choice of destination.

The married female academics, like Nusaiba, Munia, Sofia and Sama, who had to leave their spouses behind, continued to feel guilty about separating the family or uprooting the spouse from their settled profession to join their venture abroad. This feeling of guilt reflects their gendered social role (Eagly 1987), as women are expected to be at home looking after their families. The difficult decisions relating to maintaining a work-family balance lie entirely on her shoulders, for which respondent Nusaiba is seen to blame the overtly socializing culture of the country, such as unnotified social visits by friends and relatives, social gatherings and family commitments. Nusaiba's husband refrained from helping her with the decision to go abroad for her PhD by remaining silent, Namira's and Sabina's compromise in choosing study abroad destinations and Maria left hanging in her decision to go abroad for her PhD owing to an unsupportive family reinforce the same issue. Neema and Munia in this regard made a smart move by choosing the UK as their study destination as their husbands were already pursuing their studies there or had offers to study.

What is striking in this regard is that the majority of the women respondents in this study expressed their gratitude for the support they received from their spouses, family or in-laws in the process of gaining their overseas qualifications. They seemed to nurture the feeling of guilt within themselves that they had prioritized their profession and acknowledged that without support they would not be in the position that they are in. Munia says:

> I will never be able to forget my husband's contribution to my studies. He helped me out a lot. When I went for fieldwork, I could not give time to my daughter. My mom and other family members took care of her. This was a huge support for me.

Moreover, the women academics seemed aware of the prevailing hierarchical status of the male partners and seemed to respect the imposed social discourse. They seemed to believe that 'dismantling the world that is built to accommodate only some bodies' is after all a rather impractical job (Ahmed 2017: 14). Another respondent, Maisha – like Namira and Sabina – had to get married immediately on the completion of her MA degree from the UK. However, the marriage did not work out and she had to get a divorce within nine months. Apart from the psychological distress due to the far-reaching bitterness of the separation, she became subject to gender discrimination from her male colleagues at her workplace. The stigma associated with a broken marriage followed her everywhere as the prevailing conservative culture tends to denounce divorce and holds women responsible for the separation. Moreover, men around her tried to make a pass at her. Maisha shared her steps to combat this stigma:

> After my divorce, the blow did not come from my department, but the university as a whole started pointing the finger at me that I am available. People started passing comments behind my back. I joined politics just to establish an identity for myself after that.

Maisha might be the only participant who tried to stand tall against male advances. She might have figured that the only way she could avoid this male intrusion into her privacy was to have a strong position inside the university backed by political affiliation.

Participant Rashna adds another interesting dimension to how men wish to view women in Bangladeshi society. She found on her return that people still like to comment on women as a body/showpiece rather than a female professional. Her sharing of these episodes stands as evidence that she has never been asked about her work or research on return:

> Since you asked me about my experience, I have given you all this information. Otherwise, I would not have said these things publicly. And nobody wants to know what happened on return. What they want to know is why have I put on so much weight? You have become fairer/darker/why have you shortened your hair? They do not ask what have you gained from your study abroad? What was your area of research?

Once again women were identified by physical attributes in place of their intellectual blossoming, despite being members of the upper echelons of society as academia.

Glass ceiling as responsibility for work-family life balance hangs on women

> You are not getting any firm assurance from your family. The husband doesn't say you go or go ahead. He says do whatever you wish to. Or who's gonna look

after your kid? So if you are not receiving proper support, how would you go to study overseas? (Maria)

For participant Maria, there seemed to be no scope for a mutual decision on her PhD abroad as her husband became unresponsive when she insisted. In her case the male partner expected the female partner to decide that she would sacrifice the opportunity and abandon the idea of higher studies for the family's sake, reinforcing the theme of work-family life balance lying entirely on women's shoulders.

The female academics thereby were seen to be torn between whether to prioritize family or career – and in most cases, it turned out to be family. Sama went to the United States for her studies but could only decide to go when her parents volunteered to look after her baby. She went to the United States; the husband was in a different district while her baby was with her parents in another. She said:

Just imagine my condition, the struggle I had been through. My whole life was shattered in taking this decision to go abroad to study.

On her return, Sama decided not to apply for her PhD in the next few years to protect the family from the trauma of separation again. Participants like Nusaiba and Maria went through the same mental ordeal while deciding what to prioritize because their husbands were not keen on their spouses' higher education and/or career progression. Respondent Nusaiba stood first place in her MA exam and completed a second MA from the UK with a prestigious scholarship. She had to leave her child with her parents during her MA abroad. She is now thinking of abandoning her plans of a PhD not only because of her son's education but also because of insecurity related to her partner:

Well, this is such a struggle. It is like fighting against the wind. You are leaving your spouse behind and heading towards uncertainty. By the time you are back, you really do not know whether you will come back to the same person. Divorces are becoming quite common these days.

Despite all the progress, the experiences of the female respondents like Namira, Maria and Sabina suggest that restrictive gender roles and glass ceilings still permeate higher education in Bangladesh. As a result, some participants, like Namira, Sabina, Maria and Mala, have fallen prey to gender stereotyping and the fear of being negatively evaluated if they try to cross certain boundaries or break the glass ceiling, like the participants in Wesarat and Mathew (2017), Sharif (2015), and Kiaye and Singh (2013).

The participants of this study attempted to break the glass ceiling by overcoming the hurdles associated with the decision to study overseas. However, on their return, the pre-existing social roles made them vulnerable again. They once again started to feel the presence of the glass ceiling above them. Owing to the existing cultural and religious discourses, the future of their career progression then relied on their partner or family's decision. As a result, these academic women were equally vulnerable to shaming and labelling as good or bad depending on their mannerisms and behaviour, just like any other women in the country. Moreover, with every attempt to break it, the ceiling seemed to move higher for many of them, as seen in the experiences of Maria, Nusaiba and Namira. The shaming and labelling are evident in the broken marriage of Mala, the indecisiveness regarding further studies or prioritizing family issues for Nusaiba, Sabina and Namira, and the lack of family support for Maria. People judging Rashna on her appearance on return, rather than her academic pursuits and achievements, was another example of how sections of society still prioritize the looks of a woman over her educational qualifications.

Women's voice against institutional injustice

But after coming back home that level crashed drastically. It takes months to finish the same amount of work that I used to finish within weeks. The reason is that I have so many responsibilities here apart from my studies. This was like the first blow on return.

Nusaiba explains that despite leaving her husband and son behind during her time abroad for her MA, her level of productivity was very high. The same is echoed by Sabina when she says that academics usually come back strongly motivated to contribute and continue research. However, on return the academics' motivation gradually diminishes because of various social ties; as Sabina says, 'we are dragged down by too many social commitments.'

These women academics, compared to their mothers' generation, are liberated women, as they could avail the opportunity to advance their careers, for which they expressed their gratitude to their spouse and family. They attempted to remain strong in their disposition and were trying to frame a positive picture of themselves in the eyes of the researcher. This show of positivity against all odds is an indication of how complicit they are in their submission to the ongoing male hegemony. From their statements, the majority of the female academics seem to have witnessed the glass ceiling in the form of hostility from colleagues, institutions and/or unsupportive family, and embraced their positions to remain under the glass ceiling.

Neoliberal impact on feminism and experience of returnee women academics

Central to all feminist activity is the goal of changing the world by achieving gender equality. Patriarchal norms have been ingrained in Bangladeshi society in such a way that gender equality seems a far cry. Moreover, what can be discerned from some of the respondents' stories is that their academic identities developed an inherent connection to current neoliberal measures and the neoliberal values of production, consumption and competition. In this connection, Rottenberg (2014a) mentions works like Slaughter (2012) and Sandberg (2013), both of whom included a new 'discursive register' (Rottenberg 2014b: 418); a feminist subject who accepts full responsibility for her well-being and maintains a balanced work-family life. The participant academics seem to act as feminist subjects unknowingly, as they seem to embrace the idea that they really are not at a disadvantage as they can choose to further their career and study abroad. Notwithstanding the struggles they have been through, they have internalized the neoliberal belief that their success or failure depended on their individual selves, positivity, resilience and adaptability to situations (Brown 2003). They disclosed their struggle but acknowledged that they never attempted to raise their voice against such discrepancies.

Moreover, the majority (nine out of twelve) of the women academic participants in this study attempted to portray themselves as being 'positive' people. However, in the case of participants Maria and Nusaiba, this positivity was juxtaposed by words suggesting the glass ceiling (David and Woodward 1998; Sharif 2015; Wesarat and Mathew 2017). Despite facing countless difficulties, none of the academic women wanted to portray themselves as victims, nor did they wish to assert themselves as being disadvantaged or treated unfairly because of society, religion or gender issues. Rather, their stories speak of exposure to the prevailing neoliberal ethos that Bangladeshi society has progressed: that men and women are playing on the same ground and they have greater options and more freedom than women of previous generations to choose their trajectory (Baker 2010: 190). They attempted to position themselves as having 'highly individualistic selfhood, voluntaristic, intentional behaviour and choice' (Baker 2010: 190), similarly to the Australian respondents in Baker's study who were attempting to live up to neoliberal values and evade any notion of vulnerability.

Pervading neoliberal ideology coinciding with neoliberal feminist beliefs has pushed some of these female academics towards gradual submission to patriarchy and societal pressure in place of developing resilience. The female academics, whose general predisposition was to 'work hard' and 'do well' in their professional lives, blended perfectly with the neoliberal 'demands for autonomous self-motivating, responsibilised subjects' (Gill 2010: 241). As a result, participants like Nusaiba, Neema and Namira, who are working in their own spaces in their respective institutions, may be trying to remain content with whatever they have achieved, without the consciousness that there are other female professionals around them who feel the same way. With the exception of respondent Mala, none of the participants made any attempts to uphold their agency or assert their academic status.

These neoliberal subjects (individual), that is the participant women academics, have apparently without even realizing muted themselves regarding their struggles in this way (Rottenberg 2014a). Neoliberal discourses have closed down the space available for articulating any sense of unfairness or oppression in social relations and women's claim for equal rights and opportunities. If these highly educated women accept this position of being the lesser halves, then ensuring gender equality and inclusion, the fifth of the seventeen sustainable development goals set by the United Nations (United Nations Development Programme 2015), will be difficult to attain even in meritocratic academia.

Way forward

The revelation of this study calls for targeted support for female academics. The female returnees like Nusaiba, Neema and Namira, who adhered to predefined sociocultural gender roles (Eagly 1987), seemed to be suffering alone post-return from study abroad. Because of the predefined gender roles, the women academics were already stressed about pursuing their careers. On top of this, neoliberal values advocate for women to concentrate on being autonomous, strong and independent individuals rather than focusing on changing society or addressing societal injustice (see Sandberg 2013). The female participants in this study seemed to have accepted that they *'cannot have it all'* (Slaughter 2012) and abandoned thoughts of becoming changemakers. This study strongly reiterates the need to ensure gender equality and inclusion. Cases like Nusaiba and Maria only aggravate individual suffering and add to the nation's loss of intellectual faculty. To initiate the end of the 'silent suffering' of these highly educated women – who should be trailblazers in their respective areas – and to work towards empowering more and more women, this study recommends an active institute/centre for women under the University Grants Commission to ensure gender equality in academia. Well-planned social awareness programmes depicting the everyday struggle women professionals undergo could be initiated from this centre. The lived experiences of the female participants tell us that the country is in need of a more united, stronger feminist movement to bring changes that prompt gender equality and social justice.

References

Ahad, L. R. and H. Gunter (2017), 'Women in Leader Roles within Higher Education in Bangladesh', *Management in Education*, 31 (3): 135–40.

Ahmad, M. S., Z. Fakhr and J. Ahmed (2011), 'Working Women Work-life Conflict', *Business Strategy Series*, 12 (6): 289–302.

Ahmed, R. and N. Hyndman-Rizk (2018), 'The Higher Education Paradox: Towards Improving Women's Empowerment, Agency Development and Labour Force Participation in Bangladesh', *Gender and Education*. Available online: https://doi.org/10.1080/09540253.2018.1471452 (accessed 1 January 2020).

Ahmed, S. (2017), *Living a Feminist Life*, Durham, NC: Duke University Press.

Aiston, S. J. and J. Jung (2015), 'Women Academics and Research Productivity: An International Comparison', *Gender and Education*, 27 (3): 205–20.

Alandejani, J. (2013), 'Coming Home After Studying Abroad: How Saudi Female Scholars Re-adapt, Re-adjust, and Transfer Their Knowledge', PhD diss., Colorado State University, USA.

Almuarik, G. S. (2019), 'A Qualitative Study of Saudi PhD Returnees' Readjustment Experience: Their Perceptions and Impressions', PhD diss., Newcastle University, UK.

Anwar, T. (2015), 'The Bangladeshi Perspective: The Case of Married Academic Women Pursuing Foreign Degrees', MA diss., Carleton University, Canada. Available online: https://curve.carleton.ca/system/files/etd/4e962962-805b-45a3-aeef-4377e76e6b25/etd _pdf/7cc1d8e622524f70d852d7dd33c2984c/anwar-thebangladeshiperspectivethecas eofmarried_r.pdf (accessed 1 Feb 2018).

Asian Development Bank (2010), 'Country Gender Assessment Bangladesh'. Available online: https://www.adb.org/sites/default/files/institutional-document/31338/cga -women-bangladesh.pdf (accessed 30 November 2016).

Baker, J. (2010), 'Claiming Volition and Evading Victimhood: Post-Feminist Obligations for Young Women', *Feminism and Psychology*, 20 (2): 186–204.

Bombuwela, P. M. and A. C. De Alwis (2013), 'Effects of Glass Ceiling on Women's Career Development in Private Sector Organisations—Case of Sri Lanka', *Journal of Competitiveness*, 5 (2): 3–19.

Brabant, S., C. E. Palmer and R. Gramling (1990), 'Returning Home: An Empirical Investigation of Cross-cultural Re-entry', *International Journal of Intercultural Relations*, 14: 387–404.

Brabazon, H. (2021), 'The Academy's Neoliberal Response to COVID-19: Why Faculty Should be Wary and How We Can Push Back', *Academic Matters*. Available online: https://academicmatters.ca/the-academys-neoliberal-response-to-covid-19-why -faculty-should-be-wary-and-how-we-can-push-back/ (accessed 30 November 2021).

Braun, V. and V. Clarke (2006), 'Using Thematic Analysis in Psychology', *Qualitative Research in Psychology*, 3 (2): 77–101.

Braun, V. and V. Clarke (2013), *Successful Qualitative Research: A Practical Guide for Beginners*, London: Sage.

Brown, L. and J. Brown (2009), 'Out of Chaos, Into a New Identity', *Existential Analysis: Journal of the Society for Existential Analysis*, 20 (2): 341–61.

Brown, W. (2003), 'Neo-liberalism and the End of Liberal Democracy', *Theory and Event*, 7 (1): 1–19.

Chanana, K. (1994), 'Social Change or Social Reform: Women, Education and Family in Preindependence India', in C. Mukhopadhyay, C. Chapnik and S. Seymour (eds), *Women, Education and Family Structure in India*, 35–8, Boulder, CO: Westview Press.

Creswell, J. W. (2013), *Qualitative Inquiry and Research Design: Choosing Among Five Traditions*, 3rd edn, Thousand Oaks, CA: Sage.

David, M. and D. Woodward, eds (1998), *Negotiating the Glass Ceiling: Careers of Senior Women in the Academic World*, London: Falmer Press.

Eagly, A. H. (1987), *Sex Differences in Social Behavior: A Social-role Interpretation*, Hillsdale, MI: Lawrence Erlbaum.

Fraser, N. (2013), *Fortunes of Feminism: From State-managed Capitalism to Neoliberal Crisis*, London: Verso Books.

Gill, R. (2010), 'Breaking the Silence: Hidden Injuries of the Neoliberal University', in R. Ryan-Flood and R. Gill (eds), *Secrecy and Silence in the Research Process: Feminist Reflections*, 228–44, Oxford: Routledge.

Jayaweera, S. (1997a), 'Higher Education and the Economic and Social Empowerment of Women – The Asian Experience', *Compare*, 27 (3): 245–61.

Jayaweera, S. (1997b), 'Women, Education and Empowerment in Asia', *Gender and Education*, 9 (4): 411–24.

'JU Gets First Female VC' (2014), *bdnews24.com*, 2 March. Available online: https:// bdnews24.com/campus/2014/03/02/ju-gets-first-female-vc (accessed 23 February 2018).

Jung, A., H. Lee and A. Morales (2013), 'Wisdom from Korean Re-entry Counseling Professionals: A Phenomenological Study of the Re-entry Process', *International Journal for the Advancement of Counselling*, 35 (3): 153–71.

Kalam, A. (2014), 'Social Norms and Impediments of Women Development in Bangladesh', *International Journal of Social Science Studies*, 2 (2): 100–9.

Kiaye, R. E. and A. M. Singh (2013), 'The Glass Ceiling: A Perspective of Women Working in Durban', *Gender in Management: An International Journal*, 28 (1): 28–42.

Mann, S. (2010), 'A Critical Review of Qualitative Interviews in Applied Linguistics', *Applied Linguistics*, 32 (1): 6–24.

Marshall, C. and G. B. Rossman (2006), *Designing Qualitative Research*, 4th edn, London: Sage.

Mears, C. (2009), *Interviewing for Education and Social Science Research: The Gateway Approach*, Basingstoke: Palgrave Macmillan.

Meyers, M. (2013), 'The War on Academic Women: Reflections on Postfeminism in the Neoliberal Academy', *Journal on Communication Inquiry*, 37 (4): 274–83.

Miles, M. B. and A. M. Huberman (1994), *Qualitative Data Analysis: An Expanded Sourcebook*, 2nd edn, London: Sage Publications, Inc.

Morley, L. and B. Crossouard (2014), *Women in Higher Education Leadership in South Asia: Rejection, Refusal, Reluctance, Revisioning*, University of Sussex Center for Higher Education and Equity Research. Available online: https://www .empowerwomen.org/en/resources/documents/2015/10/women-in-higher-education -leadership-in-south-asia-rejection-refusal-reluctance-revisioning?lang=en (accessed 10 February 2018).

Moustakas, C. (1994), *Phenomenological Research Methods*, Thousand Oaks, CA: Sage.

Patton, M. (2002), *Qualitative Evaluation and Research Methods*, London: Sage.

Pavlenko, A. (2007), 'Autobiographic Narratives as Data in Applied Linguistics', *Applied Linguistics*, 28 (2): 163–88.

Powell, G. N. and D. A. Butterfield (2015), 'The Glass Ceiling: What Have We Learned 20 Years On?' *Journal of Organizational Effectiveness: People and Performance*, 2 (4): 306–26.

Prügl, E. (2015), 'Neoliberalising Feminism', *New Political Economy*, 20 (4): 614–31.

Rose, N. (1990), *Governing the Soul: The Shaping of the Private Self*, London: Routledge.

Rottenberg, C. (2014a), 'Happiness and the Liberal Imagination: How Superwoman Became Balanced', *Feminist Studies*, 40 (1): 144–68.

Rottenberg, C. (2014b), 'The Rise of Neoliberal Feminism', *Cultural Studies*, 28 (3): 418–37.

Sandberg, S. (2013), *Lean In: Women, Work and the Will to Lead*, New York: Alfred A. Knopf.

Sebastian, M. (2015), 'Why Moderate Feminism is Just as Bad as Radical Feminism' (Blog), Return of Kings. Available online: www.returnofkings.com/69531/why -moderate-feminism-is-just-as-bad-as-radical-feminism (accessed 08 January 2018).

Sharif, M. Y. (2015), 'Glass Ceiling, the Prime Driver of Women Entrepreneurship in Malaysia: A Phenomenological Study of Women Lawyers', *Procedia – Social and Behavioural Sciences*, 169: 329–36.

Sharma, S. and P. Sehrawat (2014), 'Glass Ceiling for Women: Does it Exist in the Modern India?', *Journal of Organization and Human Behaviour*, 3 (2–3): 9–15.

Slaughter, A. M. (2012), 'Why Women Still Can't Have It All', *The Atlantic*, 2012 Issue. Available online: https://www.theatlantic.com/magazine/archive/2012/07/why-women -still-cant-have-it-all/309020/ (accessed 10 February 2018).

Smith, P., P. Caputi and N. Crittenden (2012), 'How are Women's Glass Ceiling Beliefs Related to Career Success?', *Career Development International*, 17 (5): 458–74.

United Nations Development Programme (2015), 'Gender Inequality Index'. Available online: http://hdr.undp.org/en/content/table-4-gender-inequality-index (accessed 25 February 2018).

Valian, V. (2005), 'Beyond Gender Schemas: Improving the Advancement of Women in Academia', *Hypatia*, 20 (3): 198–213.

Wesarat, P. and J. Mathew (2017), 'Theoretical Framework of Glass Ceiling: A Case of India's Women Academic Leaders', *Paradigm*, 21 (1): 21–30.

Yasmeen, S. (1991), 'Hearing the Difference: Pakistani Feminism', *Asian Studies Review*, 15 (1): 108–10.

Yin, R. K. (2009), *Case Study Research: Design and Method*, 4th edn, Thousand Oaks, CA: Sage.

Chapter 5

Exploring Black Women Academics' Experiences in English Universities Using Critical Race Theory

Janice Johnson, Christina Schwabenland and Uvanney Maylor

Introduction

Black women remain the most marginalized and socially disadvantaged group working in academic posts within universities in England. For example, while Black people represent 3.3 per cent of the UK total population (ONS 2021), only 1.8 per cent of academic staff are Black; 0.2 per cent are senior academics and 0.06 per cent are professors (HESA 2021). Of that 0.06 per cent, twenty-five are Black women (HESA 2021). Thus, Black women remain significantly under-represented in terms of the total numbers of academic staff and seniority and progression, with a greater proportion of Black men achieving higher positions than Black women, despite the gap in numbers between men and women being minimal (HESA 2021).

The ethnic composition of English universities reflects a history of racial inequality and, although widening participation policies have had significant effect on reducing the under-representation of Black and minority ethnic students, they have had much less effect on reducing inequalities among staff (ECU 2015). Current research does not help us significantly in understanding these inequalities and/or why they continue to exist. As research into gender representation tends to focus primarily on white women while research into Black experiences concentrates predominantly on Black men, Black women are consequently left to fall in the cracks between the two (Mirza 2008).

This chapter makes a theoretical and empirical contribution to increasing our understanding about the ways in which working in higher education is experienced on a day-to-day basis by Black women academics working in England. According to Saperstein and Penner (2014), being Black means anyone having known Black ancestry. However, we accept that there are many differences between Black people. We use this term inclusively within this study, in reference to people who are descended through one or both parents from Africa or the Caribbean. Our study draws on critical race theory, which provides a framework for theorizing, examining and challenging the ways in which race can affect practice (Yosso 2005). Our findings reveal that race and racism are more salient than gender in the participants' lived experiences and provide an insight into the multilayered ways in which the frequency and depth of racism is experienced and routinely perpetuated in English higher education institutions (HEIs). We begin by outlining our theoretical framework, followed by the research study and findings and conclude by discussing the implications of our findings.

Critical race theory (CRT)

CRT was developed in the United States in the 1970s as an offshoot of critical legal studies to theorize the slow pace of racial reform (Delgado 1995). The CRT framework is based on a set of six assumptions or 'tenets' about the nature of racism and the ways in which it is socially constructed, reproduced and challenged. CRT's foundational proposition, enshrined in *tenet one*, is that racism is an everyday occurrence and endemic in American society, which 'mutates and multiplies creating a range of racisms' (Bell 2008: 624). Racism can be defined as 'culturally sanctioned beliefs, which regardless of the intentions involved defend the advantages Whites have because of the subordinated positions of racial minorities' (Wellman 1977, cited in Ladson-Billings and Tate 1995: 55). Tenet one further suggests that status, privilege and power are allocated by race, and because racism is pervasive, it is often deeper, invisible, more insidious than commonly recognized and considered normal and permanent (Delgado 1995; Ladson-Billings 1998). *Tenet two: Whiteness as property* relies upon a unique set of benefits, privileges, power, access and ideological commitments associated with whiteness and to which value is attached. Moreover, white over colour ascendancy serves important purposes for this group. White skin and whiteness are considered exclusive forms of private property, which must be 'constantly affirmed, legitimated and protected' (Harris 1993, cited in Donnor 2013: 195). *Tenet three: Counter storytelling and majoritarian narratives* is a means of amplifying and celebrating silenced voices. Counter storytelling allows minority ethnic groups to share their stories/ experiences. Storytelling is also used to analyse the myths and un-evidenced narratives suppressing Black people by providing understanding, sensitivity to and interpretations of their accounts (DeCuir and Dixson 2004). *Tenet four: Interest convergence* proposes that the interests of Black people achieving race equality will only be considered or tolerated when they converge with interests of white people in exceptional conditions. Interest convergence is the place where the interests of whites and non-whites intersect (Ladson-Billings 1998). Since racism advances the interests of whites, large segments of society have little incentive to eradicate it. *Tenet five: Critique of liberalism* challenges the neoliberalist traditional claims of, for example, legal neutrality, objectivity, colour-blindness and meritocracy as camouflages for the self-interest of dominant groups in society. Notably, critiques of racism inherently involve critiques of liberalism (Ladson-Billings and Tate 1995). *Tenet six: Intersectionality* proposes that no person has a single, easily stated unitary identity. Rather, identities are multiple and the ways they intersect require examination of race, sex, class, national origin, sexual orientation and other identity factors to understand how multiple identities play out in various settings

(Crenshaw 1991; Delgado and Stefancic 2012). An intersectional lens allows an inward critique of identity at the intersections between, for example, gender, race and class. Intersectionality as a framework captures the complexities of everyday life and identity more completely and accurately linking individual, interpersonal and social structural domains of experience (Crenshaw 1991). In short, CRT challenges the deficit view of colour and race as a disadvantage and instead focuses our attention on the cultural richness of the knowledge(s), skills and abilities of minority groups that racism acts to obscure (Yosso 2005).

CRT in English HEIs

The application of CRT has primarily been used to develop understanding about discrimination in educational contexts in the United States. Since the mid-2000s CRT has been utilized in the UK, despite the education systems in the United States and England having very different histories. Gillborn (2006, 2008), who has used CRT to study race and racism in English schools, argues that CRT's underlying assumptions and insights can be usefully transferred to the UK. This view is shared by researchers such as Warmington (2014), who used CRT to research Black British intellectuals, Housee (2008), who explored the experiences of Black lecturers in English universities, and Brah and Phoenix (2004), who investigated racial experiences in universities.

CRT values experiential knowledge and is therefore useful in understanding and providing meanings to Black women's experiences in universities (Maylor 2009). The use of voice is central to naming one's own reality and is a way that CRT links form and substance in Black scholarship (Delgado 1995). The Black voice proves challenging to the oppressor or prevailing group that seeks to justify its power with their own narratives, constructing reality in ways to maintain their privilege, regarding other experiences as outliers (Rocco, Bernier and Bowman 2014). By utilizing CRT to analyse Black women's experiences, the discussion about race in universities is made broader and deeper, not just focused on an analysis of racism alone.

Sharing stories opens possibilities for providing minorities with a forum for voice and expression, which provides greater self-insight and understanding. Stories have the capacity to reveal that others also have similar experiences and through these stories can communicate to white colleagues about things they are unlikely to know. An exchange of stories from teller to listener can thus help overcome ethnocentrism and the dysconscious conviction that there is only one way to view the world. In naming their experiences of discrimination, discrimination can be opposed, and if it is socially constructed it should also be capable of being deconstructed (Delgado and Stefancic 2012). Thus, storytelling helps the tellers to make more sense of their own story of experienced oppression and inequities, minimizing mental anguish and blame from being suffered in silence (Delgado and Stefancic 2012; Ladson-Billings and Tate 1995).

Using a CRT approach provides insight into how power and politics are being used in English HEIs to further divergence, locating Black women within the transformations and struggles taking place (Robertson 2010). Central to this chapter, therefore, is exploring the pervasiveness of racism and thus the engagement specifically with CRT tenets one, two and three in identifying the layered ways in which racism has influenced the participants' lived academic experiences.

Methodology

This chapter draws on a larger doctoral, qualitative study of seventeen Black women's experiences working in English HEIs. The study concentrated on women academics in teaching rather than in research intensive HEIs because such institutions tend to recruit greater numbers of students and staff from Black and minority ethnic backgrounds (Advance HE 2020). The participants were identified through snowball sampling, which facilitated the recruitment of Black women academics from a range of teaching HEIs. Participants had to be of African or Caribbean origin. It was not important whether they were born in the UK or not, simply that they shared this heritage. Participants were academics on permanent open-ended contracts (not visiting or hourly paid lecturers), so they were fully immersed in daily university life.

A qualitative approach was used and was more relevant (than a quantitative study) in making visible the experiences of Black women and in creating conversations and stories rich with meaning. Data were collected using semi-structured interviews over two years, in which participants were encouraged to tell their own stories (positive and negative) about working in higher education as Black women academics and about how they dealt with teaching and staff-related challenges encountered. Using semi-structured interviews allowed for further probing of the participants' accounts in areas that had not been fully explained. Additionally, this approach provided the participants with opportunities to introduce other relevant and emergent themes around their experiences. Even though a semi-structured approach to interviewing was employed, it was often abandoned in the spirit of the participants' evolving and passionate storytelling and in favour of a more conversational approach to soliciting information and the participants simply wanting to speak their truths freely and without inhibitions. Consequently, the data gathered were made significantly richer. For example, where issues of racial discrimination emerged, a few of the participants became quite emotional or upset in recounting their experiences.

Interviews were conducted at the HEIs where the participants were employed and lasted between one to two hours. The study complied with British Educational Research Association (2018) ethical guidelines including anonymization of verbatim interview transcripts and maintaining participant confidentiality in reporting of the findings.

Data analysis

The data were analysed initially through a process of in-depth reading and rereading of each transcript. To synthesize the excerpts from the transcripts into

Table 5.1 Participants' Profiles

Participant	Ethnic origin	Years in HE[a]	Role[b]	Department	Highest qualification achieved	Teaching qualification
Comfort	Nigerian	16	SL	Business	MA	PGCE; HEA
Faith	Kenyan	19	PL	Health	PhD	PGCE
Beulah	Zimbabwean	10	SL	Health	MSc	PGCE; HEA

a. Taken at the time of interview; b. L = lecturer.

meaningful data, initial categories for coding were derived from the key research themes of race and gender, allowing for connections between the threads and patterns among the excerpts to be made as the themes developed. An interpretive framework was then developed, drawing upon CRT tenets as described earlier.

In the next section we present some examples of our data drawn particularly from three of the study participants (see Table 5.1) whose experiences were most striking, who were exceptionally overt and who proved more vocal than others on certain issues expressed across the data set. Their experiences have been located within CRT tenets one and two as it became clear from the analysis that accounts about race and racism (tenet one) as well as their feelings of being considered as outsiders and being made invisible in universities (tenet two) featured most prominently in the data. Tenet three, storytelling, structures the way in which we present their accounts.

Findings

In exploring Black women's academic experiences, our research sought to ascertain whether Black women academics gave the same weight to their gendered experiences as they did to their racialized experiences but found that race matters and Blackness matters in more detailed ways (Ladson-Billings 1998). The study findings revealed that racism was happening as a normal way of life in the participants HEIs despite institutional neoliberal boasts of equity, fairness and meritocracy. The frequency and depth of racism experienced implied that racism was endemic, persistent and routinely perpetuated across faculties and subject disciplines. The participants reported little evidence of remedies or further actions taken by their institutions to address their complaints of unfair treatment. These Black women had endured experiences that white academics could not have undergone by virtue of their colour. In the following paragraph we explain why and how.

Tenet one: Permanence of racism

The application of CRT identified both overt and subtle layers of racism that revealed a murky side to HEIs and their neoliberalist policies. The participants reported offensive imagery and statements, for example:

> There were times I would come into the office and there were drawings of a monkey on my door, and it would say, 'go away, what are you doing here?' It happened to me and another colleague who was from Mauritius, a Black woman and another one was from Africa, a Black woman. When we reported these things, nothing was done. (Faith)

Highlighting that this was done more than once, and to other Black women, would indicate that racism was clearly overt, prevalent and persistent. The drawings of a monkey and the words stated could be seen as blatant acts of hate. This is despite the Race Relations Act passing into English law more than forty years ago and additional amendments made in 2000 (to challenge racial discrimination) and the 2010 Equality Act, which is the mechanism ultimately through which unequal employment experiences should be challenged. Faith's excerpt raises questions as to why the drawing was done in the first place and why no action was ever taken by the HEI concerned. It is unclear to whom these reports were made and at what level; reporting at a higher level may have resulted in a different response to this occurrence within the HEI. It could be perceived as an acknowledgement that this act of leaving a picture of a monkey on Faith's door was unimportant to whomever the report was made. If this deed was normal behaviour, requiring no further response, it demonstrated an absence of any desire for institutional change.

In using racist imagery and messages in a crude act of racial hatred, perhaps in pursuit of what may be perceived as a whiter university by the white majority, it is apparent that these Black women were told repeatedly that they did not belong in their HEIs. Images such as these may be perceived as amusing or even true by the sender and any response about the offensive nature of the images by the recipient could be construed as humourless or even touchy. Therefore, in anticipation of a likely downplayed response, it may become difficult to challenge fellow colleagues and may even serve to encourage similar behaviour.

Reflecting further on the presence of racism in the university, another participant was able to make unexpected connections from her childhood in charting her experiences in the university:

> One thing I didn't tell you which is something that I am just realizing, I was actually born in apartheid. I was born in Zimbabwe when it was Rhodesia, and I was born in a Black township, and it was illegal for me and my mum to be on another side of town at six o'clock at night . . . I spent the first five years of my life living as an inferior second-class citizen. So, when I say I feel it, I go back to that. I know when someone is trying to discriminate against me because of my race and my gender. I sense it in the manner they speak to you and all these things because I was born and socialized into that. (Beulah)

Beulah was able to make what was perceived to be sudden and important connections in terms of what it is like to be different, through making comparisons between her experiences in the university and her childhood experiences. Apartheid existed as a political system in South Africa from 1948 to 1994. It separated the different peoples living there and gave privileges to those of European origin (Encarta Dictionary online, accessed 18 September 2015). Even though Zimbabwe was not officially declared as having an apartheid system, Beulah's experiences indicate, and seem to her, that it existed, albeit informally, in the country. Her childhood experiences indicated being seen as a trespasser and being potentially detained by the police as part of her normality. In the university, this differential treatment could be perceived as her having a dissimilar and unequal status to that of her white colleagues, as well as being seen as controllable property, which coincides with the power and status that CRT's second tenet attributes to whiteness as property. Beulah implied that because of her childhood experiences she was suddenly cognisant of what was going on in the university and why it (racism) felt familiar. In 'feeling it', she also commented on sensing it in the 'manner they speak to you'. This evidence seems to support the existence of conscious or unconscious racism, or even the use of microaggressions or what could be described as dog-whistle politics. This form of micropolitics is indicative where speech is used in a coded manner to send a specific message to the intended recipient, like a dog whistle, which is unrecognized by others (Palmer Cook 2012). These messages often constitute subtle forms of racism that are hard to prove.

For the participants, there was evidence of racism operating at different levels and in different ways in the academy. In sharing their experiences, the permanence of race has been revealed overtly as well as covertly along with the failings of the neoliberalist agenda.

Tenet two: Whiteness as property

Of all the CRT tenets, whiteness as property became the area into which many of the participants' experiences appear embedded. According to Ladson-Billings and Tate (1995: 58), 'more pernicious and long lasting than the victimization of people of colour is the construction of Whiteness as the ultimate property'. In discussing the property functions of whiteness, Harris (1993: 1734), identifies what she refers to as the 'right of use and enjoyment', where privileges are given and advantages gained by virtue of being white.

Whiteness thus comes with an expectation and reliance upon a unique set of benefits and privileges associated with whiteness, which must be 'constantly affirmed, legitimated and protected' (Harris 1995, cited in Donnor 2013: 195). The use of this whiteness is interpreted as something to which value and power is seen to be attached. Hacker (1992) in an exercise with his white college students raised the question of what amount of compensation they would seek if forced to become a Black person. Students asked for fifty million dollars or one million dollars for each coming *Black* year. Hacker concluded that this exercise illustrated the material and social value that white people place on their possession of whiteness. 'The money would be used . . . to buy protection from the discriminations and dangers White people know they would face once they were perceived to be Black' (Hacker 1992: 32). Despite this quote being made in 1992, the findings from our research demonstrates it still is as relevant in 2022 as it was then. The students' comments emphasize the point that white people possess a property that Black people do not have and as a result it becomes exclusive and financially unattainable (Ladson-Billings 1998).

The unexpected and unwanted occupation of space in the university by Black women was confirmed by a white male colleague's reaction to seeing a group of Black female academics together in the same space:

> There were four of us as academic sisters [other Black women] and we were standing in this corridor, just talking and laughing and joking amongst ourselves about general things. A White colleague walked past and went into his office. He came back out about five minutes later and we were still talking. After he had done this about three times, it's almost as if he couldn't stop himself and he said, 'what are you all talking about?' I turned round and said, 'it's Black women having a conversation' and he just went bright red . . . it's almost seen as an uncomfortable situation for White people to see . . . he never came back out of his office but that did make us feel as if . . . because there are a number of us . . . was there some kind of threat? It was the deliberateness of his behaviour which made me feel that he wouldn't have been bothered with anyone else. Wouldn't have asked another group of [white] women. (Faith)

This account implies that this was an extraordinary occurrence for the white male colleague to have experienced and seemingly was not meant to happen. Puwar (2004: 51) advises that such social spaces (in this instance, the corridor) 'are not blank and open for anybody to occupy . . . some bodies have the right to belong in certain locations, while others are marked out as trespassers who are . . . out of place'. This furthers the notion that UK HEIs remain *hideously white* (term used by Greg Dyke – director general of the BBC in 2001, in describing the BBC as being 98 per cent white, Mirza 2006), and rarely open to critical gaze (Back 2004).

White colleagues, to the exclusion of non-whites, appeared to be defending academic property and space. These participants observed differences applied to their physical and emotional spaces, that is, being seen as trespassers or simply made silent. Other participants also felt that they were still trespassers where knowledge, power and access rights were vested in the white majority and could only be obtained if favoured.

These participants were apparently classified as unnatural occupants of this traditional space, which was seen as the preserve of white, middle-class males and their presence in this apparently sacred space subsequently challenged by the perceived natural occupant, the white male colleague, as unusual, out of place and creating uncomfortable or threatening situations for others (white male staff).

According to ECU (2015), feeling like outsiders in universities or feeling invisible to others can result in a natural exclusion from activities and groups and ultimately can affect career aspirations. This exclusion is also reflective of the concept of *new property* which furthers property interests away from just space and belonging into intangibles such as intellectual property and other tangibles such as jobs and contracts, as exemplified by participant Comfort whose behaviour was conditioned by 'fear' of losing her job. She said: 'they just talk at you . . . you just take it: yes sir, yes sir, three bags full . . . for fear of losing your job'. She continued:

> I'm treated as an outsider. . . . It matters to me because it tells me they [white colleagues] don't value me. It tells me I'm just a number. . . . Is there any reason why I'm being treated this way? It gives me the impression that they are trying to tolerate me rather than celebrate me.

It seemed that Comfort was now more cognisant of what was happening around her. Describing herself as inventory, having 'just a number', is reminiscent of Black property and therefore Black bodies having little identifiable value. Locke (1968, cited in Harris 1993: 1735) asserts, 'every man [*sic*] has a property in his own person'. This has been interpreted as meaning that self-ownership is necessary for identity to have value and here, we see that Comfort felt she was relegated to being just a number, removing all sense of her personal property, identity and maybe even her self-identity. This furthers the notion of possession of the right kind of property being necessary for value and worth in the university. In this situation, according to Harris (1993: 1726), 'Whiteness defines the legal status of a person as slave or free'. The women in this study were not enslaved but were treated as if they were, with their presence and right to occupy the academic space questioned.

Beulah furthered the revelation made to her by a professor in her department.

> I went to see a professor and he's from a White Irish background and I told him my issues . . . he said to me, 'you do realize why this is going on don't you?' . . . I said no . . . 'He said well I'm going to be blunt and I'm going to tell you. The main reason why you are struggling with this, you are a Black woman'. He said, 'You are Black, you are a woman but you are also Black African and historically nursing has been obviously staffed in some areas by Black people'. And he said, 'They are alright with you Beulah as long as you are on the shop floor wiping people's bottoms. You are alright to get up to matron or sister but as soon as you leave that sphere and you come into education . . . that doesn't fit in with the academic ideas about where Black people should be'. And I was absolutely gobsmacked by that, he said, 'I'm going to tell you this, so you know what you're dealing with.'

The issues being discussed were around others' perceptions of Beulah. These areas are associated with property rights which, it seems, should not be available to her. Delgado and Stefancic (2012: 27) note that if racism is deeply embedded, then the ordinary business in the organization will continue to subordinate minorities. Therefore, it could be argued that the white professor placed an emphasis on Beulah's intersectional identity – being a 'Black woman', being 'Black' and being 'Black African' and employed in nursing – and maintained that such insight was essential in comprehending how racism in universities operates. The suggestion is made that her ethnicity and place in the organization must be understood and that she would always be seen as not belonging at an academic level, but important only for doing menial work, 'wiping people's bottoms'. This professor seemed supportive and may even be giving the impression that he understood the experiences of Beulah, as coming from an Irish background he might have had a shared understanding/experience of university discrimination since, historically, Irish people living in England have experienced discrimination in employment (Garrett 2002); however, this information was not revealed.

This sense of being made to feel like unwelcomed trespassers begins to cascade down through academic ranks of the HEIs and into the student population to some of the Black students. Beulah summarized:

> There was one student . . . asking me about my journey because she was a Black student and she said, 'I remember hearing a comment where they said, "Black nurses? we expect you to be permanent members of the BBC". I said, 'BBC?' She said, 'British bum cleaners that is where you should be as a nurse.'

Evidently, the circle of white exclusivity had continued into the next generation of scholars who, despite studying for a degree, were reminded of their expected place and position in life which is undertaking unqualified, unskilled and unpleasant work. To circumvent such expectations and to better support Black women in higher education, the participants became mentors and role models to other Black women and garnered support for each other through establishing out-of-work groups and creating a sense of sisterhood. They also challenged being positioned as 'out of place' by raising their visibility within their institutions, often through over-performance in their role and by gaining higher qualifications to ensure greater credibility and acceptance in universities.

A Race at Work Report (2015) revealed that over a third of Black workers felt that they had been overlooked for promotion even though the rates of academic attainment were higher among most Black and minority ethnic groups than for white British groups. This is also evidenced in research by, for example, Gabriel and Tate (2017) and Weekes-Bernard (2017). In addition, recent collaborative research by Gyimah et al. (2022) demonstrated that in every stage of the career journey, from entering work to senior leadership, women of colour (including Black African and Caribbean women) were being locked out of reaching their true potential, which necessitates even further the need for Black women to acquire the highest academic qualifications as exemplified by Beulah.

> I received some very interesting comments about me doing a PhD. Some of them were to do with race and some of my [white] colleagues were saying, 'What is it about Africans? They seem to want to have letters after their names and some of them aren't even qualified to do that.' (Beulah)

Such a generalization made about Africans (as desiring qualifications but being uneducated to achieve them) implies that this is based on casual observations being made, where becoming qualified may be perceived as threatening to the status quo of universities. Even though Black women academics have acquired appropriate skills and qualifications to articulate and perform in their specific disciplines, therefore qualifying them as insiders, they are still seen as outsiders in universities (ECU 2009, 2015; Mirza 2008). Mirza and Reay (2000) suggest that for a Black person to become educated is to become human. For CRT scholars, removing the potential of Black people being seen as simply property provides even greater credence to Black staff raising their voices in universities and for the established university cultures to be disrupted, which may prove unacceptable to the white majority.

To address problems such as these, going forward there is an urgency for universities to create a responsibility and accountability framework that addresses racial diversity awareness and management. It is insufficient to create portfolios of policies and practices without measuring clearly evidenced effectiveness and impact. Conversely, investigations need to be undertaken to understand the failings of ineffective policies or practices, especially when they no longer offer protection to the intended beneficiaries.

There is a necessary requirement for honest conversations and discussions which assist academic employers and staff in suspending disbelief of racism, facilitating proactive diversity and inclusion changes, including allyship. Allyship requires the collaboration of a senior organizational person who advocates and actively works for the inclusion of a marginalized group through supportive personal relationships and encouraging changes to workplace policies and practices (Melaku et al. 2020). Stories about race in the workplace also have the potential to show how managers and human resources departments really think about Black women and their treatment. An ultimate challenge for universities is to create a diversity dashboard, which involves publishing their diversity statistics on their websites or on other public documents/platforms, which might lead to the emergence of diversity rankings and therefore effective change. Finally, universities should consider how racially diverse their senior management team really is and what they need to do to ensure there is progression for Black women.

Conclusion

Storytelling has been used as a medium to relate and structure the experiences of these women, allowing for a new creation of racial understanding and knowledge. The study found that for these Black women academics, being constantly reminded of their race, position and perceived capabilities created a perpetual sense of being marginalized: not trusted, feeling unwanted, unsupported, frustrated and humiliated. The participants articulated similarities and variances in their experiences which have been based on, for example, the culture prevalent within their university and their department, the behaviour and attitude of colleagues and students and even childhood recollections. In sharing their experiences, participants pronounced their struggles and strategies for challenging stereotypes and racist messages that are embedded in the psyche of white academics in higher education.

Exploring the complexities of race and racism means that there is scope for many of the issues found to be interpreted in different ways and categorized according to the CRT tenets. The findings have also shown how entrenched racism is in higher education and the extent to which achieving change will need to be a long-term goal for HEIs. Saliently, if embedded racism is to be eradicated and if Black women academics are to thrive and have positive employment experiences, then 'everything must change at once' (Delgado and Stefancic 2012: 64), otherwise HEIs will absorb the small advances made and things will regress to how they previously were.

Finally, our findings point to the need for challenges to be made to the effectiveness of existing equality, diversity and inclusion (EDI) policies formulated by HEIs, which inevitably protect white academic interests to the detriment of Black academics (Arday and Mirza 2018). More work needs to be done to improve the situation and experiences of Black women academics. HEIs must create real and safe spaces to have critical conversations around racial experiences, challenging racism and racial inequality and speaking truth to power in such conversations with colleagues and managers. Human resources departments in HEIs must champion better staff education, qualification and competence in understanding, formulating and implementing robust and effective EDI policies and documents and must sign up to the Race Equality Charter, which aims to enhance the representation and progression of Black and minority ethnic staff within higher education (Advance HE 2021). Academics must also play their part in having a more determined focus in embedding race and EDI issues in curriculum design and core teaching areas, encouraging more immersive encounters for staff with areas of race and racism to initiate and sustain change.

References

Advance HE (2020), *Equality in Higher Education Staff Statistical Report*, London: Advance HE.

Advance HE (2021), *Race Equality Charter Review*, London: Advance HE [Online]. Available online: www.advance-he.ac.uk/knowledge-hub/race-equality-charter-review (accessed 20 September 2021).

Arday, J. and H. S. Mirza (2018), *Dismantling Race in Higher Education: Racism, Whiteness and Decolonising the Academy*, London: Palgrave Macmillan.

Back, L. (2004), 'Ivory Towers? The Academy and Racism', in I. Law, D. Phillips and L. Turney (eds), *Institutional Racism in Higher Education*, 1–6, Stoke-on-Trent: Trentham Books.

Bell, D. (2008), 'Racism, the Ultimate Deception', *North Carolina Law Review*, 86: 621–34.

Brah, A. and A. Phoenix (2004), 'Ain't I a Woman? Revisiting Intersectionality', *Journal of International Women's Studies*, 5 (3): 75–86.

British Educational Research Association (2018), *Ethical Guidelines for Educational Research*. Available online: https://protect-au.mimecast.com/s/4bosCANZjQi NPpZvwFGi-_Q?domain=bera.ac.uk (accessed 10 July 2021).

Business in the Community (2015), *Race at Work Report*. [Online] Available at: https://www.bitc.org.uk/report/race-at-work-2015/ (accessed 25 May 2022).

Crenshaw, K. (1991), 'Mapping the Margins: Intersectionality, Identity Politics, and Violence Against Women of Color', *Stanford Law Review*, 43 (6): 1241–99.

DeCuir, J. T. and A. D. Dixson (2004), 'So When it Comes Out, They Aren't That Surprised That it is There: Using Critical Race Theory as a Tool of Analysis of Race and Racism in Education', *Educational Researcher*, 33 (5): 26–31.

Delgado, R. (1995), 'The Imperial Scholar: Reflections on a Review of Civil Rights Literature', in K. Crenshaw, N. Gotanda, G. Peller and K. Thomas (eds), *Critical Race Theory: The Key Writings That Formed the Movement*, 46–57, New York: The New Press.

Delgado, R. and J. Stefancic (2012), *Critical Race Theory: An Introduction*, New York: New York University Press.

Donnor, J. (2013), 'Education as the Property of Whites: African Americans' Continued Quest for Good Schools', in M. Lynn and A. Dixson (eds), *Handbook of Critical Race Theory in Education*, 195–203, London: Routledge.

ECU (2009), *The Experience of Black and Minority Ethnic Staff Working in Higher Education*, Research Report, London: Equality Challenge Unit.

ECU (2015), *Equality in Higher Education – Staff Equality Data Report for HEIs: Statistical Report Research Report*, London: Equality Challenge Unit [Online]. Available online: http://www.ecu.ac.uk/publications/equality-higher-education-statistical-report-2015/ (accessed 31 August 2021).

Gabriel, D. and S. A. Tate (2017), *Inside the Ivory Tower*. Stoke-on-Trent: Trentham Books.

Garrett, P. (2002), '"No Irish Need Apply": Social Work in Britain and the History and Politics of Exclusionary Paradigms and Practices', *British Journal of Social Work*, 32 (4): 477–94.

Gillborn, D. (2006), 'Critical Race Theory and Education: Racism and Anti-racism in Educational Theory and Praxis', *Discourse: Studies in the Cultural Politics of Education*, 27 (1): 11–32.

Gillborn, D. (2008), *Racism and Education: Coincidence or Conspiracy?* London: Routledge.

Gyimah, M., Z. Azad, S. Begum, A. Kapoor, L. Ville, A. Henderson and M. Dey (2022), *Broken Ladders: The Myth of Meritocracy for Women of Colour in the Workplace Report*. The Runnymede Trust and the Fawcett Society. London: Fawcett Society [Online] Available at https://www.fawcettsociety.org.uk/broken-ladders (accessed 29 May 2022).

Hacker, A. (1992), *Two Nations: Black and White, Separate and Unequal*. New York: Ballentine Press.

Harris, C. I. (1993), 'Whiteness as Property', *Harvard Law Review*, 106: 1707–91.

HESA (2021), 'HE Academic Staff by Ethnicity and Academic Employment 2019/20' [Online]. Available online: https://www.hesa.ac.uk/data-and-analysis/staff/table-4 (accessed 31 August 2021).

Housee, S. (2008), 'Should Ethnicity Matter When Teaching About "Race" and Racism in the Classroom?', *Race Ethnicity and Education*, 11 (4): 415–28.

Ladson-Billings, G. (1998), 'Just What Is Critical Race Theory and What's It Doing in a Nice Field Like Education?', *Qualitative Studies in Education*, 11 (1): 7–24.

Ladson-Billings, G. and F. W. Tate (1995), 'Toward a Critical Race Theory of Education', *Teachers College Record*, 97 (1): 47–68.

Maylor, U. (2009), 'What Is the Meaning of "Black"? Researching "Black" Respondents', *Ethnic and Racial Studies, Special Issue: Gender, Race and Religion: Intersections and Challenges*, 32 (2): 369–87.

Melaku, T. M., A. Beeman, D. G. Smith and W. B. Johnson (2020), 'Be a Better Ally', *Harvard Business Review*, November–December. [Online] Available at: https://hbr.org/2020/11/be-a-better-ally (accessed 1 June 2022).

Mirza, H. S. (2006), 'Transcendence Over Diversity: Black Women in the Academy', *Policy Futures in Education*, 4 (2): 101–19.

Mirza, H. S. (2008), *Race, Gender and Educational Desire: Why Black Women Succeed and Fail*, London: Routledge.

Mirza, H. S. and D. Reay (2000), 'Redefining Citizenship: Black Women Educators and "the Third Space"', in M. Arnot and J. Dillabough (eds), *Challenging Democracy: International Perspectives on Gender*, 58–73, London: Routledge Falmer.

ONS (2021), 'England and Wales 2011 Census' [Online]. Available online: https://www.ethnicity-facts-figures.service.gov.uk/uk-population-by-ethnicity/national-and-regional-populations/population-of-england-and-wales/latest (accessed 31 August 2021).

Palmer Cook, I. (2012), *Tuning the Dog Whistle* [Online]. Available online: http://www.ianpcook.com/research/ipc_dogwhistle_mw_040112.pdf (accessed 7 July 2015).

Puwar, N. (2004), 'Fish In or Out of Water: A Theoretical Framework for Race and the Space of Academia', in I. Law and I. D. Phillips (eds), *Institutional Racism in Higher Education*, 49–58, Stoke-on-Trent: Trentham Books.

Robertson, S. L. (2010), 'Corporatisation, Competitiveness, Commercialisation: New Logics in the Globalising of UK Higher Education', *Globalisation, Societies and Education*, 8 (2): 191–203.

Rocco, T. S., J. D. Bernier and L. Bowman (2014), 'Critical Race Theory and Human Resource Development (HRD): Moving Race Front and Centre', *Advances in Developing Human Resources*, 16 (4): 457–70.

Saperstein, A. and A. M. Penner (2014), 'Beyond the Looking Glass Exploring Fluidity in Racial Self-identification and Interviewer Classification', *Sociological Perspectives*, 57 (2): 186–207.

Warmington, P. (2014), *Black British Intellectuals and Education: Multiculturalism's Hidden History*, London: Routledge.

Weekes-Bernard, D. (2017), *Poverty and Ethnicity in the Labour Market Report*, Joseph Rowntree Foundation [Online] Available online: https://www.jrf.org.uk/report/poverty-ethnicity-labour-market (accessed 25 May 2022).

Yosso, T. J. (2005), 'Whose Culture has Capital? A Critical Race Theory Discussion of Community Cultural Wealth', *Race Ethnicity and Education*, 8 (1): 69–91.

Chapter 6

Bias against Women Academics in Student Evaluations of Teaching

Tarring and Feathering in Academia

Michelle Ronksley-Pavia

Prelude

In this chapter I juxtapose and situate the narrated *realities* of gendered experiences of women teaching in academia against relevant literature relating to the all too conspicuous student experience of course (SEC) and student experiences of teaching (SET) surveys and evaluations; collectively I term these student evaluations. The narrated realities (narratives), that I position alongside the exploration of associated literature are a fusion of women's voices from my own lived experiences of working and being in academia over the last ten years; voices of women heard by me, experienced by me and subsumed by me – a personalized narrative of others' happenings fused with those of my own. The fused protagonists in this composition are Shes and Hers; together, these capitalized pronouns are used as proper nouns to assist in providing voice to the many and varied experiences with which female academics contend, alongside literature pertaining to the gender bias intrinsic to student teaching evaluations. In this way, I aim to enable the narratives to convey the multiplicity of women's experiences with student evaluations, while contrasting these experiences with the findings of empirical research.

The scholarship that informs this approach is interconnected and complex, whereby as a method the writing in this chapter is both process and product. It is, therefore, difficult to tease out the overlapping collectivity of approaches and ingredients that have informed this chapter; they are fragments of autoethnography (e.g. Adams 2015), slices of collective biography (e.g. Gonick and Gannon 2013), segments of fictionalizations of real conversations (e.g. Sallis 1999), part narrative-informed reflections (e.g. Polkinghorne 1996), grazes of collective narratives (e.g. Ovchinnikov 2018), and fractions of collective stories that were never formally documented. Together, in this chapter I have chosen to write differently (Gilmore et al. 2019), not only to challenge canonical ways of writing and presenting scholarship of thoughts and ideas, but moreover in a bid to move forward in collectivizing thoughts, conversations, stories told and experienced. In doing so I hope together we may better understand the occurrences surrounding academic women and the impacts student surveys can have on us. I thus speak with one voice, informed by many.

In essence, this chapter consists of a series of two main parallel narratives: the empirical literature and the lived-experience narratives (in italicized text). The empirical literature can at times seem disconnected from the realities of how student evaluations impact on female academics. In an attempt to bridge this gap, I seek to write differently (Gilmore et al. 2019) by juxtaposing the italicized narratives alongside an encapsulated typological literature review. It is the reader's choice as to how to best connect the parallel narratives of embodied experiences and empirical literature for their own understanding, like a work of art there is no one *correct* interpretation, but many. I deliberately do not seek to deduce, as it is not my aim to analyse any of these narratives but rather to present the *truths* of each and allow the reader to interpret; bringing their own unique background and experiences to this meaning-making process. The parallel narratives can be read together as they flow through the chapter or read separately; as such, only reading the empirical literature sections, disconnected from the italicized lived-experience narratives. Next, the reader may choose to read the italicized narratives separately. Essentially, I provide three ways to read this chapter: (1) as it is set out and presented, (2) reading only the text in standard font and (3) reading only the text in italicized font.

The purpose of this chapter is to recognize and call out the ingrained bias against women that continues to be upheld in university teacher surveys, ratings and evaluations across the globe (Boring et al. 2016). I acknowledge that student evaluation data are profoundly defective and biased against women (Boring 2020; Heffernan 2021; Hornstein 2017; Langbein 2008) – cisgender, transgender, non-binary, gender-neutral, agender, gender-fluid and gender-queer individuals are likely impacted by the gender bias evident in these types of surveys. However, in this chapter I aim to focus predominantly on the fundamental bias against female academics.

Prologue

As far back as 1971 (McKeachie and Lin), it was readily recognized that higher education evaluations of teacher effectiveness by students were fundamentally affected by gender bias against female academics. Indubitably, research spanning more than fifty years continues to identify that teacher ratings are biased against female academics (see for example, Kishler Bennett 1982; Heffernan 2021). Student evaluations are also inherently prejudiced by classism, racism, sexism, homophobia, ageism and ableism and likewise subject to influences of other biases and prejudice. Yet, universities across the globe continue to rely on these flawed data to assess and rate so-called teaching quality of their academics, and indeed continue to require evaluation data for tenured, non-tenured and precariously employed academics. Moreover, these surveys play increasing roles in career advancement (or not), in terms of evaluating who is promoted, hired and dismissed (Heffernan 2021).

The reference to tarring and feathering in the title of this chapter by extension refers to severely and devastatingly criticizing an individual, to harshly shame or punish a person (Farlex Inc. 2021). Throughout history, tarring and feathering has long been associated with mob *punishment* against individuals to intimidate and humiliate them as perceived *enemies* (Bell 2013); the *Othering* of individuals. I contend that student evaluations of teaching are the modern-day equivalent simulation of tarring and feathering, where women academics in particular are the *victims* of this castigation because they are perceived by some students to have slighted them, or because students respond to some other conscious or unconscious bias through their responses to teaching evaluations. As Stark and Freishtat (2014) contend, 'anger motivates people to action more than satisfaction does' (1). Retribution for some students comes in the form of their survey responses that often humiliate and unfairly criticize female academics and their teaching practice because, for example, they were perceived to have not given *good* grades. Of course, I acknowledge that this also happens to some male academics and those of different genders, but the focus of this chapter is on the systemic bias against women in teaching evaluations.

It is empirically (and anecdotally) well recognized that student evaluations of teaching do not measure teaching *effectiveness* (Borch, Sandvoll and Torsen 2020; Boring et al. 2016; Spooren, Brockx and Mortelmans 2013) and that they are fundamentally flawed (Fan et al. 2019; Heffernan 2021).

She was trying to hold everything together . . . the session had gone well until the discussion turned to the assessment, students had not received their grades well . . . it was like an invisible switch had been flicked and the mob-mentality had materialized! She shifted uncomfortably, standing at the front of the lecture hall, a sea of angry faces, doing Her best to respond to students' concerns . . . finally the session came to an end. . . .

But She couldn't yet breathe a sigh of relief; a group of angry students remained, about a dozen, some lingering in the background, not quite sure if they wanted to be part of the pack, lingering near the exit, so they could make a quick getaway just in case the situation deteriorated. No such opportunity for Her!

The students milled around, surrounding the dais . . . the demanding envoys soon emerged . . . 'Why did our assessment feedback say this. . .', 'Why did I get this mark? I worked so hard! I put in so much effort!', 'The marking was too harsh' . . . She offered to meet with students individually to address their concerns, but She wasn't going to respond to such a barrage . . . as the group eventually started to dissipate, She caught a couple of under-the-breath comments . . . 'We'll get you in the student evaluations!', 'We know how much the university relies on those to evaluate staff!' . . . How could She address that?

She retreated to the relative safety of Her office, struggling to hold back the almost inevitable flow of tears. . . . She was not going to allow Herself to become upset . . . She'd completed Her whole doctorate without shedding a tear.

Bias against female academics is particularly prevalent when students have a tendency to evaluate the person rather than their actual teaching (Fan et al. 2019). Furthermore, time and again existent literature asserts that the widespread use of these ineffective *measures* by universities actually encourages mediocre teaching and inflation of student grades (Isely and Singh 2005; Langbein 2008; Stroebe 2020). The fact that student evaluations are used in ways that encourage grade inflation means that students hold the balance of power over the teaching of academics; thus, students can shape the teaching behaviour of academics in detrimental ways. As Stroebe (2020) points out, this type of systemic enforced influence on these evaluations, where students need good grades and academics need good student evaluations, can be used by students to 'reward lenient-grading instructors who require little work and to punish strict-grading instructors' (284). Coupled with the inherent gender bias against women in student evaluations, these types of appraisals have very little validity (if any at all), but their prejudicial outcomes continue to be used in authoritative and iniquitous ways by institutions.

Interestingly, the marketization and commercialization of higher education have seen students become akin to customers, and as Harris and González (2102) suggest, 'students have adopted that attitude [of being customers] for themselves, coming to higher education to buy the commodity of credential, rather than to learn' (6). The authors suggest that this distinction, this systemic shift from students as learners to students as customers, will intensify gender bias against women through such avenues as student evaluations. This can be especially marginalizing for women who also challenge embedded stereotypes of what it means to be a female academic with intersecting identities of disability, class, race, gender and so forth; 'if academic women become service workers who must please, rather than educate, their students, their career advancement will likely be determined to a greater extent than before by their ratings on "customer service" evaluations' (Harris and González 2012: 6). In this way, further reducing student ratings of teaching to mere ratings of 'customer service' makes such evaluations even more meaningless.

The humiliating and simulated *tarring and feathering* of female academics by cohorts of students who make mass-informed judgements about teaching is deplorable. These judgements can be coordinated in person and via social media, where students mass together to respond to perceived injustices; in some respects, this can be akin to mob behaviour, or deindividuation. The social identity model of deindividuation effects proposed by Reicher, Spears and Postmes (1995) is highly relevant here, where social identity performance stemming from students' perceptions of belonging to their social group can be quite persuading when it comes to instigating others into adopting negative views of teachers and their teaching, subsequently influencing negative evaluations of teaching, in mob-like behaviour with apparent lack of individual responsibility for their own actions. This mob mentality ensues with the adoption of emotional responses impacted by cohort mentality, instead of making rational evaluations based on individual experiences of teaching and university courses. It can be argued that the mere anonymity of teaching evaluations further perpetuates this power imbalance, which cohorts of students can hold over academics, with academics having no voice or recourse against prejudicial and, at times, personally assaultive remarks evident in these evaluations.

Sitting uncomfortably perched on the edge of Her office chair, as She knew She shouldn't as it wasn't a position conducive to good posture. . . . She re-read the anonymous student survey comment, just to double-check She hadn't initially misread or potentially misunderstood . . . 'My professor was totally wrong when She said that I had incorrectly used [the phrase] in my assignment. She needs more experience in [the world of work], She's dumb! Some feedback provided on my assessment was not necessary and came across rude. There also seems to be a misunderstanding by the professor of how this [phrase] works in the real world.' What?!! . . .

She had some idea of who this student was because She recalled this particular assignment and how one student had gone way off track. Maybe it would be better in future not to provide so much feedback to students on their assignments? Cross-referencing this qualitative comment with the quantitative ones on the survey, She could see this same student had been the only one to respond that the assessment expectations were not clear! This had brought down the overall Mean score, but then only eight of the sixty-two students had actually completed the survey! What to do with this feedback for next semester? . . .

Interlude

A recent report by the United Nations Development Programme (2020) stated that almost 90 per cent of people across the world are biased against women. Within academia globally, 43 per cent of all academics identify as women (The World Bank 2020); however, for a variety of complex reasons, in some faculties this percentage is much lower (e.g. sciences). Nevertheless, what many higher education institutions have in common is that they all use some form of teaching evaluations to assess the teaching of faculty members. Furthermore, there is a large body of research spanning almost fifty years that recognizes the gender bias against female academics inherent in teaching evaluations (Mengel, Sauermann and Zolitz 2019). This body of evidence provides substantiation of the impact of bias against women in these ratings of female academics, including significant impacts on mental health and career progression (Heffernan 2021); frequently, academics are left on their own to cope with the results of student evaluations and derogatory qualitative remarks. Some reasons put forward in the literature for gender bias in evaluations relate to aspects such as conscious and unconscious bias from students, students questioning the teaching competence of female academics, and their apparent 'lack of confidence' (Mengel, Sauermann and Zolitz 2019: 560), or appearance of being 'more shy or nervous' (560), traits purportedly associated by some students with female academics.

Her heart pounded in her chest as She downloaded the student teaching evaluations . . . trembling, Her hand moved the mouse . . . it was the same each semester, sweating palms, pounding chest – dreading the outcome of these anonymous student evaluations. Worst of all, were the comments about Her appearance – one student had once commented that She should not wear a blouse that made her bra visible. Another . . . 'Some make-up wouldn't go astray' . . . Yet another . . . 'What's with Her accent? She should speak proper English or go home!' . . . She needed to have some semblance of resilience to keep on coming back semester after semester! The feedback certainly didn't represent the whole cohort, but it was always those particularly cruel ones which remained with Her semester after semester. What was **WRONG** *with Her? No one else talked about receiving these kinds of comments in their evaluations; She must be the only one this was happening to . . . She tried to contain her shaking body, leaning against the desk for some kind of sympathetic anthropomorphistic support, in an attempt to halt Her embodied reaction . . .*

A study in the Netherlands of about 20,000 student evaluations over a five-year period (2009–13) found that female teachers received scores thirty-seven percentage points lower than male teachers (Mengel, Sauermann and Zolitz 2019). Boring (2017) analysed over 22,000 teaching evaluations conducted during a five-year period at a French university and found that male students favoured male academics and perceived these male academics as having stronger leadership skills and being more knowledgeable than female academics. Moreover, an experimental American study explored an online course where academics assumed identities of avatars with different genders. In this study, the academic with the male avatar was rated considerably higher than the academic with the female avatar, irrespective of the actual gender of the academic (MacNell, Driscoll and Hunt 2015). Taken together, these studies provide further evidence about the inherent bias against women academics clearly evident in teacher evaluations.

It was time to review the student evaluation results for Her teaching. Opening the spreadsheet, the quantitative results suggested a particularly low score this semester, 2.8 out of 5. Reading on . . . scrolling down . . . She should 'wear a dress more often', was one comment that made Her sit up abruptly in Her chair. Should She read on? How did **that** *comment remotely relate to Her teaching competence? She wondered, trying not to get too demoralized.*

She read on . . . 'In my previous time at University, I was always told by my professors that a large percentage of failing or low grades among students points to a failure on the professor's part, and therefore the professor should bear responsibility for my low grade.' She felt this one cut deep . . . the assessments were set by the Certifying Agency; She had no control over these. Maybe the next comment would be more positive . . . more rewarding for Her investment in the semesters teaching . . . Hypnotized by some kind of perverse vacillation between morbid curiosity, visceral loathsomeness at the sight of a vehicular crash scene, and somehow hoping and praying the rest wasn't as repugnant as it appeared . . . Feeling a lump developing in Her throat, would She ever be able to swallow properly again? She read on . . .

Then came the passive aggressive contradictory ones, 'She has wonderful depth of knowledge, but I do not believe She is a good fit for this course, She lacks the ability to successfully transmit knowledge to Her students'. She felt physically sick! . . . Who could She talk to about how She was feeling? . . . Her supervisor? . . . No, what if she was unaware of the evaluation outcomes? By bringing it to her attention She risked being outed as incompetent! She had to deal with it on her own . . . She internalized it, once again . . .

Studies have clearly demonstrated that had women academics been male they would have received higher scores in student evaluations; furthermore, that male teachers who were less effective than their female counterparts received higher student evaluations (Boring 2017; Boring et al. 2016; MacNell, Driscoll and Hunt 2015). The extensive literature on bias against women in these types of evaluations can be summed up by Neath's (1996) ironic number one tip to academics wanting to improve their teaching evaluations without actually improving their teaching – 'BE MALE'! Neath (1996) advises female academics to not be too 'demanding' (1365) of their students lest they be more critical on survey questions pertaining to evaluating their availability, their grading and creation of engaging content, metaphorically tarring and feathering their female teachers. Tongue-in-cheek, Neath (1996) advises female faculty to study the 'Bem Sex-role Inventory [to] learn how to be less feminine and more androgynous' (1365) so their ratings will improve!

The expectations for women in academia rarely relate to the actual subject and content of survey questions but instead relate to how women in academia are perceived, and to expectancies that they are supposed 'to be nice, caring and good-looking. Depending on their age, female professors are seen as "girlfriend" or "mother" and not necessarily as professionals' (Wagner, Rieger and Voorvelt 2016: 80). This further reproduces gender stereotyping in relation to aspects of so-called likeability and competence of females. Furthermore, these perceptions and expectations reflect the inherent bias against women across the globe recognized in the United Nations Development Programme report (2020). Yet, these significant shortcomings of student evaluations remain relatively unaddressed by universities. Indeed, typically, academics are presented with some false semblance of *control* over student evaluations, invited to set up the surveys and add questions before they are released to students to complete. However, in reality, most evaluations consist of five mandatory questions that cannot be changed or altered in any way. In particular, evaluation questions ask, 'How satisfied [you the student] is with the teaching of this staff member?' and 'How could this staff member's teaching be improved?', with the inherent (yet discounted) implication of these types of questions being that students are somehow *qualified* to evaluate these aspects of an academic's work. Borch, Sandvoll and Torsen (2020) quite rightly attempted to explore what it might mean to students to be *satisfied* with an academic's teaching, with their learning activities and so forth, and found that for the most part, students were confused about what they were actually meant to be evaluating – 'the instructor's ability to make the course exciting, the pedagogical approach, the course literature or learning activities?' (90).

She hated teaching evaluation results time! There was always this one (male) professor who gleefully shared the results of his evaluations on every social media platform he could find . . . 100% across all the questions, and scores of five out of five on each question! Time and again, he's nominated by his students for teaching awards . . . He's popular among students, he makes jokes, his lectures are just like a stand-up comedy show! He's really entertaining! He's well-known for giving good grades . . . It's all hearsay, but he's rumoured to ask his Teaching Assistants to increase his students' grades when marking . . . But She couldn't help but compare Herself to this evaluation benchmark; She'd never received 100% on any one question, let alone across them all! How does One even do that? Maybe She should try stand-up comedy?! Or give good grades all the time irrespective of work quality?! Sell Her soul to the academia 'Devil'?!

Apologue

We know that academia is a very competitive environment; academics frequently compete against each other within and across institutions for funding, awards, tenure and promotions. Student evaluations play a large role in specific aspects of an academic's competitiveness. Requirements vary from institution to institution, but generally some form of student evaluation is a requirement for promotion applications, usually across a sequence of semesters of teaching. It can be said quite equivocally that student evaluations of teaching have a persuasive impact on career progression (or not) (Mengel, Sauermann and Zolitz 2019). Furthermore, perceived low scores on survey questionnaires require responses from those academics teaching the particular low-scoring courses. This can be in the form of a comprehensive plan required to *improve* the course, as a direct result of its low score on the flawed evaluation surveys, which takes considerable effort on the part of an academic, often unsupported by university peers or management. This has been found to be particularly problematic for early-career female academics who may be required to put their efforts more into their teaching to the detriment of their research, in turn leading to fewer and potentially lower quality research outputs (Mengel, Sauermann and Zolitz 2019). The resultant course improvement process can be isolating, inducing feelings of failure and impacting on self-confidence, feeling the brunt of being ostracized due to being tarred and feathered.

It was only Her second year of university teaching, Her third semester since completing Her doctorate . . . She was so confident when opening the evaluation results that they would be good; She had invested so much into the course . . . substantial resources – videos unpacking concepts, support resources and study sheets . . . weekends spent away from Her two young children and Her partner . . . missing family outings and events . . . She'd even missed the school nativity play . . . She'd worked through the immense guilt of those missed events . . . the payoff, She told herself, would eventually be tenure. . .

She found the evaluations depressing, not at all what She had expected and secretly hoped for . . . The overall score was 2.5 out of 5 . . . But the focus was on that and that alone, no recognition of the many positive comments in students' qualitative feedback . . . no recognition that this was only the second semester this relatively new course had been offered . . . Actually, Her first time teaching this course!

*Just Her supervisor's focus on **that** question which asked, 'Overall I am satisfied with the teaching of this academic'. Even She knew that 'Satisfaction' did not equate to quality but was so very subjective! Almost 20 per cent of the 350 students had responded in the survey, a good response! But on that one 'quality' question, 6 per cent of students had selected either 'Dissatisfied' or 'Strongly Dissatisfied', coupled with those who were 'Neutral' (which somehow contributed?).*

Now She was required to create a mandatory Course Improvement Report . . . She discovered the previous (female) academic who had since left the university, had also had to produce one of these Reports . . . But it had never been passed on to Her, about potential ways to 'improve' the course! She painstakingly compiled the requisite Report . . . dutifully submitting the Report juts prior to the due date, in doing so sacrificing valuable research and writing time . . .

The next semester, the course was taken from Her and given to a professor . . . a male professor . . . She felt physically sick; She asked 'Why?' only to be met with platitudes . . . She cried, Her tears were tears of exasperation, of despair, of anger and of frustration . . . no chance to implement Her plan, no opportunity to improve and demonstrate how She had implemented student feedback and made changes to the course . . . Was She such a failure as a teacher that they had to give the course to someone else . . . a man? She grieved for the lost time, the lost opportunity, the missed research and writing deadlines, the unmet sacrifices . . .

According to Mengel, Sauermann and Zolitz (2019) there is a 'sizeable and systematic bias' (537) against female academics in student evaluations. They claim that this inherent bias affects female academics' careers in three main ways: (a) when evaluated, females appear on the surface to be systematically worse at teaching when compared to males; (b) women academics' publication outputs and publication track records are being negatively impacted by a forced focus on teaching-related activities and (c) the teaching evaluation 'gender gap' (Mengel, Sauermann and Zolitz 2019: 537) may impact on women's self-confidence and beliefs about their ability to teach. The combined impact of these three main factors may be why more women than men leave academia after graduate school (Mengel, Sauermann and Zolitz 2019). Commonly, institutions hold expectations that academics must achieve a rating of 3.75 out of 5 on surveys (Heffernan 2021), otherwise they need to show how teaching will be improved by compiling and writing a report or some form of a plan. Yet, 3.75 out of 5 is 75 per cent; even students receive a passing grade on 50 per cent for most of their assessments, so the question that needs posing is: Why are the surveys not set at 50 per cent (i.e. 2.5 out of 5)? If academics required all students to receive 75 per cent for their assessments, the pass rate and retention rate would likely fall, and universities would likely lose fees from students who could not achieve this level. Yet, academics are expected to achieve 75 per cent semester after semester. As Stark and Freishtat (2014) contend, some universities deliberately instigate 'continuous cycles of competition amongst academics by making the acceptable result one that is above the cohort's average' (Heffernan 2021: 3). In other words, irrespective of the results of the cohort, there will be 50 per cent of academics who are below the average (Stark and Freishtat 2014). Acknowledging the fundamental bias against female academics in these evaluations remains unstated in such competitive environments, and women continue to be impacted by these institutionalized misogynistic practices.

Epilogue

In academia globally, we have reached a stage of critical mass when it comes to the tide and groundswell that unequivocally confirms the prevalence of prejudice against women inherent in student evaluations. This chapter has unambiguously shown that this groundswell is based on a solid foundation of empirical research. Now is the time for critical change; our tipping point – our 'moment of critical mass, the threshold, the boiling point' (Gladwell 2000: 12) for institutional change has been reached.

Across universities, and within a broad range of topic areas taught in these institutions, student evaluations have been shown to better measure student bias against women than they actually measure teacher effectiveness (Boring et al. 2016). It is well recognized that student evaluations disadvantage female teachers in academia. The false belief in the quality of student evaluation data is rampant in universities, yet what remains unseen and unacknowledged by universities is the ingrained bias and prejudice 'that shape the views that form the [so-called objective] data' (Heffernan 2021: 3). Discriminatory student evaluations should not be used by institutions to make decisions about whom to hire, fire and promote, as this further contributes to institutionalized practices that marginalize female academics. Research has shown that gendered prejudice in student evaluations varies from course to course and from university to university, and as such the responsibility should be on universities to show that relying on these evaluations does not have a detrimental and inequitable bearing on female academics and other under-represented people (Boring et al. 2016). Universities need to introduce policies that address ingrained prejudice against women in student evaluations and ratings of teaching (Hoorens, Dekkers and Deschrijver 2021) or, better yet, get rid of them all together. But then what would they be replaced with? Better the *Devil* you know?

Gendered inequalities intrinsic in student evaluations are rendered invisible by the gender-blind systemic implementation of these surveys for evaluating the teaching and pedagogical practices of female academics. It is past time that universities recognized this ingrained bias in student evaluations. Transformation and initiation of structural change in the implementation and use of student evaluations is vital to support women academics, indeed all academics, in being the best teachers they can be, while being fully and wholeheartedly supported by their institutions in ways that do not turn a blind eye to misogynistic teaching evaluations. These forms of denial and lack of institutional recognition of inherent gender bias in teaching evaluations are suggestive of institutionalized *cultures of denial* (Cohen 2001), where the perpetuation of patriarchal practices persists through higher education practices and processes, despite apparently progressive institutional policies and initiatives purportedly taken to prevent such practices. The discernible gender bias in student evaluations has been evident for over fifty years. Women in academia contend with more than enough invisible barriers in endeavouring to achieve equity in the workplace. It is long past time to remove this visible, yet institutionally unacknowledged barrier, in the form of student evaluations, to strive to reach more equitable forms of gender parity in academia.

References

Adams, T., S. L. Holman Jones and C. Ellis (2015), *Autoethnography: Understanding Qualitative Research*, New York: Oxford University Press.

Bell, J. L. (2013), '5 Myths of Tarring and Feathering', *Journal of the American Revolution* [Online]. Available online: https://allthingsliberty.com/2013/12/5-myths-tarring -feathering/ (accessed 1 October 2021).

Borch, I., R. Sandvoll and R. Torsen (2020), 'Discrepancies in Purposes of Student Course Evaluations: What Does It Mean to be "Satisfied"?', *Educational Assessment, Evaluation and Accountability*, 32: 83–102. Available online: https://doi.org/10.1007/s11092-020 -09315-x (accessed 1 October 2021).

Boring, A. (2017), 'Gender Biases in Student Evaluations of Teaching', *Journal of Public Economics*, 145: 27–41. Available online: https://doi.org/10.1016/j.jpubeco.2016.11.006 (accessed 20 November 2021).

Boring, A. (2020), 'Surveying Student Evaluations of Teaching: Vital Tool or Flawed Methodology – What do you Think?', *London School of Economics* (blog). Available online: https://blogs.lse.ac.uk/impactofsocialsciences/2020/04/09/surveying-student -evaluations-of-teaching-vital-tool-or-flawed-methodology-what-do-you-think/ (accessed 1 October 2021).

Boring, A., K. Ottoboni, P. B. Stark and G. Steinem (2016), 'Student Evaluations of Teaching (Mostly) do not Measure Teaching Effectiveness', *ScienceOpen Research*. Available online: https://doi.org/10.14293/S2199-1006.1.SOR-EDU.AETBZC.v1 (accessed 1 October 2021).

Cohen, S. (2001), *States of Denial: Knowing About Atrocities and Suffering*, New York: Wiley.

Fan, Y., L. J. Shepherd, E. Slavich, D. Waters, M. Stone, R. Abel and E. L. Johnston (2019), 'Gender and Cultural Bias in Student Evaluations: Why Representation Matters', *PLoS ONE*, 14 (2). Available online: https://doi.org/10.1371/journal.pone.0209749 (accessed 1 September 2021).

Farlex Inc. (2021), 'Tar and Feather', *The Free Dictionary of Idioms*. Available online: https://idioms.thefreedictionary.com/tarred+and+feathered (accessed 1 December 2021).

Gilmore, S., N. Harding, J. Helin and A. Pullen (2019), 'Writing Differently', *Management Learning*, 50 (1): 3–10, doi: 10.1177/1350507618811027

Gladwell, M. (2000), *The Tipping Point: How Little Things can Make a Big Difference*, New York: Little Brown and Co.

Gonick, M and S. Gannon (2013), 'Collective Biography: An Introduction', *Girlhood Studies*, 6 (1): 7–12.

Harris, A. P. and C. G. González (2012), 'Introduction', in G. Gutiérrez y Muhs, Y. Flores Niemann, C. G. González and A. P. Harris (eds), *Presumed Incompetent: The*

Intersections of Race and Class for Women in Academia, 1–14, Boulder, CO: University Press of Colorado.

Heffernan, T. (2021), 'Sexism, Racism, Prejudice, and Bias: A Literature Review and Synthesis of Research Surrounding Student Evaluations of Courses and Teaching', *Assessment & Evaluation in Higher Education*, 46 (6): 1–11. Available online: https://doi .org/10.1080/02602938.2021.1888075 (accessed 1 December 2021).

Hoorens, V., G. Dekkers and E. Deschrijver (2021), 'Gender Bias in Student Evaluations of Teaching: Students' Self-affirmation Reduces the Bias by Lowering Evaluations of Male Professors', *Sex Roles*, 84: 34–48. Available online: https://doi.org/10.1007/s11199-020 -01148-8 (accessed 1 December 2021).

Hornstein, H. A. (2017, January 1), 'Student Evaluations of Teaching are an Inadequate Assessment Tool for Evaluating Faculty Performance', *Cogent Education*, 4 (1): 1–8. Available online: https://doi.org/10.1080/2331186X.2017.1304016 (accessed 1 October 2021).

Isely, P. and H. Singh (2005), 'Do Higher Grades Lead to Favorable Student Evaluations?' *Journal of Economic Education*, 36 (1): 29–42. Available online: https://doi.org/10.3200/ JECE (accessed 1 June 2021).

Kishler Bennett, S. (1982), 'Student Perceptions of and Expectations for Male and Female Instructors: Evidence Relating to the Question of Gender Bias in Teaching Evaluation', *Journal of Educational Psychology*, 74 (2): 170–9.

Langbein, L. (2008), 'Management by Results: Student Evaluation of Faculty Teaching and the Mis-measurement of Performance', *Economics of Education Review*, 27: 417–28. Available online: https://doi.org/10.1016/j.econedurev.2006.12.003 (accessed 1 July 2021).

MacNell, L., A. Driscoll and A. N. Hunt (2015), 'What's in a Name: Exposing Gender Bias in Student Ratings of Teaching', *Innovative Higher Education*, 40 (4): 291–303. Available online: https://doi.org/10.1007/s10755-014-9313-4 (accessed 1 October 2021).

McKeachie, W. J. and Y. Lin (1971), 'Sex Differences in Student Response to College Teachers: Teacher Warmth and Teacher Sex', *American Educational Research Journal*, 8 (2): 221–6.

Mengel, F., J. Sauermann and U. Zolitz (2019), 'Gender Bias in Teaching Evaluations', *Journal of the European Economic Association*, 17 (2): 535–66. Available online: https:// doi.org/10.1093/JEEA (accessed 21 June 2021).

Neath, I. (1996), 'How to Improve Your Teaching Evaluations Without Improving Your Teaching', *Psychological Reports*, 78 (3_suppl): 1363–72. Available online: https://doi .org/10.2466/pr0.1996.78.3c.1363 (accessed 11 June 2021).

Ovchinnikov, F. (2018), '*Collective Narrative Methodologies*'. Available online: https:// fovchik.medium.com/collective-narrative-methodology-draft-40b99bd16151 (accessed 1 June 2022).

Polkinghorne, D. E. (1996), 'Explorations of Narrative Identity', *Psychological Inquiry*, 7 (4): 363–7.

Reicher, S., R. Spears and T. Postmes (1995), 'A Social Identity Model of Deindividuation Phenomena', in W. Stroebe and M. Hewstone (eds), *European Review of Social Psychology*, 6: 161–98, Chichester: Wiley.

Sallis, E. (1999), 'Research Fiction', *TEXT*, 3 (2). Available online: http://www.textjournal .com.au/oct99/sallis.htm (accessed 1 June 2022).

Spooren, P., B. Brockx and D. Mortelmans (2013), 'On the Validity of Student Evaluation of Teaching: The State of the Art', *Review of Educational Research*, 83 (4): 598–642. Available online: https://doi.org/10.3102/0034654313496870 (accessed 21 June 2021).

Stark, P. and R. Freishtat (2014), 'An Evaluation of Course Evaluations', *ScienceOpen Research*. Available online: https://doi.org/10.14293/s2199-1006.1.sor-edu.aofrqa.v1 (accessed 25 June 2021).

Stroebe, W. (2020), 'Student Evaluations of Teaching Encourages Poor Teaching and Contributes to Grade Inflation: A Theoretical and Empirical Analysis', *Basic and Applied School Psychology*, 42 (4): 276–94. Available online: https://doi.org/10.1080 /01973533.2020.1756817 (accessed 1 October 2021).

United Nations Development Programme (2020), 'Tackling Social Norms: A Game Changer for Gender Inequalities'. Available online: https://news.un.org/en/story/2020 /03/1058731 (accessed 1 October 2021).

Wagner, N., M. Rieger and K. Voorvelt (2016), 'Gender, Ethnicity and Teaching Evaluations: Evidence from Mixed Teaching Teams', *Economics of Education Review*, 54: 79–94. Available online: http://dx.doi.org/10.1016/j.econedurev.2016.06.004 (accessed 21 June 2021).

World Bank, The (2020), 'Tertiary Education, Academic Staff (% Female)', *UNESCO Institute for Statistics*. Available online: https://data.worldbank.org/indicator/SE.TER .TCHR.FE.ZS (accessed 6 September 2021).

Chapter 7

Challenges for Chinese Women PhD Students in the United States of America

The New Foot-Binding Cloth

Jinfang (Jackie) Liu

Introduction

The United States is Chinese students' first choice for overseas education, and most international students in the United States are from China (Statista 2019). About 372,000 Chinese students were studying in the United States in 2020, with 15 per cent pursuing a doctorate (Institute of International Education (IIE) 2020; Statista 2019; Zhou 2018). Although international Chinese women doctoral students in the United States (ICWDSUS) are probably the largest international women doctoral student group there, the research on ICWDSUS is surprisingly scant. My search for the literature with the keywords 'international Chinese women doctoral students in the US' generated only one paper from the major databases (Google Scholar, ProQuest Digital Dissertations, Academic Search Premier, JSTOR, PsycINFO). As the author of the only source that I found with a focus on ICWDSUS, Kuttig (2012) was also saddened by the absence of research about this big women's group in the United States. She explained that international women doctoral students 'have been historically underrepresented in academia' (Kuttig 2012: 39). When I applied the keywords 'Chinese women in US academia', which are not focused on but have some parts about ICWDSUS, I found only six sources. All seven sources are presented in Table 7.1. Obviously, there is much to learn about ICWDSUS and the challenges for them.

Although most ICWDSUS have great academic and professional performance and notwithstanding that the United States and China are the two largest economies in the world, ICWDSUS suffer from the double portion of gender inequity and discrimination from the two strong patriarchal cultures (Gu 2016). Although the founding president of the People's Republic of China (PRC), Chairman Mao, eradicated China's 1,000-year foot-binding practice in 1949, which had disabled women from walking out of the home to work (Fincher 2014), the contemporary challenges for ICWDSUS create an invisible foot-binding cloth that constrains them from striding forward for their career advancement.

Table 7.1 Literature about Chinese Women in US Academia

Identities	Article
ICWDSUS	Kuttig, M. (2012), Doctoral Advising: A Grounded Theory Exploration of Female Mainland Chinese International Students
Chinese women graduate students and scientists in the US	Chan, I. W. (2006), Psychological Adaptation of Mainland Chinese Female International Students: A Phenomenological Inquiry
	Dickerson, Y. (2016), Chinese Female Graduate Students on US Campuses: Negotiating Classroom Silence, the Leftover Woman and the Good Woman Discourses
	Gu, D. Y. (2016), Chinese Dreams? American Dreams? The Lives of Chinese Women Scientists and Engineers in the United States
	Qin, D. (2000), Reweaving Self: Changes in Self-Understanding Among Chinese Women Graduate Students in the United States
	Qin, D. and Lykes, M. (2006), Reweaving a Fragmented Self: A Grounded Theory of Self-understanding Among Chinese Women Students in the United States of America
	Yakaboski, T. (2013), The Rest of the Story: A Qualitative Study of Chinese and Indian Women's Graduate Education Migration

The purpose of this chapter is to identify the complex challenges for ICWDSUS in order to unveil the invisible foot-binding cloth for their career development. I used Crenshaw and Bonis's (2005) concept of intersectionality to map ICWDSUS' identity from three intersected identities: Chinese women in US academia, women of colour faculty in US academia and women in the United States. Instead of Crenshaw and Bonis's (2005) horizontal intersectionality of multiple marginalized identities, the three identities are like an invisible foot-binding cloth to tie ICWDSUS layer by layer, as Figure 7.1 shows. Although ICWDSUS can feel the direct oppression from the first layer, most ICWDSUS could not identify the indirect constraints from the intersectionality of their identities as a woman and a woman of colour in the United States (layers 2 and 3). However, the invisible pressure from the second and third layers of their foot-binding cloth does suppress ICWDSUS.

I have used a solid circle to represent the first layer of foot-binding cloth that ICWDSUS have felt, and two dashed circles to represent the second and third layers that remain unknown to most ICWDSUS. With the focus on academic and career achievement as well as the lack of knowledge of gender inequity, most ICWDSUS did not pay attention to gender discrimination in the United States (Kuttig 2012). One ICWDSUS in Kuttig's (2012) research even rejected her male-dominated department's effort to make women feel comfortable for the retention of women students: She perceived women as the same as male students and did not think women need extra attention from the department. Although in Gu's (2016) research some ICWDSUS felt uncomfortable about unfair treatment in the United States, they did not know the exact problems. The seven sources about Chinese women in US academia included in Table 7.1 all took a phenomenological stance about their lives in the United States and a critical stance for Chinese culture. None of them used a lens of intersectionality to examine their discrimination in the

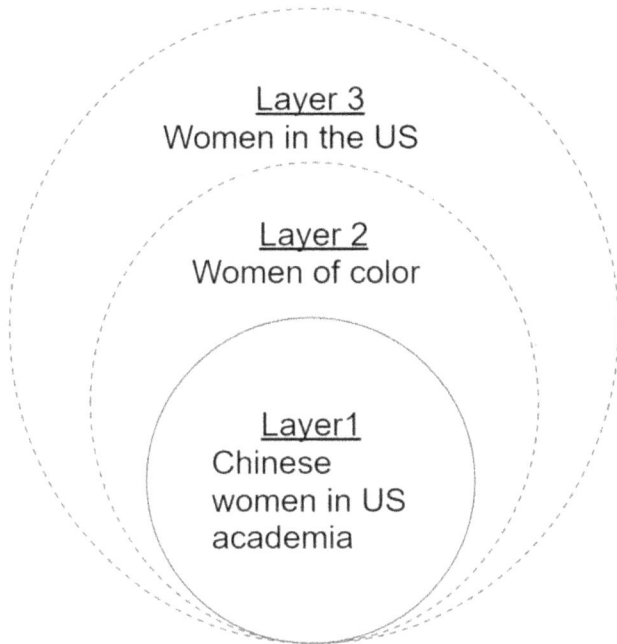

Figure 7.1 The invisible foot-binding cloth for ICWDSUS.

United States. However, this does not mean that Chinese women in the United States are immune to intersectionality. In Castro and Collins's (2021) research about Asian American women scientists, all Chinese American and other Asian American women doctoral students who were born in the United States struggled with the intersections of discrimination against them from their race, gender and studies. For ICWDSUS who were born in mainland China, the concept of intersectionality could be too new to be known. One Asian woman doctoral student in Castro and Collins's (2021: 49) research admitted that 'she had difficulty identifying other people's behaviours as discrimination'.

As American feminist Betty Friedan claimed in the *Feminine Mystique*, it is 'the problem that has no name' (Friedan 2018: 57). Therefore, when I described the invisible layer 2 and layer 3 of the foot-binding cloth, I listed the challenges for women and women of colour in the United States from current feminist studies, which are two other identities for ICWDSUS, and chose the relevant descriptions deductively from the seven sources to identify the exact problems that ICWDSUS could not name. This deductive way could not include all the challenges for ICWDSUS, and my manual connection between ICWDSUS and women of colour and women in the United States from only seven sources could be far from enough to examine the intersectionality of ICWDSUS. However, this chapter can provide a conceptual direction with a lens of intersectionality for ICWDSUS to see out of their immediate circle of the layer 1 of foot-binding cloth to discern a more

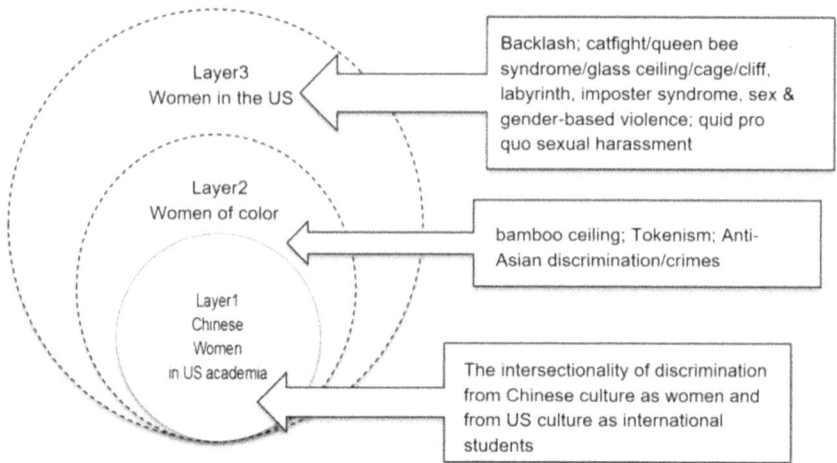

Layer3 Women in the US	Backlash; catfight/queen bee syndrome/glass ceiling/cage/cliff, labyrinth, imposter syndrome, sex & gender-based violence; quid pro quo sexual harassment
Layer2 Women of color	bamboo ceiling; Tokenism; Anti-Asian discrimination/crimes
Layer1 Chinese Women in US academia	The intersectionality of discrimination from Chinese culture as women and from US culture as international students

Figure 7.2 The details of ICWDSUS' foot-binding cloth.

complex world ahead of them, which can help them navigate better in hostile patriarchal cultures.

The rest of this chapter is presented in three sections. I use two sections to discuss the challenges for ICWDSUS from both Chinese and US patriarchal cultures, and the conclusion section to summarize the chapter. The visual in Figure 7.2 displays the details of the invisible parts of the ICWDSUS' foot-binding cloth.

Discrimination from Chinese culture

In the twenty-first century, Chinese women have faced discrimination in almost every aspect of their lives, which was in sharp contrast with Chairman Mao's slogan *women hold up half the sky* (Fincher 2014). With the focus on the economy since China's economic reform in 1978, many affirmative women's equal rights initiatives during Mao's time have been withdrawn by the government (Fincher 2014). Although one ICWDSUS in Yakaboski's (2013) research still remembered that the Cultural Revolution during Mao's era greatly promoted gender equality in China, after Mao's death, feminist values were replaced by economic values. In the 1990s, the Chinese translation of 'feminism' changed from 'Female rights-ism (*nü quan zhuyi*)', which focused on women's equal rights with men, to 'Female gender-ism (*nü xing zhuyi*)', which focused on how to live like a female in a patriarchal world (Zhang 1992). Chinese feminism has backlashed, and Chinese women who advocate for women's rights are called as *nüquanbiao* (feminist whores) (Wu and Dong 2019). This probably explains why almost all ICWDSUS in the seven sources have little knowledge about and interest in feminism and gender equality. Consequently, in contrast with China's rapid economic development which makes China the second largest economy in the world (Burden 2020), the gender equality ranking of China in the world based on the *World Gender Gap Report* has dropped rapidly from number 63 in 2006 to number 106 in 2020 out of 153 countries (World Economic Forum (WEF) 2020).

For many ICWDSUS, 'studying abroad carries more meaning than for Chinese male students' (Dickerson 2016: 31). The primary reason for ICWDSUS to earn an overseas doctorate was to leave the oppression of women in Chinese culture (Qin and Lykes 2006). Unlike men, women with the highest level of education, instead of being respected, confronted tremendous discrimination against their age, gender and personal lives (Gu 2016). In 2007, the All-China Women's Federation (ACWF) officially announced that single women older than twenty-seven were considered *leftover women,* indicating that no men wanted to marry them due to a concern of their being too old to get pregnant (Dickerson 2016). While the modern discourse of leftover women encouraged young women to get married before twenty-seven instead of pursuing ambitious career goals, the traditional Four Virtues and Three Obediences still demanded women to present diligent work, a good appearance, proper speech and gentle virtues, as well as to follow the father as a daughter, the husband as a wife and the son in widowhood (Chan 2006).

Chinese traditions still challenge women's career advancement. The ACWF found in 2011 that 61.6 per cent of men and 54.8 per cent of women held traditional opinions that men should take charge of matters outside the home and women should take charge of matters inside the home (*nan zhu nei, nü zhu wai*) (Wei 2016). Eighty-five per cent of Chinese said work-life balance was hard for working mothers and that having children negatively impacted women's career advancement (Catalyst 2020). Dickerson (2016) claimed that Chinese women graduate students in the United States struggled between their own professional identity development as international students, researchers and scholars, and discriminative women's identities from both modern and traditional Chinese culture. Single ICWDSUS were worried about dating and being *leftover*; married ICWDSUS were worried about balancing their own study and work while being 'a good wife and mother' (Gu 2016: 119).

However, regardless of a woman's identity, women's legal protection in China is lacking (Fincher 2014). For example, the Chinese Marriage Law can leave women homeless after a marriage ends or constrain women who experience domestic violence from seeking a divorce (Kuo 2020). It was not until 2016 that China passed the first domestic violence law (Fincher 2014). Unfortunately, even some ACWF women officials, who were supposed to support women, tended to blame women who were victims of domestic violence for challenging husbands at home by having a 'deficient mouth' (*zui qian*) (Yang 2007: 107). The ACWF plays 'a welfare and supportive role', instead of an advocating role for women (Sun and Li 2017: 24). Therefore, ACWF can help women participate at work, but would not advocate for women's rights in workplace gender discrimination and sexual harassment issues. Although the constitutions of China state that women and men enjoy equal rights in all areas of a socialist society, and even though there are many anti-gender discrimination laws in China, the law enforcement mechanisms to protect women's legal rights are few and are ineffective to deter gender discrimination

(Sun and Li 2017). Thus, when women sued for gender discrimination at work or sexual harassment from university professors or authorities, the men perpetrators often got no or little punishment (Gan and George 2021). It is hard to advocate for women's rights from the bottom in China: without the support of law enforcement mechanisms in the workplace, women are discriminated against during the whole process (Wei 2016). Due to the pregnancy, maternity and nursing leave that woman have to take, which bring less profit but more cost for employers, many Chinese employers directly reject female job applicants (Qin and Lykes 2006). Some Chinese universities only hire women faculty with children to guarantee that their academic productivity will not be influenced by marriage, pregnancy and maternity leave (Gu 2016). Many job advertisements include requirements for women's physical attributes (e.g. height, shape, appearance) unrelated to job duties, so many young women college students undergo cosmetic surgeries to increase their employability (Hua 2013; Wei 2016). The lack of legal protection for women in China probably already shaped the obedience of ICWDSUS, who have to accept gender discrimination.

Compared to the United States' gender pay gap of 18.5 per cent in 2019, the Chinese gender pay gap in 2019 was 21.8 per cent, which meant the average income of Chinese women was only 78.2 per cent of their male counterparts (Institute for Women's Policy Research n.d.; Zheng 2019). Smaller gender pay gaps in lower positions mask larger pay gaps in higher positions. Zweig and Ge (2018) claimed that the income gender gap among Chinese women returnees to China with doctorate degrees was the largest: women returnees with a PhD degree earned only 59 per cent of what their men counterparts received, compared to women with master's degrees earning 82 per cent of male salaries, and women with bachelor's degrees earning 95 per cent of their male counterparts' wages.

The uncertainty of Western job markets, the fast development of Chinese knowledge and an innovative economy and the Chinese government's supportive policies attract many Chinese international students to return to China (Zweig and Ge 2018). However, China has no incentives to attract women returnees, and 90 per cent of awardees of governmental incentives were men (Gu 2016). With more and more Chinese international students going back to China, many Chinese returnees have been unable to find a job (Zweig and Ge 2018). Despite the strong reverse cultural shock to the rapid development of China, Chinese overseas returnees with US doctorates often face a myriad of challenges such as higher evaluation standards, lack of support from a local network (*guanxi*), lack of knowledge of local university and organizational politics, mistrust and jealousy from local co-workers, and age and gender discrimination (Gu 2016). Most importantly, there is no tenure system in China, so professors can only be rehired if they pass the yearly evaluation based on their publications, research, service and teaching record (Gu 2016). 'Due to the institutionalized gender discriminations, lack of leadership opportunities, social stigmas towards highly educated women, and the concerns about academic freedom and dishonesty', most ICWDSUS were 'hesitant or even resistant to the idea of returning to China to work' (Gu 2016). In Gu's (2016) research, most ICWDSUS chose to stay in the United States after graduation unless they return to China to care for their parents.

The intersectionality of marginalization from the United States

Many ICWDSUS believed that they would have a good life in the United States (Dickerson 2016; Qin and Lykes 2006). Chinese doctoral students in the United States also share some part of the American dream, believing an individual can change one's social class and achieve individual success through hard work (Brazill 2021). However, few ICWDSUS know that the intersectionality of their identities as an international student, a woman and a woman of colour brings complex challenges for them in the United States. Unfortunately, despite China's being the largest population in the world, ICWDSUS were a marginalized group, whose voices were rarely heard in the United States (Kuttig 2012).

Challenges for international women graduate students

Relationship concerns

International students must cope with a multitude of challenges. Much research has shown that Chinese women international graduate students' greatest concern was their relationships, such as friendship, marriage and family relations (Chan 2006; Gu 2016; Qin and Lykes 2006). Although Chinese women international graduate students normally had great academic performance, it is not easy for ICWDSUS to establish relationships for emotional support in the United States due to the differences in culture, background and interest areas (Chan 2006).

Also, the advisor-advisee relationship is vitally important for a doctoral student's academic success. However, Chinese doctoral students and their advisors may have different expectations about the advising role. Coming from a collective culture, Chinese doctoral students expect their professors to be at the centre of their learning and to play a role as an authority and a role model (X. Li 2013). However, being from an individualistic culture, American professors serve as facilitators and expect students to be at the centre and to control their own studies. Although most Chinese women doctoral students in Kuttig's (2012) research had sincere and professional relationships with their advisors, they also claimed that their advisors could be moody sometimes and they had to see the facial expressions of the advisors before talking with them. Such advisor-advisee conflict is not rare.

Social and cultural concerns

Compared to international undergraduate students, international graduate students experience significantly more social difficulties due to religion, personal relationships and limited social and graduate student activities (X. Li 2013). The most frequently reported social-cultural challenge for international students was social alienation, wherein one felt a lack of influence over the outcome, felt meaningless and uncertain about what to do, had no sense of belonging in the host culture and felt socially estranged (e.g. loneliness and isolation) in the host country (Chan 2006). Social alienation was often 'associated with cultural differences and the discrimination and stereotypes against international students in the host country' (Xie 2007: 19). With huge cultural differences between the United States and China, all ICWDSUS in the seven sources felt that they could not integrate into American culture.

Education differences

The educational system of the United States was totally new and caused an educational shock to most international students (X. Li 2013). In contrast to the focus on passing examinations to enter the best schools in Chinese education, Western education was decentralized and student oriented with the emphasis on autonomous and interactive classroom communication (e.g. speaking up and debating in class) (X. Li 2013; Zhu 2016). Many international Chinese women graduate students did not even do the reading assignments to prepare for class discussion (Chan 2006). Chinese exam-focused pedagogy helped with the hard skills, such as academic and language capability but failed to develop the soft skills of students, such as social skills, intercultural communication, psychological readiness and knowledge about the culture of the host country and foreign universities (Zhu 2016). Without soft skills, even if Chinese students wanted to participate in class discussions, due to their lack of verbal communication skills they often chose to be silent in the classroom (Chan 2006).

Psychological barriers and lack of leisure

Due to the English language barriers, academic and career pressure, and lack of attention to an individual's psychology in Chinese traditional culture, Chinese students' mental health (e.g. anxiety, distress) is much poorer than that of most other international students (Gu 2016; Xie 2007). Chinese graduate students normally ignore work-life balance and have few leisure activities, or just unorganized, passive and solitary ones. They even feel shameful to entertain themselves (Li and Stodolska 2006). The main objective of Chinese students' social activities is not to relax but to learn about academic and career information as well as the temporary or permanent residence requirements in the United States (Li and Stodolska 2006). Chinese international students' 'mental illness is particularly urgent' (Zhu 2016: 64). All ICWDSUS in the seven sources suffered from loneliness, high stress and a lack of sense of belonging in the United States.

Career restrictions

Despite all the challenges of studying abroad, finding a good job was the ultimate goal for many international students (Xie 2007). However, many factors influenced their career placement, such as work permits and immigration restrictions in the United States, career and promotion opportunities in the job market of both the United States and the home country, living and working environments, family arrangement and expectations, transition to a new environment, reverse culture shock when returning to the home country, and other psychological issues (Chan 2006). In this fast-changing world, most of those important factors remained uncertain for a long time after graduation, which made it necessary for international students to prepare career plans for different scenarios. Married ICWDSUS' career decisions were often up to their husbands' careers (Gu 2016). Without knowing the exact number, some ICWDSUS dropped out of their doctoral programmes (Gu 2016).

Challenges for women in the United States

Unlike the direct discrimination against women in China, the microaggressions against women in the United States were indirect, implicit and sometimes invisible to many ICWDSUS (Gu 2016). As part of androcentric education in a patriarchal world, many doctoral programmes in the United States are androcentric with strong or implicit gender bias.

Backlash

Admittedly, women's empowerment movements in the past decades have greatly improved women's lives. In most countries, the new gender gap in education means more women than men have enrolled in primary, secondary and tertiary education (WEF 2020). In the United States, the gender gap in middle management has been closed (Kay and Shipman 2014). Therefore, many women of the millennial generation did not believe there was gender inequity and did not appreciate, but rather blamed, many feminists' efforts in the past as anti-family and causing tensions, which resulted in a backlash against feminism (Faludi 1991). However, instead of achieving gender equality, gender inequity has intensified in a less visible way with the interplay of power and ideology. Despite their economic success, East Asia and North America were the two slowest regions in the world in terms of gender equality progress. *The 2020 World Gender Gap Report* calculated that it would take 163 years in East Asia and 151 years in North America to close the gender gap, in contrast with '54 years in Western Europe', '107 years in Eastern Europe and Central Asia' and '140 years in the Middle East and North Africa' (WEF 2020: 6). Facing all kinds of visible and invisible challenges (e.g. burnout, depression, discrimination), Faludi (1991) warned women in the United States, 'you may be free now, but you have never been more miserable' (2).

 As mentioned earlier about the backlash of feminism in China, ICWDSUS are already the products of this backlash with little knowledge of women's rights from 'Female rights-ism (*nü quan zhuyi*)'. With Chinese androcentric education of 'Female gender-ism (*nü xing zhuyi*)', Chinese women engineers in Kuttig's (2012) study did not complain about, but appreciated, being a minority in male-dominated departments in the United States. They seemed to be content that 'in the US, female students work like male students, and male students work like animals' (Kuttig 2012: 104). Many ICWDSUS did little to change their unfair treatment but rather changed their career aspirations to accept their unfair treatment (Kuttig 2012).

Sex and gender-based violence and quid pro quo sexual harassment

Women are often the first targets of attack by criminals and one out of three women has experienced sexual violence (World Bank 2019). Compared to male international students, female Chinese international students were more vulnerable to crimes. In Gu's (2016) research, some ICWDSUS experienced sexual harassment from co-workers, peers, professors, advisors and their professional networks in various forms. Compared to physical or verbal sexual harassment behaviours, *quid pro quo* sexual harassment was most destructive for ICWDSUS' career, when prospective employers, supervisors or advising professors used the recommendation or termination of scholarship and employment to push ICWDSUS to submit to unwelcome sexual favours (Gu 2016).

Catfight and queen bee syndrome

According to the backlash discourse, one outcome of the *backlash, catfight* culture, in which women viciously compete against other women, makes women rob women of the social, economic and political power gained from past women's movements and strengthens patriarchal orders (Tanenbaum 2003). Although female friendship is vital for well-being, providing women with strong mental support and role models to cope with societal pressure, their first enemy is also women. Klein (1991) claimed that it is 'suicidal politics' for 'women to disown one another,' which makes individual women even more vulnerable to struggle alone in a hostile patriarchal world. Patriarchal culture has often avoided putting men as the enemy of women and has promoted women who follow traditional patriarchal values to put down other progressive women, such as using mothers-in-law to suppress daughters-in-law (Kabeer 1999). With more educated and capable women taking leadership roles, many men now support women leaders, but women often put down other women. *Queen bee syndrome* has been used to describe the phenomenon where senior women leaders disaffiliate from or put down their female subordinates to prevent them from career advancement (Seo, Huang and Han 2017). Unfortunately, modern education is also based on androcentric culture with an emphasis on competition and individualism, and women are educated to compete for limited leadership opportunities (Seo, Huang and Han 2017).

From the seven sources in Table 7.1, I found no discussion about the phenomena of either catfight or queen bee syndrome. Admittedly, from a collective culture, the individualism and competitiveness among Chinese women could be less strong than for women from individualistic cultures. However, in addition to the dearth of research about ICWDSUS, social isolation from American culture, marginalized positions, and the few numbers of ICWDSUS in their fields has probably disconnected the ICWDSUS from many women for potential catfight and queen bee syndrome. Loneliness is the norm for ICWDSUS (Chan 2006; Gu 2016; Kuttig 2012; Qin and Lykes 2006); however, although most Chinese value friendship and only have Chinese friends, women graduate students in Chan's (2006) research also pointed out the superficial and reciprocal nature of their relationships with other Chinese women. As everyone is busy with their own work and studies, few ICWDSUS have trustworthy friends with whom to share deep thoughts (Chan 2006).

Glass ceiling/cage/cliff, labyrinth and imposter syndrome

There are many metaphors that describe the barriers to women's development. *Glass ceiling* means the invisible barriers in organizations that block women from top leadership positions and put women in staff positions (Warrell 2013). Once their oppression from the external world is internalized, women will develop feelings of worthlessness that deter them from pursuing further and higher professional and life goals, holding them back in a figurative *glass cage*. Compared to men, women have significantly lower leadership self-efficacy (Hackett and Betz 1981). Manese, Sedlacek and Leong's (1988) study found that women international students in the United States were less confident and less likely to act on strong beliefs or to take leadership roles but were more easily discouraged. With few women in leadership roles to serve as role models and little encouragement for women's leadership practices from families and communities, it is hard for a woman to increase her leadership experiences and self-efficacy or even to envision herself as a leader (Hackett and Betz 1981). Even high-achieving women, who have successfully overcome the glass ceiling, often suffer from *imposter syndrome* and regard their accomplishments as phony, so they fear failure and often have higher anxiety and depression as well as low self-confidence.

In Gu's (2016) research, all ICWDSUS performed well in research and publications in highly competitive male-dominated fields, but constantly suffered from *imposter syndrome*, feeling 'not good enough' or fearing being regarded as 'stupid or unqualified' (133). Many ICWDSUS felt extremely nervous about seeking scholarly assistance from advisors and others, with the concern of being regarded as 'dumb' (Gu 2016; Kuttig 2012).

During periods of crisis or times when there is a higher chance of failure, women or minorities are more likely to be appointed as leaders than white men, 'not because they are expected to improve the situation, but because they are seen to be good people managers and can take the blame for organizational failure' (Ryan, Haslam, Hersby, and Bongiorno 2011:470). This phenomenon was called the *glass cliff* (Ryan, Haslam and Postmes 2007). If a woman leader failed to change the crisis, she was an easy scapegoat; if she saved the situation, after the crisis, she was likely to be replaced by a man. Either way, the woman leader, chosen during an organizational crisis, often fell from her elevated position quickly. Although none of the ICWDSUS in the seven sources in Table 7.1 mentioned leadership, their marginalized positions, social isolation from US culture, lack of feminist knowledge and acceptive attitude towards discrimination (Kuttig 2012) could make them easy scapegoats in the US patriarchal world.

Considering the 'complexity and variety of challenges for women' in their career journey from the bottom to the top, Eagly and Carli (2012) claimed the glass ceiling metaphor is now 'more wrong than right', the barriers for women being more like a labyrinth from both external and internal worlds of a woman. However, with a focus on academic and career commitment in the United States, sources of discrimination – whether from a woman's external world or the psychological challenges from her inner world – have been ignored by ICWDSUS (Kuttig 2012). The good academic performance of ICWDSUS can involve the cost of sacrificing their women's rights and psychological well-being.

Challenges for women of colour

Concrete/bamboo ceiling

While white women fought to smash the glass ceiling, due to the racism and stereotypes in the United States, women of colour often faced a *concrete ceiling* (for Black women) or *bamboo ceiling* (for Asian), both of which were almost impossible to crack down (Hyun 2005). Although most Asian American students, especially women students, displayed great academic performance, most Asian staff were in entry-level positions. Hyun (2005) coined the term 'bamboo ceiling' to describe the slow career progress and barriers of Asians for leadership positions in the United States, due to many subjective stereotypes against Asians, such as lack of assertiveness of leaders. Most ICWDSUS in Gu's (2016) research complained about the stereotypes their male colleagues and professors held against them as being docile and submissive, which appeared not only during daily interactions but also during conference presentations and workplace and academic collaborations.

Tokenism

Predominantly white institutions tend to marginalize and tokenize women of colour faculty and staff with little support and coaching for their work and promotion but expect them to be role models to complete heavy workloads for their race, gender and profession (Thomas and Hollenshead 2001). Many ICWDSUS in Gu's (2016) research were often given heavy and challenging workloads at the last minute without much supervision or resources; even though some ICWDSUS proactively reached out to their supervisors for help, some supervisors still perceived this as an offer to do an errand (e.g. get coffee) for them. ICWDSUS often had to do extra work with less pay as 'cheap labour' with the hope of gaining a H1B visa for legal status in the United States, but some employers refused to help with visa issues or permanent residency after exploiting their labour; even those who got permanent residency had few promotional opportunities (Gu 2016: 126).

Anti-Asian discrimination and crimes

One of the worst hardships for international students in the United States was discrimination from local American educators, classmates and contacts, ranging from ignoring to verbally or even physically insulting and confronting (Xie 2007). Anti-Asian discrimination always exists in the United States and Chinese students face unique anti-Asian discrimination, such as being suspected as spies for China (Brazill 2021). In 2011, a UCLA student took to YouTube to criticize the Asian groups on campus. In 2019, Dr Neely in Duke University demanded that Chinese graduate students stop speaking Chinese with their Chinese peers on the campus and used the loss of internship opportunities to threaten them (Brazill 2021). Since the trade war between the United States and China in 2016, many Chinese scholars have become victims of political conflicts between the United States and China – from being required to renew visas every year, their visas being cancelled, being questioned by the Federal Bureau of Investigation or even being banned from entering the United States (Rong 2021). Some Asian women, including Chinese women, have become victims of the increasingly intense anti-Asian hate crimes in the United States (Kanthor 2021). None of the seven sources mentioned the anti-Asian discrimination in the United States. Although it must be hard for a marginalized ICWDSUS to share their thoughts about the anti-Asian racism in the United States, further research is needed to unveil the intersectionality of challenges for ICWDSUS by adding a new identity as Asian women in the United States.

Conclusion

This chapter has summarized the challenges faced by ICWDSUS from both Chinese and US cultures, supporting the metaphor of foot-binding that limits ICWDSUS' career development. As Figure 7.2 shows, today's foot-binding cloth for ICWDSUS is probably much thicker and trickier than the old ones. Compared to the gender discrimination from Chinese culture, the indirect intersectionality of discrimination from US culture can be more cunning, escaping the radar of ICWDSUS without being discerned. Although ICWDSUS know little about their challenges from layer 2 and layer 3, it can be assumed that challenges for ICWDSUS as women of colour and women in the United States must be more complex than what I found from current limited research.

Unfortunately, the total published research about ICWDSUS is probably less than most ICWDSUS' own publications. ICWDSUS' unbalanced career development patterns, with strong academic commitment and little knowledge about women's rights and the intersectionality of discrimination, challenge the sustainable development of ICWDSUS' career. Admittedly, the foot-binding cloth of challenges for ICWDSUS needs to be addressed by educators, policymakers and management from both the United States and China. However, situated as they are in two patriarchal cultures and androcentric education systems, ICWDSUS should not passively wait for the changes from patriarchal institutions but should take ownership of their lives to navigate their career path to untie the foot-binding cloth layer by layer from different patriarchal cultures. I hope that in the future, despite different research specialties, more ICWDSUS will join me to reflect on the same research question about how to untie or loosen the foot-binding cloth to help them stride further and higher in their career journeys.

References

Brazill, S. C. (2021), 'Narrative Inquiry into Chinese International Doctoral Students' Journey: A Strength-Based Perspective', *International Journal of Doctoral Studies*, 16: 395–428.

Burden, L. (2020), 'China's Economy Set to Overtake US Earlier Due to COVID Fallout', *Bloomberg*, 25 December. Available online: https://www.bloomberg.com/news/articles/2020-12-26/covid-fallout-means-china-to-overtake-u-s-economy-earlier (accessed 20 January 2022).

Castro, A. and C. Collins (2021), 'Asian American Women in STEM in the Lab with "White Men Named John"', *Science Education (Salem, Mass.)*, 105 (1): 33–61.

Catalyst (2020), 'Women in the Workplace: China', *Catalyst*, 14 April. Available online: https://www.catalyst.org/research/women-in-the-workforce-china/ (accessed 20 January 2022).

Chan, I. (2006), 'Psychological Adaptation of Mainland Chinese Female International Students: A Phenomenological Inquiry', Doctoral diss., University of Tennessee, Knoxville.

Crenshaw, K. and O. Bonis (2005), 'Mapping the Margins: Intersectionality, Identity Politics, and Violence against Women of Color', *Cahiers du Genre*, 39 (2): 51–82.

Dickerson, Y. Z. (2016), 'Chinese Female Graduate Students on US Campuses: Negotiating Classroom Silence, the Leftover Woman and the Good Woman Discourses', Doctoral diss., Syracuse University, Syracuse.

Eagly, A. H. and L. L. Carli (2012), 'Women and the Labyrinth of Leadership', in W. E. Rosenbach, R. Taylor and M. A. Youndt (eds), *Contemporary Issues in Leadership*, 147–62, New York: Westview Press.

Faludi, S. (1991), *The Undeclared War Against American Women*, New York: Crown.

Fincher, L. H. (2014), *Leftover Women: The Resurgence of Gender Inequality in China*, London: Zedbooks.

Friedan, B. (2018), *The Problem That has no Name*, Docklands: Penguin Books.

Gan, N. and S. George (2021), 'An Intern Took On One of China's Biggest TV Stars in a Landmark #MeToo Case. She Lost, but Vowed to Fight On', *CNN*, 15 September. Available online: https://edition.cnn.com/2021/09/15/china/xianzi-zhu-jun-sexual-harassment-case-mic-intl-hnk/index.html (accessed 20 January 2022).

Gu, D. Y. (2016), *Chinese Dreams? American Dreams?: The Lives of Chinese Women Scientists and Engineers in the United States*, Berlin: Springer.

Hackett, G. and N. E. Betz (1981), 'A Self-efficacy Approach to the Career Development of Women', *Journal of Vocational Behavior*, 18 (3): 326–39.

Hua, W. (2013), *Buying Beauty: Cosmetic Surgery in China (Vol. 1)*, Hong Kong: Hong Kong University Press.

Hyun, J. (2005), *Breaking the Bamboo Ceiling: Career Strategies for Asians*, New York: HarperCollins e-books.

Institute of International Education (2020), 'Open doors 2020: 2020 FACT SHEET: CHINA', *Open Doors*. Available online: https://opendoorsdata.org/fact_sheets/china/ (accessed 20 January 2022).

Institute for Women's Policy Research (n.d.), 'The Gender Wage Gap by Occupation 2019', *Institute for Women's Policy Research*. Available online: https://iwpr.org/iwpr -issues/employment-and-earnings/the-gender-wage-gap-by-occupation-2019/#_edn2 (accessed 20 January 2022).

Kabeer, N. (1999), 'Resources, Agency, Achievements: Reflections on the Measurement of Women's Empowerment', *Development and Change*, 30 (3): 435–64.

Kanthor, R. (2021), 'Chinese Students in the US Grapple With the Rise in Anti-Asian Hate Crimes', *The World*, 8 April. Available online: https://www.pri.org/stories/2021 -04-08/chinese-students-us-grapple-rise-anti-asian-hate-crimes (accessed 20 January 2022).

Kay, K. and C. Shipman (2014), 'The Confidence Gap', *The Atlantic*, May. Available online: https://www.theatlantic.com/magazine/archive/2014/05/the-confidence-gap/359815 (accessed 20 January 2022).

Klein, R. (1991), 'Passion and Politics in Women's Studies in the 90s', *Women's Studies International Forum*, 14 (3): 125–34.

Kuo, L. (2020), 'Anger in China at Law Ordering "cooling-off" Period before Divorce', *The Guardian*, 29 May. Available online: https://www.theguardian.com/world/2020/may /29/anger-in-china-at-law-ordering-cooling-off-period-before-divorce (accessed 20 January 2022).

Kuttig, M. (2012), 'Doctoral Advising: A Grounded Theory Exploration of Female Mainland Chinese International Students', Doctoral diss., University of Rochester, Rochester.

Li, M. Z. and M. Stodolska (2006), 'Transnationalism, Leisure, and Chinese Graduate Students in the United States', *Leisure Sciences*, 28 (1): 39–55.

Li, X. (2013), 'The Academic and Social Integration of Chinese Doctoral Students into US Universities and the Role of the Chinese Students and Scholars Association (CSSA)', Doctoral diss., University of California, Los Angeles.

Manese, J. E., W. E. Sedlacek and F. T. Leong (1988), 'Needs and Perceptions of Female and Male International Undergraduate Students', *Journal of Multicultural Counseling and Development*, 16 (1): 24–9.

Qin, D. (2000), 'Reweaving Self: Changes in Self-understanding Among Chinese Women Graduate Students in the United States', Doctoral diss., Boston College, Boston.

Qin, D. and M. Lykes (2006), 'Reweaving a Fragmented Self: A Grounded Theory of Self-understanding Among Chinese Women Students in the United States of America', *International Journal of Qualitative Studies in Education*, 19 (2): 177–200.

Rong, X. (2021), 'Chinese Students in the US Caught Up in Geopolitics and Trump's Immigration Crackdown', *Documented*, 8 January. Available online: https:// documentedny.com/2021/01/08/chinese-students-caught-up-in-geopolitics-and -trumps-immigration-crackdown/ (accessed 20 January 2022).

Ryan, M. K., S. A. Haslam and T. Postmes (2007), 'Reactions to the Glass Cliff: Gender Differences in the Explanations for the Precariousness of Women's Leadership Positions', *Journal of Organizational Change Management*, 20 (2): 182–97.

Ryan, M. K., S. A. Haslam, M. D. Hersby and R. Bongiorno (2011), 'Think Crisis–Think Female: The Glass Cliff and Contextual Variation in the Think Manager–Think Male Stereotype', *Journal of Applied Psychology*, 96 (3): 470–84.

Seo, G., W. Huang and S. H. C. Han (2017), 'Conceptual Review of Underrepresentation of Women in Senior Leadership Positions From a Perspective of Gendered Social Status in the Workplace: Implication for HRD Research and Practice', *Human Resource Development Review*, 16 (1): 35–59.

Statista (2019), 'Number of College and University Students From China in the United States From Academic Year 2008/09 to 2018/19', *Statista*. Available online: https://www.statista.com/statistics/372900/number-of-chinese-students-that-study-in-the-us/ (accessed 20 January 2022).

Sun, J. Y. and J. Li (2017), 'Women in Leadership in China: Past, Present, and Future', in Y. Cho, R. Ghosh, J. Y. Sun and G. N. McLean (eds), *Current Perspectives on Asian Women in Leadership*, 19–35, Cham: Palgrave Macmillan.

Tanenbaum, L. (2003), *Catfight: Rivalries Among Women – From Diets to Dating, From the Boardroom to the Delivery Room*, New York: Harper Collins.

Thomas, G. D. and C. Hollenshead (2001), 'Resisting From the Margins: The Coping Strategies of Black Women and Other Women of Color Faculty Members at a Research University', *The Journal of Negro Education*, 70 (3): 166.

Warrell, M. (2013), 'Glass Ceiling or Glass Cage? Breaking Through the Biggest Barrier Holding Women Back', *Forbes*, 4 August. Available online: https://www.forbes.com/sites/margiewarrell/2013/08/04/glass-ceiling-or-glass-cage-breaking-through-the-biggest-barrier-holding-women-back/#6ad925c53101 (accessed 20 January 2022).

Wei, N. (2016), 'A Study of Employment Discrimination against Women in China from a Comparative Perspective', MA diss., University of Oslo, Oslo.

World Bank (2019), 'Gender-Based Violence (Violence Against Women and Girls)', *The World Bank*, 25 September. Available online: https://www.worldbank.org/en/topic/socialsustainability/brief/violence-against-women-and-girls (accessed 20 January 2022).

World Economic Forum (2020), 'The Global Gender Gap Report 2020', *World Economic Forum*. Available online: https://www.weforum.org/reports/gender-gap-2020-report-100-years-pay-equality (accessed 20 January 2022).

Wu, A. X. and Y. Dong (2019), 'What is Made-in-China feminism(s)? Gender Discontent and Class Friction in Post-socialist China', *Critical Asian Studies*, 51 (1): 1–22.

Xie, B. (2007), 'Chinese International Students' Perceptions and Attitudes Toward Seeking Psychological Counseling Services: A Qualitative Exploration', Doctoral diss., University of Minnesota, Twin Cities.

Yakaboski, T. (2013), 'The Rest of the Story: A Qualitative Study of Chinese and Indian Women's Graduate Education Migration', *Journal About Women in Higher Education*, 6 (2): 166–84.

Yang, J. (2007), 'Zuiqian "Deficient Mouth": Discourse, Gender and Domestic Violence', *Gender and Language*, 1 (1): 107–18.

Zhang, J. Y. (1992), *Dangdai Nvxing Zhuyi Wenxue Piping* [Critique on Modern Feminist Literature], Beijing: Beijing University Press.

Zheng, Y. (2019), 'Chinese Women Earn a Fifth Less Than Men and the Gap is Widening Fast, Survey by Online Recruiter Boss Zhipin Finds', *South China Morning Post*, 7 March. Available online: https://www.scmp.com/business/china-business/article

/2188933/chinese-women-earn-fifth-less-men-and-gap-widening-fast (accessed 20 January 2022).

Zhou, Y. (2018), 'The Impact of Chinese Students in the US, Charted and Mapped', *Quartz*, 2 October. Available online: https://qz.com/1410768/the-number-of-chinese -students-in-the-us-charted-and-mapped/ (accessed 20 January 2022).

Zhu, J. (2016), *Chinese Overseas Students and Intercultural Learning Environments*, London: Palgrave Macmillan.

Zweig, D. and Z. Ge (2018), 'How Chinese Students Who Return Home After Studying Abroad Succeed – And Why They Don't', *SCWP*, 27 July. Available online: https://www .scmp.com/comment/insight-opinion/asia/article/2157081/how-chinese-students-who -return-home-after-studying (accessed 20 January 2022).

Chapter 8

Gender Inequality in the Higher Education Workplace

Demanding a Seat at an Antiquated Table

Rebekah Bray and Shelly Shaffer

Introduction

> I've definitely been in so many meetings or environments in which I felt immediately uncomfortable. Like this is not – we're not communicating in a way that's respectful or productive, and really feeling like you just need to stand up and say, 'Thank you, but I can't engage in this way.' (Hannah*, interview) (*all names are pseudonyms)

At one of my weekly meetings at UX, I (Rebekah Shaffer) witnessed an interruption. A female colleague tried to explain the reasoning behind a decision made by an office on campus, when she was abruptly interrupted and talked over by a male colleague. She sat in stunned silence, as the man put his hand up to quiet her. She locked eyes with me as we let his disrespect wash over us. Never having witnessed him interrupting a male colleague, I couldn't help but wonder if this man felt entitled to interrupt because of whom he was interrupting: a woman.

Working in higher education, we (both authors) have witnessed female staff and faculty experience discrimination and mistreatment by men. As women who value education and a society focused on gender inequality, we believe in a higher education workplace where access, inclusivity and encouragement for women compare to the same opportunities for men. Although progress has been made over the years in terms of gender equality in education and in the workplace, women still fight not only for a seat at the academic table, but also for a higher rung on the professional ladder.

The purpose of this research was to add to the literature by investigating the experiences of women working at a university in the North-western United States, UX. We explored their experiences related to gender through survey and interview data, hoping to uncover whether women at UX had gender inequality experiences.

Women in higher education

According to Beddoes and Schimpf (2016), Cundiff et al. (2018) and Wheat and Hill (2016), women have made serious strides in academia and hold more tenure-track faculty and high-level administrative positions than ever before. Despite this tremendous progress, the under-representation of women in upper ranks of faculty and administration continues to run rampant and is even more pronounced for women of minority racial and ethnic status (Beddoes and Schimpf 2016; Cundiff et al. 2018; Hymowitz and Schellhardt 1986). Wheat and Hill (2016) studied women in higher education administration and noted that women were less likely to hold senior administrative positions such as academic dean, vice-president, provost or president. Beddoes and Schimpf (2016) claimed that one of the major contributing factors to female under-representation in higher education was 'gender-blindness', which referred to the fact that most department heads were white men (36). These male leaders erroneously thought that they were treating women fairly, but their unacknowledged biases contributed to a male-centred working environment. Visible under-representation (Beddoes and Schimpf 2016; Cundiff et al. 2018; Hymowitz and Schellhardt 1986; Wheat and Hill 2016) was also related to a significant pay gap between men and women who did the same job (Cundiff et al. 2018; Hegewisch and Barsi 2020).

Not only have women been severely under-represented in senior-level positions in higher education institutions, but the personal experiences of women have also been under-represented in the research about leadership and power in higher education. Enke (2014) claimed that the experiences of women leaders have rarely been included in scholarship. Wheat and Hill (2016) noted that gender differences in leadership roles were not studied until the 1970s and connected the lack of gender-related research, as well as the current and historical absence of female leadership at the university level, to this finding. This lack of data perpetuates beliefs about the 'effectiveness, competency, and legitimacy' of women leaders, as well as the value of their work (Enke 2014: 202).

Challenges for women in higher education

Although women were often innovative, productive and successful leaders, they experienced barriers to their progress and advancement, which perpetuated gender under-representation (Teague 2015). External obstacles such as lower salaries, appointments at lower ranks, slower rates of promotion, lower rates of retention and less recognition were prevalent within higher education (Dominici, Fried and Zeger 2009). Kersh (2018) observed that women administrators in higher education were often affected by factors such as leadership issues, multiple-role management, discrimination and marginalization and role insufficiency, which led to increased stress, health risks and mental health issues in women occupying these roles. Chuang (2015) found that family and time constraints, cost and work constraints, lack of support systems and the lack of career advice and resources also impacted women's experiences.

Despite deterrents and challenges, Chuang (2015) and Beddoes and Schimpf (2016) believed that to increase the number of women who successfully advanced into leadership positions in higher education, universities must address the barriers and obstacles that continue to hamper women's advancement, such as lack of professional development, lack of professional mentorship and biases and discrimination related to gender. Turner, Norwood and Noe (2013) claimed that the perpetuation of barriers caused additional challenges for women, including discouraging women from pursuing leadership routes.

Gender stereotypes and cultural assumptions about leadership potential and effectiveness were some of the most destructive root causes of under-representation of women in higher education (Chuang 2015; Dominici, Fried and Zeger 2009). In places like Hong Kong and Australia, Aiston and Yang (2017) and Noble (2014) found a lack of reliable data about women in higher education, as well as cultural barriers about women's ambition and qualifications. However, Hackett, Betz and Doty (1985) and Shepherd (2017) noted that women's missing agency likely comes from internal factors, as well as from a lack of confidence, leading women to voluntarily opt out of senior-level positions. While some universities have made efforts to destroy gender inequality, the contributions of women have continued to be unrecognized or were unfairly measured against the work of male colleagues (Lipton 2017). Across Africa, women at universities have experienced under-representation because of patriarchal practices, customs, traditions and cultural stereotypes that further work against women seeking leadership or management positions, despite being qualified (Eboiyehi, Fayomi and Eboiyehi 2016).

Regarding systemic structures that stood in the way of women's success in higher education workplaces, Gouthro, Taber and Brazil (2018) pointed to the perpetuation of economic and policy pressures which limited the value of critical, creative thinking and often led to cuts in disciplines that tended to have a greater concentration of women faculty.

Cassidy, Faucher and Jackson (2014) concluded that female faculty, both those in permanent and non-permanent positions, were more likely to be targeted by bullying than male faculty. Similarly, female faculty tended to carry the long-term effects of being bullied with them throughout their careers (Cassidy, Faucher and Jackson 2014). Women in university workplaces were often the recipients of bullying that included (a) positionality, (b) differences (age, gender, race, religion, sexual orientation, etc.), (c) jealousy, (d) clandestine decision-making, (e) accountability and leadership and (f) victim blaming (Sedivy-Benton et al. 2014).

Strategies leading to success

While many issues face women in the higher education workplace today, a rising number of proactive strategies and coping mechanisms are being used by women to increase health, work and personal success. Kersh (2018) suggested that women working in higher education saw external workplace stressors as challenges rather than as threats, and that they employed various coping strategies to overcome, resolve or redirect challenges, including active coping, humour, mental disengagement, use of emotional support, acceptance of the situation, positive reinterpretation and venting of emotions. Similar to Kersh (2018), Murphrey et al. (2016) suggested that strategies that involved interaction with other individuals were more effective for women. Edds-Ellis and Keaster (2013), Murphrey et al. (2016), O'Connor (2019) and Parker (2015) found mentorship created a positive climate for female leadership development, improved readiness for leadership roles and increased the number of female leaders in higher education. O'Connor (2019) noted that developing a positive climate meant hiring leaders for senior positions who had a history of fighting gender inequality and focusing on gender-sensitive budgeting and policies. In addition, Teague (2015) argued the importance of leaders who came prepared with a diverse set of experiences, viewpoints and backgrounds.

Cundiff et al. (2018) and Dominici, Fried and Zeger (2009) argued that the gender biases were often the result of undetected stereotypes, claiming that interventions could 'educate individuals about the subtle nature of bias so they are better able to detect, report, and avoid bias', which could eventually lead to more success for women in the higher education workplace (614). Dominici, Fried and Zeger (2009) claimed that 'recognizing the root causes of under-representation of women in leadership positions – that is, the gender stereotypes that exist – is the first concrete step toward the elimination of the obstacles women face' (2). Lester (2008) argued similarly that progress would only be made once gender roles and norms were exposed and destroyed.

Beddoes and Schimpf (2016) claimed that examining the discourses of higher education can help us to understand why inequalities exist and persist. Teague (2015) listed a number of other action steps that positively influenced women in higher education, which included raising awareness and ensuring accountability. Both Teague (2015) and Turner, Norwood and Noe (2013) believed that it was critical to offer guidance to women who wanted to prepare themselves for leadership so that they recognized and valued their skills and talents. Schoening (2009) argued that institutional policies like increasing family-care and disability leave, stopping the tenure clock, creating modified duties and temporary part-time appointments, childcare policies and setting clear standards could improve the occupancy and sustainability of women in senior faculty and administrative positions. Finally, Edwards (2017) found a need for regular, effective training connected to a myriad of university activities, like the submission of grant applications and promotion and performance reviews.

Description of the project

Drawing upon the review of the literature and personal experiences, this study examined the experiences and beliefs of women working at a Masters' University in the North-western part of the United States, UX. This research project was guided by three research questions:

1. What are the experiences of women in the higher education workforce at UX?
2. Do women face inequalities in the workforce at University X?
3. What strategies do women at UX use to overcome gender inequality?

This study employed a mixed-methodology design, with data collected via a quantitative survey and qualitative semi-structured interviews. Collecting both qualitative and quantitative data allowed the researchers to investigate the general and specific experiences of women working at UX.

Description of the site and participants

UX is a four-year public Masters university in the North-western United States. It is known for its rural setting and diverse population of approximately 12,000 students and 2,500 employees. Employees work in various offices and positions across the university's three campuses.

In order to distribute an anonymous survey to female employees at UX, I (Rebekah) conducted a convenience sampling of UX's female employees. I spent several days scouring UX's website, gathering the names and email addresses of every female employee I could find. I searched through each college, department and office page until I was confident that I had accessed every viewable UX page that listed employees. I will note here that I had no other criteria in the selection of subjects other than (a) being a woman listed on UX's site, and (b) having a readily available email address. I did not use any other method for finding female UX employees and I did not include student workers. In total, I collected the names and email addresses of 497 women who worked at UX and I distributed the survey to each of them. In the end, I received 148 completed surveys. Table 8.1 shares the self-reported positions of survey respondents.

Overall, respondents were highly educated. Almost 65 per cent had graduate degrees: forty-four held a doctoral or professional degree (29.93 per cent) and

Table 8.1 Survey Respondents

Position	Number of respondents	Percentage
Senior-level administration	3	2.07%
Administration	44	30.14%
Senior-level classified	5	3.42%
Classified	36	25.34%
Department chair	1	0.68%
Full professor	10	6.85%
Associate professor	7	4.79%
Assistant professor	12	8.22%
Lecturer or quarterly faculty	21	14.38%
Other	6	4.11%

Table 8.2 Interview Participants

Participant[a]	Role
Patricia	Faculty member, age: early to mid-40s
Jeri	Classified administrative support, age: late 20s/early 30s
Hannah	Faculty member, age: late 30s/early 40s
Ava	Classified staff, age: mid-40s
Alex	Upper-level administration, age: late 50s
Melinda	Classified administrative support, age: mid/late 20s

[a.] All names are pseudonyms.

fifty-one held a master's degree (34.69 per cent). Another 29.93 per cent had a college degree: forty-one with a bachelor's degree (27.89 per cent) and three with an associate degree (2.04 per cent). Just 8 of the 147 respondents had less than an associate degree.

The semi-structured interview was designed to be a follow-up to the survey in order to investigate specific participant experiences in the UX workplace. To solicit interviewees, I included my contact information at the end of the survey. I was contacted by more than ten women interested in participating in the interview. I selected the first six women to respond, again using convenience sampling to select participants. Only gender was considered in the selection of interview participants, and no data concerning race or ethnicity were collected. See Table 8.2 for a description of participants.

Data collection

The survey included twenty-two questions investigating experiences and perceptions of gender in the workplace. The survey itself allowed for full anonymity, not asking any questions pertaining to participants' identities. A Likert scale was used for sixteen of the twenty-two questions, which allowed the participants to gauge the rating of their response. The survey also included two demographic questions that asked the respondent to select their type of position at UX, as well as their highest level of schooling completed. At the end of the survey, contact information was provided for those who were interested in a follow-up interview. Readers can access the survey questions using the following link: https://tinyurl.com/yfvytyb9.

According to the Robert Wood Johnson Foundation (2008), semi-structured interviews allow for the use of an interview guide while still providing the opportunity to stray from formality and 'identify new ways of seeing and understanding the topic at hand'. For this project in particular, the idea of using a formal interview guide with several questions that would be asked of all interviewees while having the freedom to explore the experiences and ideas of the interviewees on such a hot-button issue seemed like the best of both worlds. To access the list of structured interview questions, please visit https://tinyurl.com/nmcp3rca.

Data-analysis strategies

This survey was distributed via Survey Monkey and participants were provided two weeks to complete the survey and contact the researcher about the interview. Of the 497 women who received the survey, 147 women responded, an approximately 30 per cent response rate. Descriptive statistics of the survey's responses were taken from Survey Monkey's analytics and calculated by hand (see Table 8.3).

Each interview was recorded and later transcribed. Responses were coded using open coding by both researchers and then umbrella categories were created, grouping codes into categories or axial codes (Corbin and Strauss 2007). Merriam (2009) claimed that names of the categories can come from at least three sources: 'the researcher, the participants, or sources outside the study such as the literature' (184). The final codes we used were taken directly from participant interview transcripts. Table 8.4 shows the axial codes and open codes that were discovered from the interview data.

Findings

The findings fell into four categories: progressive, boys' club, troublemaking and empower. These categories were determined after a close examination of the data and determining the relationship to the study questions.

Table 8.3 Survey Descriptive Statistics

Question	Respondents	Range	Mean	Std. Deviation
1	147	4	1.91	0.70
2	147	5	2.93	1.12
3	146	5	2.63	1.01
4	147	5	2.73	1.05
5	147	4	1.88	0.58
6	146	3	1.06	0.31
7	147	5	2.39	1.08
8	146	5	2.51	1.07
9	147	5	2.44	1.13
10	146	5	2.08	1.06
11	147	5	4.64	0.66
12	145	5	2.94	1.03
13	146	4	1.59	0.70
14	145	5	2.47	1.17
15	144	3	2.17	0.97
16	146	2	1.61	0.49
17	67	3	1.60	0.71
18	146	2	1.62	0.49
19	68	3	1.90	0.93
20	146	4	2.52	1.26
21	145	10	4.89	2.79
22	146	6	2.18	1.08

Note: This table shares the number of responses for each survey question, along with the range, mean and standard deviation.

Table 8.4 Coding

Umbrella category	Codes within the category
Progressive	Other roles, balancing, unrealistic expectations, carrying unequal loads
Good Old Boys	Pay, boys' club, men more credible, exclusive
Troublemaking	Bitch, assertiveness, perceptions, troublemaker, reporting, emotional
Empower	Female leaders (visibility/lack of visibility), mentorship, lack of knowledge/training, power/empower, ally, collaboration

'We're supposed to be progressive'

Women in the study identified balancing several roles, including home and workplace; unrealistic expectations for women versus men; unequal roles between men and women doing the same job; and gendered roles in the workplace. Each of these findings fits into the *progressive* category because women were frustrated that the university did not support equality in the workplace or their outside-of-work roles – ideals those in higher education would expect to see represented in the setting. Jeri expressed this during an interview: 'I'm in academia. We're a university. We're supposed to be progressive and we're not.'

Participants shared frustration due to juggling multiple roles both at work and at home. Being a wife, mother or primary caregiver carried its own expectations that often created a tug-of-war with work expectations. Hannah shared that she felt unable to back away from her work in order to have children, pursue creative projects or conduct research without disappointing her department: 'I was told early on "No, you can't leave."' According to Patricia, balancing the multiple roles was an unfair expectation for women:

> So, it just does feel like there's maybe some flexibility that might be needed, and I don't know if that's a gender-related thing. But it's – it is something that could help the busy women that are trying to balance their families and their jobs and, you know, all of these things. . . . And I feel like women do more of that balancing than men.

Patricia noted that beyond work at the university, women were often expected to go home, attend school events, cook dinner and clean the house. The expectations of balancing a teaching load with these other responsibilities seemed impossible for some faculty, including Patricia.

Participants shared experiences where workloads and the expectations for women were different on the job compared to men. Hannah claimed: 'There is a disparity that I feel is gendered in the amount of service that female faculty contribute versus men. In my own experience, there – my male colleagues understand how to implement boundaries really early on and don't budge.' Hannah shared, 'I do have more boundaries, because I had children and I have to,' but she often felt tension about these boundaries – even leading to job insecurity. Hannah said duties just 'piled on, piled on, piled on' and because of the vulnerability of her programme and position, she felt unable to refuse additional work. Patricia also said, 'I think some of the expectations as far as – just the amount of busyness – could be not friendly for women that have families' and 'the workload. It feels unequally distributed.' In fact, 54 per cent of women surveyed reported that they felt they must perform better than their male counterparts to be promoted to the same position. Only 18 per cent of respondents disagreed or strongly disagreed with this statement, revealing that the majority of women surveyed believed that they must outperform their male counterparts to be chosen for promotion. This reflected a feeling among participants that more work was being done by women compared to men in the same roles.

Workplace gendered roles were often the norm in several of our participants' experiences. Being charged with decorations and party planning was an expectation. Melinda commented on being her department's 'token vagina' after hearing a male colleague's comment, 'We want you to be a part of this so you can give us, help us give a feminine touch.' She was angry and appalled by the assumption that because she was female, she cared about parties and decorating. Jeri expressed frustration after discussing the #MeToo movement with colleagues. She didn't like the phrasing 'look at us as a sister . . . [or] as a mother' because that seemed to support gendered thinking; rather, she said, 'Just treat us like human beings.'

Good old boys

An interesting finding was the interviewees' perceptions of UX's administration. More than half of the interviewees brought up the existence of a 'boys' club' (Jeri), 'the old boys' club' (Patricia) or 'the good old boys' (Ava) within upper administration on the other hand; others argued that actually a larger number of women occupied upper administrative roles (i.e. university president, vice-president(s) and dean). Ava noted:

> There are still some, what I guess could be construed as something like the 'good old boys'. That they really kind of stick close together and promote who they promote, not necessarily based on qualifications, but can be construed as how you identify. In this case most likely, I mean male.

Alex shared:

> I think it's important to pay attention to who you automatically choose in your inner circle, and I think by and large – I think there's a quote-unquote natural tendency to choose people who are like you.

Both Jeri and Patricia acknowledged that some women were in leadership roles at the top, but both questioned these leaders' legitimacy and power. Jeri shared, 'We do have leadership that is women. Like we do have some. I mean we have token ones.' Patricia said, 'The president is more of a token figure anyways.' Alex stated, 'Whatever power the president has, it's very quiet.' In contrast, Melinda felt that the many women leaders at UX created a gender imbalance towards men:

I don't think that my perspective is reality, because I only see the high-level executives on campus who are predominantly female. So, like I would say there's gender inequity in the sense that there's too many females. There's an unbalance of females, I would say, not too many, because you can't have too many. It's just not balanced.

The mixed perceptions of the women in top leadership positions were evident in the interviews with the women at UX. Though some felt marginalized by the men at the top, others felt women leaders were rampant at the university, albeit in positions for show rather than of actual power.

In response to the question, 'Do you believe women are as capable as men of serving in senior executive positions at UX, whether faculty or administration?' over 99 per cent strongly agreed or agreed in women's capabilities to perform senior leadership roles. Only 1 of the 147 total survey takers disagreed with this statement. In terms of capability and positional superiority, 94 per cent of respondents either disagreed or strongly disagreed that men were superior to women. On the other hand, 73 per cent of women surveyed shared the perception that some men they knew at UX felt they were superior to women. Building on this, Alex, Ava, Hannah, Jeri, Melinda and Patricia all found themselves in situations where they thought that they had either witnessed or personally experienced gender bias by male co-workers. Alex blamed cultural norms: 'A tall man with a deep voice is going to be more commanding than a small woman with a high-pitched voice.' Interviewees pondered how different situations would have played out if they were men: 'I wonder if it would be different for a man, because he would manage it differently, right?' (Hannah). Survey respondents were mixed on whether they were treated differently in the workplace than their male counterparts; 41 per cent of respondents strongly agreed or agreed that they were treated equally, while 38 per cent reported unequal treatment. In addition, many respondents believed that UX should be doing more to promote gender equality in the workplace (37 per cent).

When considering differences in pay between men and women in the workplace, the boys' club again played a role. Having worked in a sector of the university that deals with finances and payroll, Ava noted that she was privy to seeing inequalities when it came to pay. 'I would tell women to come in here and reach for the stars when it comes to stuff like that, because chances are even what you ask for are still not going to be as much as some people around here. I just want to put it that way.' Despite this, when asked about pay differences between genders, just 42 per cent of survey respondents believed that pay inequality existed between males and females who had the same credentials and 22 per cent of respondents disagreed that a gender pay gap existed.

Troublemaking

The theme of troublemaking appeared in several interviews. This umbrella category includes female faculty perceptions about reporting sexual harassment and discrimination, and negative labelling.

Women were often conflicted over reporting discrimination and harassment due to fear of repercussions towards their promotion and reputation at the workplace. Jeri spoke of a specific workplace scenario where she was belittled and yelled at, forced to agonize over whether or not to report the situation while weighing the risks of becoming a *troublemaker.*

> I have to be very careful in my position because if I say the wrong thing or if I go and make an issue of it, how is that going to hurt my career? And you can't make those enemies. Especially even though they may not be here at that time, that reputation goes around, and I don't want to be known as a troublemaker.

Jeri went on to say:

> You shouldn't have to feel fear every day. . . . And not just for your safety, but is somebody going to yell at me today? Is somebody going to speak to me in a certain way . . . that they wouldn't speak to me if I was a different gender?

In thinking about reporting, both Ava and Jeri had trouble identifying whom they could contact for issues of inequality or discrimination.

The survey asked respondents whether they had experienced gender discrimination and harassment. When asked, 'Have you ever been a victim of gender discrimination in [UX's] workplace environment?' more than 70 per cent of respondents were either *not sure* or reported they *had not* been victims of discrimination. Only 29 per cent revealed that they had been victims of discrimination in the workplace. When asked if they had been harassed or bullied due to their gender, almost 70 per cent of survey respondents reported *no*, with only 22 per cent reporting they had been harassed or bullied.

Another finding was the perceived correlation between being labelled a *bitch* or *emotional* versus being *successful* or *opinionated.* Interviewees seemed to find common ground in the frustration that stemmed from this common dichotomy. Melinda said:

> As a society, we're still not accepting of women being dominant leaders. I mean, there's that classic that if a man is assertive, he's seen as a powerful leader. If a woman is assertive, she's seen as a bitch. I think the problem for women in leadership is that they can be portrayed as catty or bitchy, when really if a man said the exact same thing, he would be seen as making a difference.

Similarly, Jeri said:

> I think that they also need to realize that there's the fine line of being – how do I want to phrase this? You can't be so hard that you're perceived as a bitch. If I was abrasive, then I would be a bitch. Nobody would want to work with me.

The perceptions of others made a huge impact on how women spoke and acted in the workplace. Being stigmatized by a label was something that most of the women wanted to avoid. At times, women also felt like their decisions were questioned. Hannah noted wanting to make a decision and 'not feeling like we have to explain ourselves or overly lay out the justification more so than our peers or male colleagues would need to . . . to not question the decisions that we make as much'.

Empower

There was a common thread among all interviewees regarding power. Participants often reported feeling disempowered in the workplace but, in contrast, feeling empowered by their success in their personal lives. Women also compared their power to men at the university and found differences.

Participants often felt supported in their respective positions but were mostly unaware of whether UX promoted professional development and success for women in the workplace. When asked if women were encouraged to apply for senior faculty or administrative positions, seventy-eight respondents strongly agreed/agreed, while twenty-three women disagreed/strongly disagreed. Regarding career development opportunities, respondents indicated similar answers: seventy-nine women agreed/strongly agreed while thirty disagreed/strongly disagreed. Women surveyed were split about equal opportunities, with about 33 per cent agreeing/strongly agreeing and 33 per cent disagreeing/strongly disagreeing. When asked whether gender will make a difference in their ability to advance their career, 40 per cent reported it would be *harder*, 3 per cent claimed it would be *easier* and 58 per cent indicated it *won't make much difference*.

Participants identified a need for support. Women often referred to finding a mentor to act as a guide through the inevitable rocky terrain of being a woman in leadership. Despite research claiming that mentorship and collaboration is a key component for women's success in higher education, only 38.78 per cent (fifty-seven) of women surveyed at UX reported they had worked with a mentor during their time at the university. Of those fifty-seven women who had worked with a mentor, more than half (thirty-six) had a female mentor. Respondents had also served as mentors to other women (56/147), with 33/57 (or 48.53 per cent) reporting having worked with female mentees. Hannah shared:

> It's hit or miss. I think mentorship in general at [UX] is really sporadic. That's what, you know. You can have someone that really mentors you and facilitates, then you could have somebody who's not interested in helping anymore, and that might be for really good reasons. That might be because it's a revolving door, right? And they're just like [sigh]. They've been burned so many times that they put up their walls and boundaries and then, you know, their way of surviving and, you know, it's not personal but it feels personal.

Patricia brought up the point that women often took on leadership roles without the official title or pay, and these women often served as mentors to other women. Patricia felt that UX did have 'women that are around and that are leaders and that are kind of showing that for other women on campus. They're just not officially in like a leadership position . . . they are leaders, but they're not being like paid to be a leader'. Mentoring seemed to be desired, but not often provided or available, at least officially by UX.

Discussion and implications

For women hoping to learn more about the experiences of women in higher education, our study adds to the research centred on personal experiences of female staff and faculty in university settings, as per Emke (2014). While some findings support the prior research, others provide direction for further exploration.

The study connected to prior research about unequal expectations and balancing roles in the workplace and at home. For example, like participants in Kersh (2018) and Chuang (2015), our participants struggled balancing work and home expectations. Both Hannah and Patricia expressed frustration at trying to balance the unrealistic expectations of workload with personal pursuits and family, often comparing their experiences to male colleagues. Hannah's inability to step away from job duties to pursue creative opportunities also compared to the findings in Gouthro, Taber and Brazil (2018). Like the women mentioned in the studies of Chuang (2015), Dominici, Fried and Zeger (2009), Kersh (2018) and Teague (2015), women working at UX also faced issues in balancing social and work roles, being listened to or taken seriously as a legitimate professional, being promoted to new positions, being charged with far greater amounts of work and experiencing pay inequalities.

Beyond gendered expectations related to job duties, our study revealed that women in higher education, especially in male-dominated departments, were often tokenized. Like women in studies by Aiston and Yang (2017), Eboiyehi, Fayomi and Eboiyehi (2016) and Noble (2014), cultural factors impacted the way women were treated in the workplace. Women in our study experienced unfair expectations by male colleagues to 'provide a feminine touch' on planning and events in the department. These patriarchal expectations were not part of the job duties ascribed to these women; however, they were expected to perform the task simply due to gender. Also, women in leadership roles were often viewed as having less power than their male counterparts.

While the data overwhelmingly showed that most women felt they were just as capable to serve in leadership positions as their male counterparts, more than half also felt like they must perform better in order to be promoted to the same position, as per Lipton (2017). Additionally, similar to the findings of Cundiff et al. (2018) and Dominici, Fried and Zeger (2009), several of our interviewees noted that gender stereotypes and assumptions worked against gender equality, bringing into question the competence, abilities and leadership qualities of women in the higher education workplace.

There seemed to be a common thread regarding professional development opportunities for women in the workplace at UX. Similar to O'Connor (2019) and Teague (2015), our participants recognized the importance of women mentors already in leadership positions. Almost 40 per cent of those surveyed had been in a mentorship programme in the past; data hinted at the idea that women working at UX might be interested in a more robust mentorship programme. Studies by Edds-Ellis and Keaster (2013), Murphey et al. (2016), O'Connor (2019) and Parker (2015) all found comparable data that suggested the importance of mentorship, specifically same-gendered mentorship. In addition to mentorship programmes, support groups, trainings and workshops would support UX's women in the workplace, all of which are in tandem with the research of Edwards (2017), Teague (2015) and Turner, Norwood and Noe (2013).

Though our research was limited to studying the experiences of a small sample of women from a regional university in the North-western United States, we feel it contributes to the growing field of studies about women's experiences in the higher education environment. We have learned that gender continues to play a major role in the experiences of women in this domain.

References

Aiston, S. J. and Z. Yang (2017), '"Absent Data, Absent Women": Gender and Higher Education Leadership', *Policy Futures in Education*, 15 (3): 262–74.

Beddoes, K. and C. Schimpf (2016), 'What's Wrong with Fairness? How Discourses in Higher Education Literature Support Gender Inequalities', *Discourse: Studies in the Cultural Politics of Education*, 39 (1): 31–40.

Cassidy, W., C. Faucher and M. Jackson (2014), 'The Dark Side of the Ivory Tower: Cyberbullying of University Faculty and Teaching Personnel', *Alberta Journal of Educational Research*, 60 (2): 279–99.

Chuang, S. (2015), 'Deterrents to Women's Participation in Continuing Professional Development', *New Horizons in Adult Education & Human Resource Development*, 27 (2): 28–37.

Corbin, J. and A. Strauss (2007), *Basics of Qualitative Research: Techniques and Procedures for Developing Grounded Theory*, 3rd edn, Thousand Oaks, CA: Sage.

Cundiff, J. L., C. L. Danube, S. A. Shields and M. J. Zawadzki (2018), 'Testing an Intervention for Recognizing and Reporting Subtle Gender Bias in Promotion and Tenure Decisions', *The Journal of Higher Education*, 89 (5): 611–36.

Dominici, F., L. P. Fried and S. L. Zeger (2009), 'So Few Women Leaders', *Academe*, 95 (4): 25–7.

Eboiyehi, C. O., I. Fayomi and F. A. Eboiyehi (2016), 'From Exclusion to Discrimination: Gender Inequality in the Senior Management of Nigerian Universities', *Issues in Educational Research*, 26 (2): 182–205.

Edds-Ellis, S. and R. Keaster (2013), 'Same-gendered Leadership Mentoring in Postsecondary Education', *Journal of Academic Administration in Higher Education*, 9 (1): 1–8.

Edwards, J. (2017), 'Narrating Experiences of Sexism in Higher Education: A Critical Feminist Autoethnography to Make Meaning of the Past, Challenge the Status Quo and Consider the Future', *International Journal of Qualitative Studies in Education*, 30 (7): 621–34.

Enke, K. (2014), 'Conceptions of Power Among Senior Women Administrators at Liberal Arts Colleges in the Upper Midwestern United States', *NASPA Journal About Women in Higher Education*, 7 (2): 199–225.

Gouthro, P., N. Taber and A. Brazil (2018), 'Universities as Inclusive Learning Organizations for Women? Considering the Role of Women in Faculty and Leadership Roles in Academe', *The Learning Organization*, 25 (1): 29–39.

Hackett, G., N. E. Betz and M. S. Doty (1985), 'The Development of a Taxonomy of Career Competencies for Professional Women', *Sex Roles*, 12 (3–4): 393–409.

Hegewisch, A. and Z. Barsi (2020, March 24), 'ESME, Fact Sheet: The Gender Wage Gap by Occupation 2019', Institute for Women's Policy Research. Available online: https://iwpr.org/iwpr-issues/employment-and-earnings/the-gender-wage-gap-by-occupation-2019/#_edn2 (accessed 15 April 2020).

Hymowitz, C. and T. D. Schellhardt (1986), 'The Glass Ceiling: Why Women Can't Seem to Break the Invisible Barrier that Blocks Them from the Top Jobs', *Wall Street Journal*, 24 March: 61.

Kersh, R. (2018), 'Women in Higher Education: Exploring Stressful Workplace Factors and Coping Strategies', *NASPA Journal About Women in Higher Education*, 11 (1): 56–73.

Lester, J. (2008), 'Performing Gender in the Workplace: Gender Socialization, Power, and Identity Among Women Faculty Members', *Community College Review*, 35 (4): 277–305.

Lipton, B. (2017), 'Measures of Success: Cruel Optimism and the Paradox of Academic Women's Participation in Australian Higher Education', *Higher Education Research & Development*, 36 (3): 486–97.

Merriam, S. B. (2009), *Qualitative Research: A Guide to Design and Implementation: Revised and Expanded from Qualitative Research and Case Study Applications in Education*, San Francisco, CA: Jossey-Bass.

Murphrey, T. P., S. F. Odom, V. McKee and C. C. Wilkens (2016), 'A Qualitative Examination of Success Factors for Tenure-Track Women Faculty in Postsecondary Agricultural Education', *Journal of Agricultural Education*, 57 (4): 54–67.

Noble, C. (2014), 'Gender Equity in Australian Universities: The Many Paradoxes of Securing Senior Leadership Positions', *Forum on Public Policy*, 2014 (1): 1–9.

O'Connor, P. (2019), 'Gender Imbalance in Senior Positions in Higher Education: What is the Problem? What Can be Done?' *Policy Reviews in Higher Education*, 3 (1): 28–50.

Parker, P. (2015), 'The Historical Role of Women in Higher Education', *Administrative Issues Journal: Connecting Education, Practice, and Research*, 5 (1): 3–14.

Robert Wood Johnson Foundation (2008), 'Semi-Structured Interviews'. Available online: http://www.qualres.org/HomeSemi-3629.html (accessed 30 April 2019).

Schoening, A. M. (2009), 'Women and Tenure: Closing the Gap', *The Journal of Women in Educational Leadership*, 7 (2): 77–92.

Sedivy-Benton, A., G. Strohschen, N. Cavazos and C. Boden-McGill (2014), 'Good Ol' Boys, Mean Girls, and Tyrants: A Phenomenological Study of the Lived Experiences and Survival Strategies of Bullied Adult Educators', *Adult Learning*, 26 (1): 35–41.

Shepherd, S. (2017), 'Why are There so Few Female Leaders in Higher Education: A Case of Structure or Agency?' *Management in Education*, 31 (2): 82–7.

Teague, L. J. (2015), 'Higher Education Plays Critical Role in Society: More Women Leaders Can Make a Difference', *Forum on Public Policy Online*, 2015 (2): 1–20.

Turner, P. K., K. Norwood and C. Noe (2013), 'A Woman with a Plan: Recognizing Competencies for Ascent to Administration in Higher Education', *NASPA Journal About Women in Higher Education*, 6 (1): 22–47.

Wheat, C. A. and L. H. Hill (2016), 'Leadership Identities, Styles, and Practices of Women University Administrators and Presidents', *Research in the Schools*, 23 (2): 1–16.

Chapter 9

A Joint Autoethnographic Account of Two Young Women in Academia

On Overcoming Imposter Syndrome

Catherine Wilkinson and Samantha Wilkinson

Introduction

This chapter adopts an intersectional lens – focusing on the intersection of age and gender – to present a joint autoethnographic account of two young women lecturers at different higher education institutions (HEIs) in the UK. Herein, we, twin sisters, build on previous autoethnographic publications written while employed in our first lecturing positions (S. Wilkinson 2019; C. Wilkinson, 2020). Now employed as a reader (Catherine) and a senior lecturer (Samantha), we reflect on excerpts from personal research diaries recorded between January 2019 and April 2021, considering strategies for overcoming feelings of being imposters.

This chapter contributes a nuanced account to existing work on imposter syndrome and women in academia, using the lens of intersectionality and the methodological approach of joint autoethnography. Many autoethnographies in academia are narratives of struggle. For instance, Wright (2016) positions herself as an accidental academic, focusing on working-class cultural and economic barriers. The author, reflecting on the unplanned nature of her journey to becoming a scholar, calls for educators to encourage more deliberate academic pursuits for those belonging to lower socioeconomic groups. Tienari (2019) offers an autoethnographic account of moving from a Finnish-speaking business school to a Swedish-speaking one in Helsinki, Finland. The author tells of the sense of guilt he felt as a Finnish speaker who works in English, for not contributing in Swedish and for enacting an identity of an outsider in his community. Much less often seen in the literature are joint autoethnographies. For an exception we refer the reader to Anderson, Goodall and Trahar's (2020: 393) collaborative autoethnography of academia, which they term a 'powerful conversation'. Through this process the authors 'challenged generalisations, explored emotions and illuminated further [their] complex identities as women in academia' (Anderson, Goodall and Trahar 2020: 393). Likewise, through this chapter we argue for the usefulness of joint autoethnography as a multivocal and reflexive methodological approach.

This chapter is structured as follows. First, we provide a position statement. We then review existing literature on imposter syndrome in higher education. Second, we present key debates in the literature concerned with women in academia, with an emphasis on what adopting an intersectional approach can bring to these debates. Then, we detail the methodological approach adopted in this chapter: joint autoethnography. Following this, we discuss key themes identified through our analysis: practical and purposeful solutions; and changing life circumstances: putting things into perspective. We conclude with recommendations for practice, or more specifically institutional change, and recommendations for future research to further understandings of the gendered and aged experiences of academic women, beyond the experiences we present herein.

Position statement

We both began our PhDs in 2012, submitting them and being conferred in 2015. Having completed our PhDs, we moved into temporary research roles. Within one year of working in these roles, we secured lecturing posts in 2016 before moving on to secure positions as Senior Lecturers, and Catherine more recently as a Reader. At the time of writing this chapter, we are thirty-two years old. However, we reflect on our field diaries recorded when we were twenty-nine to thirty years of age. Certainly, in the UK higher education system we are considered young for a tenured Reader and Senior Lecturer.

Imposter syndrome in higher education

'Imposter syndrome', a term coined in 1978 by Clance and Imes (1978), refers to a psychological phenomenon characterized by intense feelings of intellectual fraudulence. Imposter syndrome suggests that you believe your success was down to luck and that soon your lack of ability will be exposed as underserving of your position (Kauati n.d.). Pressures of perfectionism, increasing social comparisons and a fear of failure are suggested to contribute to imposter syndrome (Sakulku 2011). Imposter syndrome has been well documented in the academy, ranging from research studying the incidence and impact of the phenomenon (Hutchins and Rainbolt 2017) to a focus on imposter syndrome as related to doctoral students (Craddock et al. 2011) and teaching evaluations (Brems et al. 1994).

For the individual who experiences it, imposter syndrome can be debilitating. It can have wide-reaching career implications. Laux (2018) reports on flawed perceptions of the promotion process and implications of this for women academics experiencing imposter syndrome. Further, Robertson (2017) tells how the anxiety and stress provoked by imposter syndrome can lead people to give up their academic careers. Imposter syndrome can have wider implications beyond the workplace, including sleep disruption (C. Wilkinson 2020).

While some literature has focused on documenting the experiences of imposter syndrome (e.g. C. Wilkinson 2020) or determining what triggers it (Hutchins and Rainbolt 2017), other literature has focused on detailing the overcoming of imposter syndrome. Presenting a critical autoethnography, Edwards (2019) gives voice to her intersectional lived experiences as a young, Black woman in the predominately middle-aged, white, male academy. Edwards (2019: 18) explores how she overcame imposter syndrome and stereotype threat by reconceptualizing the definition of a scholar to both 'survive and thrive' in the academy. Martinez and Forrey (2019) discuss how new librarians rarely feel fully prepared for academic library instruction. Tracking their first year as new instruction librarians, the authors illuminate how imposter syndrome impacts library instruction and provide suggestions for what academic libraries can do to mitigate feelings of fraudulence among their employees. In a discussion of 'dealing' with imposter syndrome, Robertson (2017) provides a practical guide to overcoming it for ourselves and our colleagues: have empathy (as a manager) and appreciation; promote self-awareness and introspection; seek accurate feedback on your performance; mentor or peer with whom you identify and have understanding of imposter syndrome.

Such literature focused on sharing experiences of overcoming imposter syndrome is important as there may be strategies identified that other academics working in HEIs can implement or adapt. It is to this specific body of literature concerned with imposter syndrome that this chapter contributes, with an emphasis on the experiences of two women in academia.

Women in academia

Patriarchy and hegemonic forms of masculinity are privileged in academia. Scholars (e.g. Howe-Walsh and Turnbull 2016; Nielsen 2016) highlight a gendered dimension to the commodification of academia, with women disproportionately experiencing job insecurity and limited promotion opportunities. Earlier research by Groot (1997) highlights that the growth of the competitive, individualistic and output-oriented aspects of academic life and activity links to male privilege, while women tend to value cooperative, collective and process-oriented ways of working. Consequently, a female colleague cooperating with colleagues rather than focusing solely on career opportunities may not fare well (Groot 1997). Those who will be successful are able to neglect or marginalize activities which are invisible to performance measures (Willmott 1995), restricting their work to activities providing the greatest measurable, visible output; for instance, publications (Leahey 2006) and funding.

Black and Garvis (2018) compiled an edited collection on the lived experiences of women in academia. The collection explores issues related to gender roles, family-making, work-life balance and motherhood, among others. While this collection is comprehensive, the stories of women explored in the individual chapters focus predominantly on unidimensional aspects of their identities.

Adopting an intersectional lens, in this chapter we argue that our experiences of imposter syndrome as women academics cannot be understood by engaging with gender alone; our experiences are more nuanced and complex than this. As such, we share our gendered experiences alongside the intersection of another axis of difference: age. Despite its importance as a key characteristic, the intersectionality literature has paid little attention to age (Holman and Walker 2020), in comparison to other axes of difference such as race and sexual orientation. The literature which does exist focuses predominantly on ageing or older bodies (e.g. Meliou and Mallett 2021) and less so on younger bodies, or bodies that look young. This is another identified scholarly void that this chapter aims to fill.

Having provided an overview of literature related to imposter syndrome and women in academia, we detail the methodological approach adopted in the study on which this chapter is based.

Methodology

This chapter reports on a joint autoethnography undertaken by the authors. Joint autoethnography, sometimes termed collaborative autoethnography, is a 'multivocal approach' (Lapadat 2017: 589) in which two or more researchers work together to share personal encounters and interpret the pooled autoethnographic data. This chapter builds on existing published autoethnographic work by the authors (S. Wilkinson 2019; C. Wilkinson 2020), which reflected on early data from our research diaries. These papers include honest accounts of our lived experiences of imposter syndrome in our first lecturing positions in UK HEIs. Now, Catherine employed as a Reader and Samantha as a Senior Lecturer, we draw on more recent entries from our personal research diaries and adopt an intersectional lens as we explore how we overcame our feelings of being imposters. We argue that joint autoethnography is a valid methodology through which to achieve the kind of reflexivity required to reflect on and represent our roles as young women academics.

Diary-keeping

From January 2019 to April 2021 we recorded, in individual personal diaries, observations, thoughts, feelings and interactions of our everyday experiences (Dewalt and Dewalt 2002) in academia. In our diaries, we were concerned with the ordinary, banal everydayness of events and interactions, paying attention to taken-for-granted practices in our roles. Our diaries contained subjective accounts that we reflected upon, individually and together, periodically. Journaling is recognized as evoking conversations with self (Hiemstra 2001). Like Travers (2011), we found the process of keeping our diaries cathartic.

Data analysis

We adopted an interactive, thematic approach to analysing our diary entries. We analysed by hand as we believed this would facilitate greater closeness to the data, considering this 'human as analyst' (Robson 2011: 463) stance important due to the autoethnographic nature of our study, whereby 'the Self of the researcher is integrated into the research' (Woods 1996: 51).

After reading through our data set multiple times, first we undertook open coding, using verbatim words from our diary entries. We dismissed any preconceived data categories and loosened the initial focus of the study in an effort to 'generate as many codes as possible' (Emerson, Fretz and Shaw 1995: 152). We used memos to comment on parts of our diaries that intrigued us, or that we considered particularly important. This was followed by a second coding of data (axial coding). MacLure (2008: 174) speaks of the pleasure derived from manual analysis, particularly 'poring over the data, annotating, describing, linking, bringing theory to bear, recalling what others have written, and seeing things from different angles'. Crucially, this enabled us to ask questions about what had emerged through the data. As a result, we changed and made links between some codes, and dropped and added others. We returned to the data multiple times, adopting a process of constant comparison, grouping some of the open codes together under a single code and comparing our individual analyses to ensure thorough interrogation of data and thematic concordance (Silverio, Wilkinson and Wilkinson 2020). In what follows, we introduce you to the key themes yielded from selective coding.

Findings and discussion

The key themes identified in our analysis are practical and purposeful solutions and changing life circumstances: putting things into perspective. We discuss these respectively herein.

Practical and purposeful solutions

One of the themes identified through our diary excerpts was the practical and purposeful solutions we intentionally implemented to give us confidence in our roles. See the following excerpt from Samantha's personal research diary:

> When I first started lecturing, I worried that I was not smart enough (physically) and felt I should wear something (e.g. formal wear) that set me apart from typical student attire, but now I have found that I am at my best when I am comfortable and being me. I wore trainers, jeans and a casual jumper regularly that had the slogan 'sushi and Savvy B [sauvignon blanc]' – for some this may not seem professional, but for me it was comfortable and gave me confidence. (Samantha, personal research diary, January 2019)

Samantha's discussion of the clothes she wears contributes to Scott's (2007) discussion of having 'lecture trousers' prepared as a tool for overcoming stage fright and performance anxiety as a university lecturer. Strategically choosing clothing to wear could be seen as a way in which Samantha played with her 'personal front' (Goffman 1959). Under the student gaze, Samantha decided not to wear formal clothing; instead, she performed 'another' femininity, opting for jeans and a jumper. As Thrift (2008) argues, clothing produces particular corporeal stances. Likewise, Gokanksel (2009) claims that dress acts upon the body; it transforms the self physically and emotionally. Wearing fashionable, casual clothes is one way in which Samantha learned to deploy her body in an attempt to 'fit in' (Thurnell-Read 2011), rather than distancing herself as 'other' (as may have been the case if she turned up in a suit). This dress code also assisted in making Samantha feel comfortable which she feels, in turn, enabled both herself and students to relax (Leyshon 2002). This is also something that C. Wilkinson (2020) reflected on in her early lecturing days and is evident still in her more recent diary excerpts:

> Knowing I was teaching in a large lecture theatre today with around 100 students, I made a very conscious decision about what to wear. I chose a high neck and long sleeved jumper and jeans. This outfit meant I had less skin on show and I felt less conspicuous to the student body. My outfit was not feminine in any way, and this is something I have increasingly noticed – whilst I own many feminine, floral blouses or pink coloured items of clothing, these never make it into the lecture theatres. (Catherine, personal research diary, March 2020)

Catherine's reflection in the previous diary excerpt relates to Perrone's (2010: 730) argument that 'we negotiate our gender and sexual identities, and shift our personalities and style of dress to represent ourselves in the most appropriate and comfortable manner'. Overall, we can be seen to explore, negotiate and notably minimize femininity through our dress. For Catherine, she appreciates that feminine clothes may position her as inferior (see Mpame 2020) and so she avoids these.

Interestingly, Samantha discusses other strategies she employed to feel empowered when teaching, focusing not on herself but on the space around her, realizing she could control this to her advantage:

> One thing I have found that makes me feel empowered, powerful and confident in my role is my command over the space. I always check out a teaching room the day before, so that I can suss out where I will stand, and what facilities the room has. At the start of the teaching session, I experiment with lighting so the room feels comfortable to me – I feel more confident in a darker room; and rearrange furniture and I often intentionally do this as a display as students are entering the room. (Samantha, personal research diary, March 2019)

While there has been extensive research undertaken into the relationship between the student and the classroom environment (see, for instance, Ivory's 2011 study into the impact of dynamic furniture on classroom performance), Samantha's excerpt highlights that the relationship between the lecturer and the classroom environment is also worthy of attention. For Samantha, being and looking like a young academic – who is often confused with students by other students and academics (see also C. Wilkinson 2020) – moving the furniture is a non-verbal signal that she is not a student. Furthermore, the moving of heavy furniture (such as tables) goes against the frailty myth relating to female physical inferiority and the historic phenomenology of the feminine body as 'not capable of lifting and carrying heavy things' (see Young 1980: 142), and Samantha admits that she often intentionally does this as a 'display' to students.

During the undertaking of our joint autoethnography, the COVID-19 pandemic struck in the UK, and in March 2019 our respective institutions moved teaching online. Despite not having presence in a physical classroom, Catherine documents how she still found ways to prepare, and therefore control, the virtual teaching environment:

> When teaching today via Zoom I joined the virtual teaching session 15 minutes before the scheduled start time. I did this so I could ensure I could see what myself and my background looked like to students and to make any adjustments. Adjustments I made included moving the laptop further away from me to avoid such a close-up image of myself and ensuring that the area surrounding contained items I would want students to see and that contributed to, rather than detracted from, my professionalism. For instance, I would ensure that books I have published featured on a bookshelf behind me, and that washing was not drying on the radiator behind me. (Catherine, personal research diary, April 2020)

Catherine can be seen to find alternative ways to 'rearrange the furniture' in the virtual classroom, considering this important in distinguishing herself from the student body. Importantly, Catherine indicates that she does not want items associated with domestic chores on display and continues in her personal research diary that laundry on show 'brings to mind the gender gaps regarding domestic responsibilities' and provides the illusion to students that she 'cannot juggle the work-life balance' (Catherine, personal research diary, April 2020). Others have reflected that the intrusion into our home lives afforded by virtual learning can breach privacy and highlight inequalities, particularly among the student body. For instance, Thiago, a PhD student, reflects: 'I see most of my professors with their backgrounds full of books, like how academics should be. But some of my PhD mates have been attending meetings in their backyards or with their fishing tanks behind them, which makes me feel less exceptional' (see Bogossian 2020). Thus, importantly, while Catherine showcases her books in an attempt to reduce her own feelings of being an imposter, this may result in students feeling inadequate.

While the excerpts we have shared in this section are intentional strategies adopted by us to overcome imposter syndrome, our personal research diaries revealed that a change in personal life circumstances contributed to combatting our feelings of imposter syndrome. We turn to discuss these next.

Changing life circumstances: Putting things into perspective

The second theme identified through analysis of our personal research diaries related to how changing life circumstances, namely getting married, becoming pregnant, having a baby and also losing our mum 'put things into perspective' and helped to create a sense of detachment whereby we 'cared less' about others' perceptions of us as frauds (Catherine's personal research diary, October 2019). The following quotation from Catherine makes this clear in relation to returning to work after the death of our mum in September 2019:

> Today was my first day back at work after taking a short period of sick leave following the death of my mum. It was the first time I hadn't suffered from nerves before or during lecturing – I felt apathetic almost. Students and staff had been informed of the reason for my absence and I received many compassionate nods, gestures and well wishes. I found that students behaved differently around me, there was less chatter when I was talking and students were generally better behaved in my presence. I wondered if this is because, being a similar age to many of my students, they could put themselves in my position and feel the pain of losing their mum at a young age. (Catherine, personal research diary, October 2019)

It is clear that the apathy Catherine describes in the previous excerpt is attributed to the new-found perspective gained following the loss of her mum to cancer. Discussing cancer, bereavement and work in the academy, Martin (2021) considers the unwanted 'bereaved mother/cancer survivor tag' she acquired following the death of her son to cancer and her own cancer battle, and the implications of this on the social and personal construction of identity and sense of self. Like Martin (2021), Catherine too carried an unwanted label, that of the 'bereaved daughter'. For Catherine, she carried the lived experience of the loss of her mum at work in a form of 'embodied storytelling' (Letherby and Davidson 2015: 343). Through not concealing emotions, Catherine presented her authentic self to the student body (van de Port 2004), and students appeared to respond empathetically to this. Catherine reflects that it was potentially her age, which was comparable to that of her students, which enabled this empathy to be developed.

A similar sentiment of 'putting things into perspective' is echoed by Samantha in relation to returning to work after a period of maternity leave with her first child:

> After having a baby, my priorities have changed and whilst I love my job and it is important to me, my child's happiness is at the top of my agenda. I now do not fret and worry about every aspect of my job, and whether I am good enough. I get on with it. I also find I use time much more efficiently now, and spend

less time over-thinking / analysing and just 'get on with it'. (Samantha, personal research diary, November 2020)

Existing research has questioned how new working mothers develop their embodied selves in what are highly competitive working lives (Huopalainen and Satama 2019). Craft and Maseberg-Tomlinson (2015) present an in-depth view of the transition of returning to work after maternity leave. Craft notes facing challenges both with the prioritization and fulfilment of her academic work, and with childcare and household responsibilities. For Samantha, prior to becoming a mother, academia was at the top of her list of priorities, yet now her child's health and happiness take precedence. While, for some academics, academic motherhood can lead to questioning their competency and feeling inadequate in both their personal and professional lives (Hirakata and Daniluk 2009), for Samantha becoming a mother made her more efficient at work, spending less time worrying, and this led to increased feelings of competence and diminished feelings of imposter syndrome.

Interestingly, Catherine hints that being pregnant was related to her feelings of unbecoming an imposter:

Now that I am pregnant and 'showing' I feel I have more credibility in teaching the subject of Early Childhood Studies. This is especially so as I am not a practitioner / former practitioner, and so my only knowledge of early childhood and of how children aged 0-8 develop, learn and think is through reading books and journal articles. Being pregnant has presented a rite of passage where I am transitioning to someone with that first-hand knowledge. (Catherine, personal research diary, March 2021)

Catherine's reflection on her pregnant body contributes to recent research by Ollilainen (2020) which explores pregnancy in academia and the notion of 'ideal bodies at work'. While Catherine would agree with Ollilainen (2020) that the pregnant body disrupts the masculine disembodied ideal academic worker norm, for Catherine this was positive in helping her to convey her subject knowledge (of early childhood studies) through her body. Further, reflecting on the intersection of age, Catherine felt that becoming pregnant presented a rite of passage to an 'older', more mature self, which would be recognized by students. This resonates with Kindelsperger's (2017) observation that, when teaching while pregnant, the tone of her classroom shifted. Like Kindersperger (2017: 130), Catherine believes that she and her students 'saw each other as more fully human and respected each other as people with lives and valuable knowledge that is often untapped in the classroom'.

Similar to Catherine's reflections on pregnancy earlier, Samantha discussed in her personal research diary how becoming married presented a significant life event, shaping her perceptions of herself as older:

Today I returned to work as a married woman. I wore my wedding ring proudly and couldn't help but twiddle it when I was teaching. This was largely unintentional – the ring became a prop which I could hold and play with when I was nervous, but there was also an intentional aspect to this display. I wore the ring with the knowledge that it signalled to students a move to a new chapter in my adult life. I felt more powerful and confident wearing the ring. (Samantha, personal research diary, May 2019)

Samantha can be seen to consider herself as growing out of impostership (see also Mainali 2020). She believed that being married helped to position herself as a woman in mid-life transition (Brown 1982). Much existing academic literature discusses the negative implications of marriage for women in academia, including presenting a barrier to obtaining tenure-track employment (Wolfinger, Mason and Goulden 2008). Yet, for Samantha, as a young woman academic, marriage presented a transition to 'true' adulthood, which separated her from the majority of the student body and thus gave her more confidence in her position.

Having presented our findings and discussion, we now conclude this chapter.

Conclusions and recommendations

This chapter has reported on research using a joint autoethnographic approach to explore the lived experiences of imposter syndrome, and specifically of 'unbecoming' imposters, for two young women in academia in the UK. Adopting an intersectional lens, we included excerpts from personal research diaries recorded between January 2019 and April 2021.

This chapter makes the following contributions to existing literature. First, it contributes to existing work on imposter syndrome and women in academia with a focus on intersectionality. This intersectional lens enabled understanding of the complexities of how we, as young women, are positioned and position ourselves within academia. As well as offering a more nuanced approach than the exploration of our gendered identities alone, intersectionality offers a way of explaining the complexity of our lived experiences. Second, with this chapter we have promoted the underutilized method of a joint autoethnography and argued for its usefulness as a multivocal and reflexive methodological approach. With the exception of Anderson, Goodall and Trahar's (2020) collaborative autoethnography of their experiences as women in academia, we are not aware of studies in this area using a joint autoethnographic approach and found no literature which uses a joint ethnographic approach to explore experiences of imposter syndrome, something typically considered personal and individualized.

Recommendations

Through our narrative presented in this chapter, we have developed a collective understanding of how both gender and age are shaped by, and shape, structures, systems and practices in academia. We propose the following recommendations for practice and institutional change:

- Internal and external programmes designed to address the under-representation of women in leadership positions in the sector, such as Aurora (Advance HE's leadership development initiative for women), should take into consideration other intersectional aspects of identity, alongside gender.
- HEIs should run training sessions on imposter syndrome. This training should explore and evaluate how imposter syndrome affects an individual while also focusing on strategies to overcome it.

We also propose the following recommendations for future research:

- Future research should consider other intersectional facets of identity in relation to imposter syndrome and women in academia, including class, disability and sexuality.
- To allow for a comparative perspective, it would be interesting to see a joint autoethnography of the experiences of imposter syndrome in the academy co-authored by a male and a female academic.

Through implementing these recommendations, researchers can further understandings of the experiences of academic women, yond the experiences we have presented herein.

References

Anderson, J., H. Goodall and S. Trahar (2020), 'Women in Powerful Conversation: Collaborative Autoethnography and Academia', *International Journal of Qualitative Studies in Education*, 33 (4): 393–403.

Black, A. L. and S. Garvis, eds (2018), *Lived Experiences of Women in Academia: Metaphors, Manifestos and Memoir*, Oxon: Routledge.

Bogossian, T. (2020), 'What Should Be Behind Me When I'm Teaching?' [Online]. Available online: https://thiagobogossian.wordpress.com/2020/05/14/what-should-be-behind-me-when-im-teaching/ (accessed 07 July 2021).

Brems, C., M. R. Baldwin, L. Davis and L. Namyniuk (1994), 'The Imposter Syndrome as Related to Teaching Evaluations and Advising Relationships of University Faculty Members', *The Journal of Higher Education*, 65 (2): 183–93.

Brown, B. E. (1982), *Married, Academic, Women in Mid-life Transition*, unpublished doctoral thesis, Temple University.

Clance, P. R. and S. A. Imes (1978), 'The Imposter Phenomenon in High Achieving Women: Dynamics and Therapeutic Intervention', *Psychotherapy: Theory, Research & Practice*, 15 (3): 241–7.

Craddock, S., M. Birnbaum, K. L. Rodriguez, C. Cobb and S. Zeeh (2011), 'Doctoral Students and the Imposter Phenomenon: Am I Smart Enough to be Here?', *Journal of Student Affairs Research and Practice*, 48 (4): 429–42.

Craft, C. M. and J. Maseberg-Tomlinson (2015), 'Challenges Experienced by One Academic Mother Transitioning From Maternity Leave Back to Academia', *NASPA Journal About Women in Higher Education*, 8 (1): 66–81.

Dewalt, K. M. and B. R. Dewalt (2002), *Participant Observation: A Guide for Fieldworkers*, Plymouth: AltaMira Press.

Edwards, C. W. (2019), 'Overcoming Imposter Syndrome and Stereotype Threat: Reconceptualizing the Definition of a Scholar', *Taboo: The Journal of Culture and Education*, 18 (1): 18–34.

Emerson, R., R. Fretz and L. Shaw (1995), *Writing Ethnographic Fieldnotes*, Chicago: The University of Chicago Press.

Goffman, E. (1959), *The Presentation of Self in Everyday Life*, London: Penguin Books.

Gokanksel, B. (2009), 'Beyond the Officially Sacred: Religion, Secularism, and the Body in the Production of Subjectivity', *Social & Cultural Geography*, 10 (6): 657–74.

Groot, J. (1997), 'After the Ivory Tower: Gender, Commodification and the "Academic"', *Feminist Review*, 55: 130–43.

Hiemstra, R. (2001), 'Uses and Benefits of Journal Writing', *New Directions for Adult and Continuing Education*, 90: 19–26.

Hirakata, P. E. and J. C. Daniluk (2009), 'Swimming Upstream: The Experience of Academic Mothers of Young Children', *Canadian Journal of Counselling*, 43 (4): 283–94.

Holman, D. and A. Walker (2020), 'Understanding Unequal Ageing: Towards a Synthesis of Intersectionality and Life Course Analyses', *European Journal of Ageing*, 18 (2): 239–55 .

Howe-Walsh, L. and S. Turnbull (2016), 'Barriers to Women Leaders in Academia: Tales From Science and Technology', *Studies in Higher Education*, 41 (3): 415–28.

Huopalainen, A. S. and S. T. Satama (2019), 'Mothers and Researchers in the Making: Negotiating "New" Motherhood Within the "New" Academia', *Human Relations*, 72 (1): 98–121.

Hutchins, H. M. and H. Rainbolt (2017), 'What Triggers Imposter Phenomenon Among Academic Faculty? A Critical Incident Study Exploring Antecedents, Coping, and Development Opportunities', *Human Resource Development International*, 20 (3): 194–214.

Ivory, D. M. (2011), 'The Impact of Dynamic Furniture on Classroom Performance: A Pilot Study', MSc diss., University of Puget Sound.

Kauati, A. (n.d.), 'The Imposter Syndrome and Academic Life' [Online]. Available online: http://www.interparadigmas.org.br/wp-content/uploads/2015/06/N1.EN_.KAUATI .pdf (accessed 29 June 2021).

Kindelsperger, A. (2017), '"Unexpected" Opportunities: Teaching While Pregnant', *Counterpoints*, 486: 129–33.

Lapadat, J. C. (2017), 'Ethics in Autoethnography and Collaborative Autoethnography', *Qualitative Inquiry*, 23 (8): 589–603.

Laux, S. E. (2018), 'Experiencing the Imposter Syndrome in Academia: Women Faculty Members' Perception of the Tenure and Promotion Process', PhD diss., Saint Louis University.

Leahey, E. (2006), 'Gender Differences in Productivity: Research Specialization as a Missing Link', *Gender & Society*, 20 (6): 754–80.

Letherby, G. and D. Davidson (2015), 'Embodied Storytelling: Loss and Bereavement, Creative Practices, and Support', *Illness, Crisis & Loss*, 23 (4): 343–60.

Leyshon, M. (2002), 'On Being "in the field": Practice, Progress and Problems in Research With Young People in Rural Areas', *Journal of Rural Studies*, 18 (2): 179–91.

MacLure, M. (2008), 'Classification or Wonder? Coding as an Analytic Practice in Qualitative Research', in R. Coleman and J. Ringrose (eds), *Deleuze and Research Methodologies*, 164–83, Edinburgh: Edinburgh University Press.

Mainali, S. (2020), 'Being an Imposter: Growing Out of Impostership', *JNMA: Journal of the Nepal Medical Association*, 58 (232): 1097–9.

Martin, N. (2021), 'Cancer, Bereavement and Work', in N. Brown (ed.), *Lived Experiences of Ableism in Academia: Strategies for Inclusion in Higher Education*, 283–300, Bristol: Bristol University Press.

Martinez, J. and M. Forrey (2019), 'Overcoming Imposter Syndrome: The Adventures of Two New Instruction Librarians', *Reference Services Review*, 47 (3): 331–42.

Meliou, E. and O. Mallett (2021), 'Negotiating Gendered Ageing: Intersectional Reflexivity and Experiences of Incongruity of Self-Employed Older Women', *Work, Employment and Society*. Available online: https://doi.org/10.1177/0950017021994489 (accessed 12 November 2021).

Mpame, C. L. (2020), 'Clothing: A Statement of One's Gender Identity', PhD diss., Memorial University of Newfoundland.

Nielsen, M. W. (2016), 'Limits to Meritocracy? Gender in Academic Recruitment and Promotion Processes', *Science and Public Policy*, 43 (3): 386–99.

Ollilainen, M. (2020), 'Ideal Bodies at Work: Faculty Mothers and Pregnancy in Academia', *Gender and Education*, 32 (7): 961–76.

Perrone, D. (2010), 'Gender and Sexuality in the Field: A Female Ethnographer's Experience Researching Drug Use in Dance Clubs', *Substance Use & Misuse*, 45 (5): 717–35.

Robertson, J. (2017), 'Dealing With Imposter Syndrome', in J. Roberton, A. Williams, D. Jones, L. Isbel and D. Loades (eds), *EqualBITE: Gender Equality in Higher Education*, 146–51, Rotterdam: Sense Publishers.

Robson, C. (2011), *Real World Research*, West Sussex: John Wiley & Sons.

Sakulku, J. (2011), 'The Impostor Phenomenon', *International Journal of Behavioral Science*, 6 (1): 75–97.

Scott, S. (2007), 'College Hats or Lecture Trousers? Stage Fright and Performance Anxiety in University Teachers', *Ethnography and Education*, 2 (2): 191–207.

Silverio, S. A., C. Wilkinson and S. Wilkinson (2020), 'Further Uses for Grounded Theory: A Methodology for Psychological Studies of the Performing Arts, Literature, and Visual Media', *Qualitative Methods in Psychology Bulletin*, 29: 8–19.

Thrift, N. (2008), *Non-representational Theory: Space, Politics, Affect*, London: Routledge.

Thurnell-Read, T. (2011), '"Common-sense" Research: Senses, Emotions and Embodiment in Researching Stag Tourism in Eastern Europe', *Methodological Innovations Online*, 6 (3): 39–49.

Tienari, J. (2019), 'One Flew Over the Duck Pond: Autoethnography, Academic Identity, and Language', *Management Learning*, 50 (5): 576–90.

Travers, C. (2011), 'Unveiling a Reflective Diary Methodology for Exploring the Lived Experiences of Stress and Coping', *Journal of Vocational Behaviour*, 79: 204–16.

van de Port, M. (2004), 'Registers of Incontestability: The Quest for Authenticity in Academia and Beyond', *Etnofoor*, 17 (1–2): 7–22.

Wilkinson, C. (2020), 'Imposter Syndrome and the Accidental Academic: An Autoethnographic Account', *International Journal for Academic Development*, 25 (4): 363–74.

Wilkinson, S. (2019), 'The Story of Samantha: The Teaching Performances and Inauthenticities of an Early Career Human Geography Lecturer', *Higher Education Research & Development*, 38 (2): 398–410.

Willmott, H. (1995), 'Managing the Academics: Commodification and Control in the Development of University Education in the UK', *Human Relations*, 48 (9): 993–1027.

Wolfinger, N. H., M. A. Mason and M. Goulden (2008), 'Problems in the Pipeline: Gender, Marriage, and Fertility in the Ivory Tower', *The Journal of Higher Education*, 79 (4): 388–405.

Woods, P. (1996), *Researching the Art of Teaching: Ethnography for Educational Use*, Oxon: Routledge.

Wright, R. R. (2016), 'Comics, Kitsch, and Class: An Autoethnographic Exploration of an Accidental Academic', *International Journal of Qualitative Studies in Education*, 29 (3): 426–44.

Young, I. M. (1980), 'Throwing Like a Girl: A Phenomenology of Feminine Body Comportment Motility and Spatiality', *Human Studies*, 3 (1): 137–56.

Chapter 10

Women in Supramolecular Chemistry

Narratives of Resilience and Community Building in a Gender-Constrained Field

Jennifer Leigh, Jennifer Hiscock, Anna McConnell, Cally Haynes, Claudia Caltagirone, Marion Kieffer, Emily Draper, Anna Slater, Larissa von Krbek, Kristin Hutchins, Davita Watkins, Nathalie Busschaert Katrina (Kate) Jolliffe and Michaele Hardie

Women in science

Women have always been interested in science (Fara 2018). However, historically and to this day they have faced barriers that have blocked them from succeeding and progressing. In 2018, the Royal Society of Chemistry (RSC) conducted a review on diversity (and the lack thereof) in the chemical sciences (RSC 2018), and followed this with a report on the particular challenges for women in terms of their progression and retention (RSC 2019a). The RSC found that women faced a multitude of small obstacles throughout the publishing process leading to their publishing less, in lower impact journals, and being cited less than men (RSC 2019b). This catalogue of small barriers could be considered as a series of microaggressions, a term used by Sara Ahmed (2012, 2017) and other critical race scholars. In the United States, various programmes have been funded to combat the attrition of women from the sciences with varying amounts of long-term success (Rosser 2017). While the numbers demonstrate that more women are recruited into undergraduate courses, internationally the growth at the most senior levels is disappointing, and in some subjects and in some universities the numbers of senior women in science are in attrition (Mason and Ekman 2007; Rosser 2017). When considering the lack of progress on gender balance in science, it is important to note that gender cannot be considered in isolation, and that gender is not binary. Women and other marginalized genders face intersectional barriers. 'Intersectionality' is a term first used by Kimberlé Crenshaw (1989) to describe the racism and sexism faced by Black women. Protected characteristics, including sexuality, race, ethnicity, religion, and disability, all result in barriers that compound to prevent an individual from reaching their full potential.

There is a notable lack of diversity within academia (Fryberg and Martinez 2014; Shelton, Flynn and Grosland 2018), and even more so within science; people of colour and those marginalized due to other protected characteristics such as sexuality or disability are all minority groups (CRAC 2020; McWhinne 2017; McGee and Robinson 2020; RSC 2018). Since the 2020 #BlackLivesMatter protests brought attention to the lack of diversity in society, more Black scientists have written about their experiences and the lack of diversity around them (see for example Coughlan 2021; Makgoba 2020; Prasad 2021; Vaughan 2020). As a result, we are also slowly beginning to see more awareness around the lack of visibility and opportunity for those who are marginalized due to other reasons, for example, disabled scientists (Brock 2021; Hiscock and Leigh 2021; Sarju 2021; Vasquez 2020). However, increased awareness is not enough: there is still a need for effective action and change.

Indeed, despite over fifty years of attention to gender imbalance, the elephant in the room (or the laboratory) is that women are still a marginalized group in science (Caltagirone et al. 2021b). What is striking in the literature is a distinct lack of narratives from women in STEM, with only a few notable exceptions, such as those from Ellen Daniell (2006), Rita Colwell (Colwell and Bertsch McGrayne 2020), Mary-Ann Mason (Mason and Ekman 2007) and Sue Rosser (2004, 2012). There is, however, work published *on* women in STEM, for example their history (Fara 2018), discussing their career paths (Thege et al. 2014) and reflections on this as told to others (Gornick 2009). Work of this kind, which reports on women rather than having them share their own stories often includes a critical commentary. This critical commentary can manifest in an emphasis on appearance, judgement on choices and a superficiality in responses, presumably due to a lack of specificity in the questions or understanding of the context of working within science.

Community and academic identity

The idea of community, and more specifically, feminist community, as an important factor of academia is not new (Stiver Lie and O'Leary 1990). Early-career academics are often urged to find networks and communities to engage with as a source of support for their own sense of well-being (Boynton 2020; Clark and Sousa 2018). However, guides on developing an academic career in general (Becher and Trowler 1989; Fanghanel 2012), and particularly those aimed at women that also discuss the impact of motherhood on careers (Crimmins 2019; Evans and Grant 2008; Murray and Mifsud 2019; Shelton, Flynn and Grosland 2018), often tend to focus on, and are written by, those in the social sciences. Work that centres on women in science (Daniell 2006; Colwell and Bertsch McGrayne 2020; Mason and Ekman 2007; Rosser 2004, 2012) also champions the importance of community and the need for women in science to find a network of trusted peers and mentors, and then in turn to act as mentors for others. However, this is more easily said than done, particularly when one of the consequences of being in a minority group is isolation.

The international Women in Supramolecular Chemistry (WISC) network was launched in November 2019, with the aim to build a sense of community and kinship in order to promote the retention and progression of women in supramolecular chemistry. Its ethos is to take an area-specific approach, embedding qualitative research approaches to community-led initiatives (Caltagirone et al. 2021b) and to 'call in' the community to support its own, rather than calling out reprehensible behaviour (Caltagirone et al. 2021a). WISC has a website signposting resources (WISC 2020), a mentoring programme, regular events in the form of webinars, conference talks and workshops and a range of community support clusters. Board members of WISC have led on two journal special issues to date, one targeted at mentors and mentees (McConnell et al. 2020) and the other on women in supramolecular chemistry (Caltagirone et al. 2022).

All WISC's activities have been community led and are open to all within the supramolecular community regardless of gender, though they are targeted at women and other minorities. WISC also has a programme of research. This includes surveys on barriers to progression (Caltagirone et al. 2021b) and experiences through COVID-19 (Leigh et al. 2022). Less conventionally, it also includes funded work exploring experiences of women principal investigators and their research groups that utilizes embodied inquiry (Leigh and Brown 2021), video as method (Harris 2016), rhythm analysis (Lyon 2019) and ongoing collaborative autoethnography (Bochner and Ellis 2016).

This chapter is a significant contribution to work on feminist resilience narratives and communities, because it captures the voices of women in STEM. We want to highlight the importance of community and how scientists can utilize social science methodologies for processing, sharing and learning from experiences. Traditionally, those in STEM disciplines do not use qualitative methods. In addition, and unlike traditional research in this area, this chapter does not report social science researching *on* those in STEM, but reports social scientists working collaboratively *with* supramolecular chemists. To the best of our knowledge this example is the first of its kind to be promoted within the literature. There is an assumption within science (particularly in supramolecular chemistry), that due to the so-called 'leaky pipeline' (RSC 2019a), corresponding authors and team leaders are men, or women without caring responsibilities. There is a culture of silence around the active or unintentional sexism that women who stay experience. Those who speak out tend either to have left academia completely (Daniell 2006), reorientating themselves into administration or 'gender studies' (Mason and Ekman 2007; Rosser 2012) or feel they have nothing to lose because they are towards the end of their careers and safe enough to bear the repercussions (Colwell and Bertsch McGrayne 2020; Gornick 2009; Monosson 2008). WISC triangulates research findings to create and tell a story that evokes (Wilson 2018) women's experiences in STEM (Leigh et al. 2022) while protecting them from the dangers of whistleblowing (Bjørkelo 2013). In order to do this, we intentionally incorporate a range of methods that are inclusive and intersectional (Evans-Winters 2019) and use the creation of fictional vignettes

(Clough 2002; Leavy 2016; Philips and Kara 2021) as a reflective aid to processing experiences, as well as prompts for discussion, dissemination and education.

This chapter combines empirical findings on perceptions of women in chemistry working to develop their academic identity and develop independent research, as well as surviving through and beyond the impact of the global COVID-19 pandemic. The collaborative autoethnography sheds light on the hitherto invisible narratives of some of these women. The aim of this publication is to inspire others to succeed, to reach out, and to build communities and resilience.

Supramolecular chemistry

Supramolecular chemistry is an interdisciplinary field within chemistry that incorporates elements of physical, organic, and inorganic chemistry alongside materials science. It focuses on the study of non-covalent interactions between molecules and has applications in industry, engineering, and medicine. However, despite its scale and scientific diversity, there is a significant lack of representation for women. From 2000 to 2022 only five women were awarded one of the three significant annual prizes in supramolecular chemistry. Only two women have won the RSC's Bob Hay lectureship prize for Supramolecular Chemistry in the period 1991–2021. Similarly, in that time only two women have won the Izatt-Christenen Award, and only one woman has won the Cram Lehn Pedersen Prize in Supramolecular Chemistry 2011–21 (ISMSC 2021). Men outnumbered women speakers four to one at the 2019 International Supramolecular and Macrocyclic Chemistry Conference. Excitingly, there is now a growing body of evidence that the culture is changing, in part due to WISC's visibility and efforts. The RSC Special Interest Group in this area now has more women members on its committee than the total number of women it has previously had since this group was first initiated over ten years ago.

At the time of writing, we are still living in and with the repercussions of a global pandemic. The majority of laboratories have been shut down at some point in the last eighteen months, which has had a negative impact on the mental health of many scientists (Abbott 2021). The Higher Education sector is struggling, with increases in workload, redundancies (Gewin 2021) and cuts to research funding (Butler and Yancy 2020; Estermann et al. 2020). Many of those with caring responsibilities were expected to juggle childcare, home-schooling, or care of others while continuing to work. Not all of those with caring responsibilities are women; however, it is widely recognized that women bear the brunt of the 'second shift' (Agarwal 2021; O'Reilly and Green 2021). Being a mother and an academic is not easy (Evans and Grant 2008). For those in a laboratory and working in a gender-constrained field these difficulties are amplified (Monosson 2008). Many young women in science believe that it is not possible to have a career and a family, often because they do not see the role models who have carved out that path for them to follow (Caltagirone et al. 2021b). The long-term impact of the COVID-19 pandemic on women and other minority groups is yet to be seen. However, there is already evidence to show that women's publication rates have been affected (Flaherty 2020; Viglione 2020), that women bore an unfair burden (Gabster et al. 2020) and that mothers in particular have been impacted negatively (Kovarovic et al. 2021; O'Reilly and Green 2021). During this time, WISC decided to focus on experiences through the pandemic, as labs reopened, and people struggled to return to the norm. In surveys and as ongoing discussions in our collaborative autoethnography group, we asked: How will community play a part in how women in chemistry process their experiences of being chemists without laboratories, and negotiate how their careers and opportunities may change as a result?

Collective qualitative research methods

One of the key elements of WISC's research ethos was to work collectively and collaboratively within an inclusive and intersectional feminist ethos (Evans-Winters 2019). An embodied and creative approach (Leigh and Brown 2021) foregrounds lived experiences and allows participants to express what is otherwise hard to put into words (Brown and Leigh 2018). In order to facilitate this, creative methods (Kara 2015) were used as part of regular reflective meetings with research groups led by women, and a collaborative autoethnography (Bochner and Ellis 2016; Chang, Ngunjiri and Hernandez 2016) of thirteen international research group leaders. Research group meetings were held every two weeks, while the collaborative autoethnography meetings were held monthly. At each meeting people would be invited to draw, mark-make, or bring an image or object as a metaphorical representation (Lakoff and Johnson 2003), or offer their reflective thoughts on a prompt or theme decided by the group at the previous meeting. This process allowed them to share stories and connect with each other on an embodied and emotional level despite meetings happening online. The collaborative autoethnography group also discussed findings from the surveys and research group meetings and prepared documents for dissemination collaboratively.

Prior to the project starting, there was a fair amount of apprehension around using social science research approaches and the level of communication and collaboration that would be required. Initially, the plan had been to include six women in the collaborative autoethnography, however, this expanded to thirteen over the course of the first twelve months. The onset of COVID-19 meant that people were struggling and reached out to each other for help. The reflective projects introduced participants to creative ways of reflecting, sharing and processing their experiences. Participants commented:

> It feels so good to speak about my feelings with you! Thanks a lot for let [*sic*] me be part of this.

> Just to say it was lovely to talk to you all and I really appreciate the invitation to join the conversation . . . talking about it helps us to reflect on our choices and reasons, and what we might change for the future.

The group found a sense of shared ownership and recognition from the undertaking of these sessions, valuing the impact they had on their lives and approach to work. Sharing experiences and recognizing those of others allowed them to feel less isolated, as well as providing a valuable source of information and solutions to common challenges. Some of the themes discussed were around burnout and overwork, imposter syndrome, and mothering (Leigh et al. 2022). Being a mother in academia is challenging (Evans and Grant 2008; Mason and Ekman 2007), and much work around navigating academia as a woman focuses on this (Crimmins 2019; Shelton, Flynn and Grosland 2018). Emily Monosson described motherhood as the 'elephant in the laboratory' (Monosson 2008), for example pregnancy in the lab is a subject that is barely discussed (Slater et al. 2022). Combining the challenges of mothering through COVID-19 (O'Reilly and Green 2021; Kovarovic et al. 2021) with the challenges of being a woman in science was an epic undertaking. WISC's second survey, which focused on experiences through COVID-19, found that those most negatively affected were those who had caring responsibilities, regardless of gender (Leigh et al. 2022). However, it needs to be recognized that for a long time the proportion of women with children in science has been far lower than the proportion of men (Mason 2013; Mason and Ekman 2007).

Impact of WISC's approach

From the very beginning, WISC has sparked interest within the supramolecular and wider chemistry and scientific communities. The website had over 1,000 hits from 40 countries worldwide in its first 18 months and the Twitter handle @SupraChem gained over 1,100 followers (2021). The first tweet launching the network received over 26,000 impressions in its first week. The second WISC survey QR code received nearly 50,000 impressions. The pinned tweet which links to the *Angewandte Chemie* paper had over 14,000 impressions and nearly 300 engagements in the first 3 months. WISC uses Twitter to engage with the supramolecular and wider community, and interactions there have led to collaborations with Empowering Female Minds in STEM (EFeMS), and have encouraged members to join the mentoring programme as mentees and mentors and to access the website for support clusters and online resources. WISC's paper in *Angewandte Chemie*, 'An Area-Specific, International Community-Led Approach to Understanding and Addressing Equality, Diversity, and Inclusion Issues within Supramolecular Chemistry', has an altmetric score of 105. Since publication, it has been placed in the top 5 per cent of research of its type. It was picked up by seven international news outlets, resulting in articles published in *Chemistry World*, *ScienMag*, *EurekaAlert*, *Chemistry Views* and *Phys.org*. In terms of attention on Twitter, to date the paper has garnered tweets from 142 users from the United States, Australia, Mexico, Canada, India and Europe, with an upper bound of nearly 470,000 followers. Further articles continued to make an impact, including a comment for *Nature Reviews Chemistry* on pregnancy in the lab, which attracted 2.7 million views on Twitter in its first week online.

Feedback and comments on WISC from WISC members and the supramolecular community have included the following:

> This is a wonderful initiative, and I would be absolutely delighted to contribute to it at any capacity!

> I think continuing to increase the visibility of women scientists in supramolecular chemistry (at all levels) helps to inspire the next generation/progression of younger female members of the field.

> I think that the WISC Network is one of the best initiatives in Science to promote gender equality and inclusiveness. Retention and progression of women in Science is crucial for a better society.

The first online survey had 100 responses, (81 per cent women); the second 104 (68 per cent women). Both had international reach, with respondents from places including the UK, Europe, India, and the United States. The surveys were aimed at supramolecular chemists who were studying or working at postgraduate level and above. The first survey's respondents were; MSc students 5 per cent, PhD students 30 per cent, post-docs 24 per cent, research fellows/independent researchers 41 per cent and others 4 per cent. The second survey's respondents were; 4 per cent MSc students, 35 per cent PhD students, 11 per cent post-docs, 44 per cent research fellows/independent researchers and 10 per cent other. Both surveys had a very high completion rate, with respondents answering all questions in full.

The mentoring network currently comprises nineteen mentees (thirteen PhD students, four post-docs, two independent early-career researchers) based in the UK, the United States, India, Austria, Germany, and Australia, forming the basis of six mentoring groups. Interest in joining the mentoring programme and the community support clusters increased with the WISC Skills Workshop in September 2021.

Comments from members of the mentoring programme include:

> Having resources and mentors are [*sic*] exceptionally important. I find myself seeking advice from those who have been in my shoes.

> I have found that regular mentoring and support makes a world of difference in terms of career development.

What's next?

As always, WISC aims to maintain and expand the network's activities, visibility and reach. The first WISC Skills Workshop (2021, Cagliari) for early-career researchers provided an introduction to standard experimental techniques and a platform for promoting inclusion and diversity in supramolecular chemistry. Over 200 people registered for the hybrid event, with 50 attending in person. Delegates came from across five continents and nineteen countries. Evaluation feedback was very positive, with 100 per cent saying that they would attend another event:

> I really enjoyed all the presentations and the WISC event that allowed us to voice our thoughts and hearing about all the support that WISC is offering.

> The hybrid of online and in person was really good and should stay in the future to help those with caring responsibilities.

Within the scope of this workshop, WISC are launching a new community cluster and research focus to support First Generation Chemists. These community clusters are a safer space where individuals with specific needs, experiences, or pressures can come together and find support from peers. It is envisioned that this initiative will expand the network's impact and create a community for students and early-career researchers who are first in their family to study in Higher Education. In addition, we plan to recruit more mentees and mentors to the mentoring network and work to increase the visibility of and activities for the other two community support clusters on Parenting, and Disability/Chronic Illness/Neurodivergence. Finally, we launched a Public Engagement channel (@SupraLab1) in 2022, with content uploaded onto platforms including YouTube, Instagram and TikTok. The channel is aimed at a young audience without a science degree, humanizing work in a research lab.

Currently, most WISC members are based in the UK and Europe. WISC aims to expand the reach of the network by increasing its visibility in other countries. For example, WISC would like to increase its presence and number of members in the United States by working with US-based Advisory Board members. Together with the First Generation cluster, this will further WISC's ability to support marginalized women working in the supramolecular chemistry community.

Challenges

The main challenges that WISC has faced are to do with the scarcity of time and resources. WISC is run by volunteers. The Board comprises women in their early-to-mid-career phases, who are working to support WISC in their own time and not as part of paid employment. The majority of the Board are in academia on research and teaching contracts, with pressure to produce world-leading research outputs, run research teams, teach large cohorts of undergraduate and postgraduate students, supervise PhD students, and complete service requirements at their own institutions. The academics are all in supramolecular chemistry, with the exception of the social scientist expert who researches embodiment, creative methods, and academic identity. WISC also has Board members working in industry, again with teams to run and deadlines to meet.

The Board includes members who have disabilities/chronic illnesses/ neurodivergences and spans a number of religious and cultural backgrounds. Five of the members have young families. One challenge has been a lack of perceived diversity in the Board as all are white presenting. This has been addressed somewhat by members of the Advisory Board and participants in collaborative projects, however, ensuring diversity in terms of race that is not tokenistic is important to WISC. We have recently begun work with Empowering Female Minds in STEM, a non-profit working across Africa, and will be inviting more representatives from Africa to our Advisory Board to join those from the UK, the United States, Australia, and India. WISC has also taken the lack of women and Black visibility in science communication and outreach work as the heart of a project looking to build capacity and increase the visibility of Black women in science.

WISC started off as a small network, however, due to interest and enthusiasm from the supramolecular community, it has grown and expanded at a much faster rate than anticipated. In addition to the mentoring programme, community clusters, skills workshop and webinars (in collaboration with RSC's virtual MASC group), the network Board is also involved in several research and writing projects, including surveys, collaborative autoethnography, research papers, a short book and several book chapters. These activities all take time, and as such one challenge that the team has faced is ensuring that WISC is supported and that their own careers are not put on hold as a result. Time and resources are scarce within academia, and the majority of the Board fit in work for WISC around their day-to-day workloads and home life.

COVID-19 has proved challenging for WISC. Planned workshops and panel events had to be cancelled or moved online during 2020/1. Although much of WISC's activities take place online, the reflective and community elements are hard to reproduce virtually. Similarly, invited sessions at large international conferences and outreach events, where WISC might meet more people and attract new members and volunteers, were cancelled or made online in 2021. Accessing activities has been made more challenging for some participants due to lack of internet/privacy. Although we would like our research and surveys to be representative of the supramolecular community, we are aware that our samples are limited to those who chose to engage with us. We attract a higher proportion of responses from women than would be expected given the demographics of the community.

Conclusion

We wanted to understand how community plays a part in how women in chemistry process their experiences of being chemists without laboratories, and how they negotiate their careers and opportunities. This work is still ongoing. The collaborative autoethnography has been very valuable for those involved. These active WISC members have benefitted from an increased sense of community and support, and a decreased sense of isolation and loneliness, which positively contributes to their sense of well-being. The ability to connect and share experiences in a safer space was particularly important for these women through COVID-19, as they faced unprecedented challenges in running their research groups. Similarly, the research group members who are part of regular reflective meetings have reported feeling better supported. The model we have developed is being adapted to address retention issues in doctoral training partnership programmes and will inform a forthcoming 'toolkit' for surviving in the laboratory, aimed particularly at those who are already marginalized in some way. We strongly believe that the development of a sense of community is vital in the drive to retain women and other marginalized groups within STEM and to support the progression of those who choose to remain.

In this chapter we have contextualized the absence of voices of women in STEM in the literature before outlining the work of WISC, findings from its surveys, and its progressive use of creative, qualitative research approaches with women in STEM. Our intention is to support the supramolecular community, to produce a framework that other areas of STEM can follow and to shed light on the unique experiences of women in supramolecular chemistry at this time.

References

Abbott, A. (2021), 'COVID's Mental-Health Toll: How Scientists Are Tracking a Surge in Depression', *Nature*, 3 February. Available online: https://www.nature.com/articles/d41586-021-00175-z (accessed 25 January 2022).

Agarwal, P. (2021), *(M)Otherhood: On the Choices of Being a Woman*, Edinburgh: Canongate Books.

Ahmed, S. (2012), *On Being Included: Racism and Diversity in Institutional Life*, Durham, NC: Duke University Press.

Ahmed, S. (2017), *Living a Feminist Life*, Durham, NC: Duke University Press.

Becher, T. and P. Trowler (1989), *Academic Tribes and Territories*, 2nd edn, Buckingham: Open University Press.

Bjørkelo, B. (2013), 'Workplace Bullying After Whistleblowing: Future Research and Implications', R. T. Lee and C. M. Brotheridge (eds), *Journal of Managerial Psychology*, 28 (3): 306–23. Available online: https://doi.org/10.1108/02683941311321178 (accessed 25 January 2022).

Bochner, A. and C. Ellis (2016), *Evocative Autoethnography: Writing Lives and Telling Stories*, London: Routledge.

Boynton, P. (2020), *Being Well in Academia*, Abingdon: Routledge.

Brock, J. (2021), '"Textbook Case" of Disability Discrimination in Grant Applications', *Nature Index*, January. Available online: https://www.natureindex.com/news-blog/textbook-case-of-disability-discrimination-in-research-grant-applications (accessed 25 January 2022).

Brown, N. and J. Leigh (2018), 'Creativity and Playfulness in HE Research', in J. Huisman and M. Tight (eds), *Theory and Method in Higher Education Research*, vol. 4, 49–66, Bingley: Emerald.

Butler, J. and G. Yancy (2020), *Mourning Is a Political Act Amid the Pandemic and Its Disparities*. Available online: https://discoversociety.org/2020/04/10/covid-19-what-it-means-to-think-violently/ (accessed 25 January 2022).

Caltagirone, C., E. Draper, M. Hardie, C. Haynes, J. Hiscock, K. Jolliffe, M. Kieffer, J. Leigh and A. McConnell (2021a), 'Calling in Support', *Chemistry World*, March. Available online: https://www.chemistryworld.com/opinion/supramolecular-community-calls-in -support-for-gender-equity/4013248.article (accessed 25 January 2022).

Caltagirone, C., E. Draper, J. Hiscock, M. Hardie, C. Haynes, K. Jolliffe, M. Kieffer, A. McConnell and J. Leigh (2021b), 'An Area Specific, International Community-Led Approach to Understanding and Addressing EDI Issues within Supramolecular Chemistry', *Angewandte Chemie International Edition*, 60 (21): 11572–9. Available online: https://onlinelibrary.wiley.com/doi/10.1002/anie.202015297 (accessed 25 January 2022).

Caltagirone, C., E. R. Draper, J. S. Leigh, C. J. E. Haynes, J. R. Hiscock and A. J. McConnell (2022), 'Editorial: International Women of Supramolecular Chemistry', *Frontiers in Chemistry*, 10. Available online https://www.frontiersin.org/articles/10.3389/fchem .2022.854085/full (accessed 15 May 2022).

Chang, H., F. Ngunjiri and K.-A. Hernandez (2016), *Collaborative Autoethnography*, Abingdon: Routledge.

Clark, A. and B. Sousa (2018), *How to Be a Happy Academic*, London: Sage.

Clough, P. (2002), *Narratives and Fictions in Educational Research*, Maidenhead: Open University Press.

Colwell, R. and S. Bertsch McGrayne (2020), *A Lab of One's Own: One Woman's Personal Journey through Sexism in Science*, New York: Simon & Schuster.

Coughlan, S. (2021), 'Only 1% of UK University Professors Are Black', *BBC News*, 19 January. Available online: https://www.bbc.co.uk/news/education-55723120 (accessed 25 January 2022).

CRAC (2020), 'Qualitative Research on Barriers to Progression of Disabled Scientists', London. Available online: https://royalsociety.org/-/media/policy/topics/diversity-in -science/qualitative-research-on-barriers-to-progression-of-disabled-scientists.pdf. %0A (accessed 25 January 2022).

Crenshaw, K. (1989), *Demarginalizing the Intersection of Race and Sex: A Black Feminist Critique of Antidiscrimination Doctrine, Feminist Theory, and Antiracist Politics*, 139–67, Chicago: University of Chicago Legal Forum.

Crimmins, G., ed. (2019), *Strategies for Resisting Sexism in the Academy: Higher Education, Gender and Intersectionality*, Cham: Palgrave Macmillan.

Daniell, E. (2006), *Every Other Thursday: Stories and Strategies from Successful Women Scientists*, New Haven: Yale University Press.

Estermann, T., E. B. Pruvot, V. Kupriyanova and H. Stoyanova (2020), 'The Impact of the COVID-19 Crisis on University Funding in Europe: Lessons Learnt from the 2008 Global Financial Crisis', European Universities Research Association. Available online: https://eua.eu/resources/publications/927:the-impact-of-the-covid-19-crisis-on -university-funding-in-europe.html (accessed 25 January 2022).

Evans, E. and C. Grant, eds (2008), *Mama PhD: Women Write about Motherhood and Academic Life*, Pisctataway, NJ: Rutgers University Press.

Evans-Winters, V. (2019), *Black Feminism in Qualitative Inquiry*, Abingdon: Routledge.

Fanghanel, J. (2012), *Being an Academic*, Abingdon: Routledge.

Fara, P. (2018), *A Lab of One's Own: Science and Suffrage in the First World War*, Oxford: Oxford University Press.

Flaherty, C. (2020), 'No Room of One's Own', *Inside Higher Ed*. Available online: https:// www.insidehighered.com/news/2020/04/21/early-journal-submission-data-suggest -covid-19-tanking-womens-research-productivity (accessed 25 January 2022).

Fryberg, S. and E. Martinez, eds (2014), *The Truly Diverse Faculty: New Dialogues in American Higher Education*, Basingstoke: Palgrave Macmillan.

Gabster, B. P., K. van Daalen, R. Dhatt and M. Barry (2020), 'Challenges for the Female Academic During the COVID-19 Pandemic', *Lancet*, 395 (10242): 1968–70. Available online: https://doi.org/10.1016/S0140-6736(20)31412-4 (accessed 25 January 2022).

Gewin, V. (2021), 'The Hashtags That Brought Black Scientists Together', *Nature*, August. Available online: https://www.nature.com/articles/d41586-021-02223-0 (accessed 25 January 2022).

Gornick, V. (2009), *Women in Science: Then and Now*, 25th anniversary edn, New York: The Feminist Press.

Harris, A. (2016), *Video as Method: Understanding Qualitative Research*, Oxford: Oxford University Press.

Hiscock, J. and J. Leigh (2021), 'Teaching with and Supporting Teachers with Dyslexia in Higher Education', in N. Brown (ed.), *Lived Experiences of Ableism in Academia: Strategies for Inclusion in Higher Education*, 249–63, Bristol: Policy Press.

ISMSC (2021), 'ISMSC Prizes', Brigham Young University. Available online: https://www .chem.byu.edu/alumni/ismsc/awards/ (accessed 25 January 2022).

Kara, H. (2015), *Creative Research Methods in the Social Sciences: A Practical Guide*, Bristol: Policy Press.

Kovarovic, K. 'Fire', M. Dixon, K. Hall and N. Westmarland (2021), 'The Impact of COVID-19 on Mothers Working in UK Higher Education Institutions', Durham. Available online: https://www.dur.ac.uk/resources/lets.network/MothersinHEandCovid-19ReportbyMAMSNetworkJune2021.pdf (accessed 25 January 2022).

Lakoff, G. and M. Johnson (2003), *Metaphors We Live By*, 2nd edn, Chicago: University of Chicago Press.

Leavy, P. (2016), *Fiction as Research Practice: Short Stories, Novellas, and Novels*, Abingdon: Routledge.

Leigh, J. and N. Brown (2021), *Embodied Inquiry: Research Methods*, London: Bloomsbury.

Leigh, J., J. Hiscock, A. McConnell, C. Haynes, C. Caltagirone, M. Kieffer, E. Draper, A. Slater, L. von Krbek, K. Hutchins, D. Watkins and N. Busschaert (2022), *Women In Supramolecular Chemistry: Collectively Crafting the Rhythms of Our Work and Lives in STEM*, Bristol: Policy Press.

Leigh, J. S., J. R. Hiscock, S. Koops, A. J. McConnell, C. J. E. Haynes, C. Caltagirone, M. Kieffer, E. R. Draper, A. G. Slater, K. Hutchins, D. Watkins, N. Busschaert, L. von Krbrek, K. A. Jolliffe and M. J. Hardie (2022), 'Managing Research Throughout COVID-19: Lived Experiences of Supramolecular Chemists', *CHEM Cell Press*, 8: 299–311.

Lyon, D. (2019), *What Is Rhythmanalysis?*, London: Bloomsbury.

Makgoba, M. (2020), 'Black Scientists Matter', *Science* 369 (6506): 884. Available online: https://doi.org/10.1126/science.abe3234 (accessed 25 January 2022).

Mason, M. A. (2013), 'In the Ivory Tower, Men Only: For Men, Having Children Is a Career Advantage: For Women, It's a Career Killer', *Slate*, June.

Mason, M. A. and E. M. Ekman (2007), *Mothers on the Fast Track: How a New Generation Can Balance Family and Careers*, Oxford: Oxford University Press.

McConnell, A., C. Haynes, C. Caltagirone and J. Hiscock (2020), 'Editorial for the Supramolecular Chemistry: Young Talents and Their Mentors Special Collection', *ChemPlusChem*, 85 (12): 2544–5.

McGee, E. O. and W. H. Robinson, eds (2020), *Diversifying STEM: Multidisciplinary Perspectives on Race and Gender*, New Brunswick, NJ: Rutgers University Press.

McWhinne, S. (2017), *The Demographics and Research Interests of the UK Astronomy and Geophysics Communities 2016*, London: Royal Astronomical Society.

Monosson, E., ed. (2008), *Motherhood, the Elephant in the Laboratory: Women Scientists Speak Out*, Ithaca, NY: Cornell University.

Murray, R. and D. Mifsud, eds (2019), *The Positioning and Making of Female Professors*, Cham: Palgrave Macmillan.

O'Reilly, A. and F. J. Green, eds (2021), *Mothers, Mothering, and COVID-19: Dispatches from a Pandemic*, Ontario: Demeter.

Philips, R. and H. Kara (2021), *Creative Writing for Social Research: A Practical Guide*, Bristol: Bristol University Press.

Prasad, A. (2021), 'Why Are There Still so Few Black Scientists in the UK?', *The Observer*, 10 April. Available online: https://www.theguardian.com/science/2021/apr/10/why-are-there-still-so-few-black-scientists-in-the-uk (accessed 25 January 2022).

Rosser, S. (2004), *The Science Glass Ceiling: Academic Women Scientists and the Struggle to Succeed*, New York: Routledge.

Rosser, S. (2012), *Breaking into the Lab: Engineering Progress for Women in Science*, New York: New York University Press.

Rosser, S. (2017), *Academic Women in STEM Faculty*, Basingstoke: Palgrave Macmillan.

Royal Society of Chemistry (2018), *Diversity Landscape of the Chemical Sciences*, London: Royal Society of Chemistry.

Royal Society of Chemistry (2019a), *Breaking the Barriers: Women's Retention and Progression in the Chemical Sciences*, London: Royal Society of Chemistry.

Royal Society of Chemistry (2019b), *Is Publishing in the Chemical Sciences Gender Biased? Driving Change in Research Culture*, London: Royal Society of Chemistry.

Sarju, J. (2021), 'Nothing About Us Without Us – Towards Genuine Inclusion of Disabled Scientists and Science Students Post Pandemic', *Chemistry–A European Journal*, 27 (41): 10489–94. Available online: https://doi.org/https://doi.org/10.1002/chem.202100268 (accessed 25 January 2022).

Shelton, S. A., J. E. Flynn and T. J. Grosland, eds (2018), *Feminism and Intersectionality in Academia: Women's Narratives and Experiences in Higher Education*, Basingstoke: Palgrave Macmillan.

Slater, A. G., C. Caltagirone, E. Draper, N. Busschaert, K. M. Hutchins and J. Leigh (2022), 'Pregnancy in the Lab', *Nature Reviews Chemistry*, 6: 163–4.

Stiver Lie, S. and V. O'Leary, eds (1990), *Storming the Tower: Women in the Academic World*, London: Kogan Page.

Thege, B., S. Popescue-Willigmann, R. Pioch and S. Badri-Hoher, eds (2014), *Paths to Career and Success for Women in Science: Findings from International Research*, Wiesbaden: Springer VS.

Vasquez, K. (2020), 'Excluded from the Lab', *Chemistry World*, Opinion: 9 December. Available online: https://www.chemistryworld.com/opinion/disabled-scientists-excluded-from-the-lab/4012695.article (accessed 25 January 2022).

Vaughan, A. (2020), 'Only 10 Senior Black Researchers Awarded UK Science Funding Last Year', *New Scientist*, 15 December. Available online: https://www.newscientist.com/article/2262849-only-10-senior-black-researchers-awarded-uk-science-funding-last-year/ (accessed 25 January 2022).

Viglione, G. (2020), 'Are Women Publishing Less during the Pandemic? Here's What the Data Say', *Nature*, 581 (7809): 365–6. Available online: https://doi.org/10.1038/d41586-020-01294-9 (accessed 25 January 2022).

Wilson, S. (2018), 'Haunting and the Knowing and Showing of Qualitative Research', *The Sociological Review*, 66 (6). Available online: https://doi.org/10.1177/0038026118769843 (accessed 25 January 2022).

WISC (2020), 'WISC: Women in Suprachem'. Available online: https://www.womeninsuprachem.com/ (accessed 25 January 2022).

Chapter 11

Feminist Online Communities

The Story of the Women in Academia Support Network (WIASN) – A Tale of Resistance and Online Activism

Kelly Pickard-Smith, Eleonora (Ele) Belfiore and Amy Bonsall

In the beginning

This chapter offers a reflective and inevitably subjective account of the experiences of the six women who got together on a Facebook group one evening and unwittingly ended up leading a global network of several thousand members – the Women in Academia Support Network (WIASN) – while inadvertently also positioning themselves as online community managers and online activists within the British and international higher education sector.

Therefore, in line with the personal and narrative slant of this chapter, we start by telling the story of how this Facebook group came about one evening almost five years ago. The story is directly lifted from the WIASN Facebook group, where it was first shared in 2017 in response to members' queries as to the origin of the group, only to be returned to regularly and further contributed to up until the present day. This is the genesis story of WIASN, which colourfully describes how being silenced and being expected to self-censor is part of everyday life for women in academia. This story, while intentionally light-hearted and humorous, serves as a serious provocation ahead of our later discussion of how, in taking advantage of the global connectivity of social media (Facebook), academic women can organize collective resistance to gender inequality in higher education and research.

Soup Boy: A genesis story

2017

Maxine: Once upon a time there lived a group of very clever women who liked to meet at the village well and complain about the rubbishness of their lives. It all sounded very grumbly at the well, but it gave the women of the village the chance to vent, and then they could get on with the drudgery of their lives.

One day, during a meeting at the well, a handsome knight came past and heard the grumbling. He said, 'STOP! Your grumbling is wrong. It hurts my feelz'. The women were grateful to the very clever stranger. They stopped grumbling and started to stroke the poor knight and his wounded feelz.

But three shrill women would not stroke his feelz. They shouted and said it wasn't fair that the knight's feelz took priority over the women's only outlet for the drudgery. But the man said they were wrong. So they were banished. The women then founded Flossieville and invited all their friends and lived happily ever after.

Kelly: True story.

As they were banished the Knight Strokers sought to entice the shrill women back to the well with promises of good feelz by way of a trade – the shrill women's academic rucksacks for magic beans (designer bags), which would endear all menfolk academics to the women by way of the shiny, shiny bag. The shrill women thought 'this is bs' – The end.

Catherine: That's accurate.

Amy: Amazeballs. A perfect description.

And he can keep his shitty home-made soup as well.

Eleonora: This is great, but . . . but . . . BUT . . . **Maxine,** you haven't explained about THE SOUP!!!!!!!!! I'll do it for you: the knight with all the legitimate feelz explained that he couldn't possibly have a sexist bone in his knightly body because he was one of these modern men who – CAN YOU BELIEVE IT? – looks after the children sometimes and helps out in the kitchen. Indeed, as the caring women and the shrill ones argued on the wall of the Facebook group, our knight had disappeared from the scene (having dropped his bombshell), because HE WAS MAKING SOUP (FROM SCRATCH!!!) FOR HIS FAMILY. From that day onwards, he was known, among the three shrill flossies, as SOUP BOY. If you have spotted here and there mysterious references in Admin's comment to Soup Boy, that's him, our knight with all the allowed feelz . . .

From then on, when in doubt about posting something on social media, we ask ourselves: 'Would this upset Soup Boy's feelz?' If the answer is 'Yes', WE POST!!

I know, I'm quite pleased with that one . . . #SoupBoy

Kelly: Abridged version. Women discuss valid experiences. Man takes mic and says their experience jars his feelz and he shouldn't have to listen to it. Drops mic and leaves to make soup.

2019

Eleonora: I think Maxine's original post needs an update: 'The women then founded Flossieville and invited all their friends and lived happily ever after. And, two years later, there was 10,669 of them.'

2020

Kelly: This, my friends, is what we WIASN admin commonly refer to as a 'Soup Boy'. A self-professed woke feminist man who makes soup and all – who just doesn't actually like to practise the actual feminism.

This group started because a guy in another group said our stories about misogyny made him feel bad because, you know, not all men. Women were being asked to temper stories and consider his feelings of having to listen to them because he was 'woke' – apparently. I mean he could make home-made soup and everything, so basically, he totally understood us (*more sarcasm). Btw we call men like this 'soup boys'.

2021

Eleonora: Amy is doing Soup Boy's origin story in her podcast – I love it!!!!

The story we have presented is the reproduction of a digital/online Facebook conversation between ourselves as the founders of WIASN, and originally took place in 2017. It has been revisited on several occasions, over time, when new members ask about the genesis of the Facebook group and when the topic of male allyship comes up in discussion threads. The conversation was not anonymized, since WIASN is now a charity (as well as a searchable Facebook group) and our names are, therefore, in the public arena. The story of WIASN has also been related at conferences and elsewhere and is now part of the 'official' history of the group, even though this is the first time that this origin story is reproduced in written form and subjected to academic reflection.

The genesis of the WIASN group story began in a different Facebook academic group, in which a male member, who described himself as an 'ally' of women, took offence against terms such as 'mansplaining' and recurring negative posts about sexism in academia, because 'not all academic men' are bad (and especially not *him*). The constant negativity made him feel bad, and why should he have to read negative comments about men when he is such a good ally? This performative male allyship was an attempt to silence women and centre the male experience (of both academic life and of the Facebook group) and made the group feel unsafe for women who were seeking advice and support to deal with the discrimination and poor treatment they regularly faced in academia. In response, a lively debate ensued, which saw many apologize to the male member for the upset caused him by women sharing their own lived experience, resulting in the indignant exodus of the would-be WIASN admin team from the group. Women in Academia Support Network was created that very evening driven by an impulse of righteous anger. Over time, it has blossomed into a professional learning network where women academics can discuss any aspects that relate to or impact their academic life. This is a vocally trans women and non-binary inclusive space where members' experiences are unapologetically at the centre of everything. Through the years, 'Soup Boy' has become almost a stand-in for the patriarchy and the importance of organizing ourselves, as academic women, to resist and rebel against narratives in which women's voices are subjugated, dismissed or rendered invisible. What comes next is a discussion of how Facebook, while not a problem-free tool, can be utilized effectively to organize academic women, globally, to resist and remake academia in new, more equitable ways.

Facebook: A brief introduction

Facebook is a social media platform that began in 2004 and was originally intended to connect students at Harvard in an online game based on the social sharing of pictures of female students to be rated 'hot or not'. Facebook then expanded to the local geographical area of its operation, the Ivy League and then US and Canadian colleges, then UK universities in 2005, before wider global expansion in 2006. Beginning as a network of individual users only, Facebook's first community pages did not appear until 2011, but now in 2022, Facebook groups are well established and have a variety of uses and focuses, from support groups to hobbies, local interest and more. 'Community management' is the term Facebook uses to describe the labour of looking after these communities, carried out by 'group admins'. Online community management is a rapidly growing area of expertise that has been capitalized on by industry as a marketing tool, so much so that Facebook, for instance, is now offering certified Digital Community Management courses. Community management is one of the fastest growing of the new social media/digital occupations, as either paid or voluntary work. Arguably, Facebook community management is now one of, if not the largest voluntary sectors in the world. Currently, 1.8 billion people use Facebook groups every month, and there are more than 70 million admins and moderators. According to a 2021 YouGov survey, in eleven out of the fifteen countries studied, the largest proportion of respondents stated that the most important social group to which they belong is a primarily online one. The study concluded that Facebook groups tend to attract members and leaders who are marginalized in the physical realities they find themselves in, and who use the platform to build new kinds of communities that would be difficult to form otherwise. The report further suggests that these Facebook groups are significant contemporary organizations that can generate impact and provide their members with a strong sense of community and belonging. Many groups have community managers administering groups larger than the organization for which they work or the towns and cities in which they live.

Currently, WIASN has over 12,000 members from over 100 countries, whose career level ranges from PhD student to vice chancellor. As group community managers we, in our role of WIASN admins, have oversight of a community much larger and, in some cases, more diverse than the institutions in which we work. However, Facebook is no panacea, and it is not lost on WIASN that Facebook was conceptualized for use in higher education to objectify women and that it remains a largely sexist space. Considering also the limitations to accessing the platform from certain areas of the globe and the ongoing concerns over Facebook's undue political influence and its power to shape and manipulate public opinion, there is no doubt that serious questions and real tensions remain in using the platform. However, our experience also shows the possibility of exploiting the affordances of the medium of Facebook for progressive ends by subverting its original conception as a tool to foster female oppression in order to actively counter it. In the following sections of the chapter, we reflect on how this might be possible, connecting our personal experience to the extant literature on digital communities and activism.

Digital community: On becoming digital academics

What follows is a discussion of how digital/virtual communities on Facebook might come together and how digital academic personas might be developed. We take as a starting point Rheingold's (1993) classic definition of virtual communities: 'Virtual communities are social aggregations that emerge from the Net when enough people carry on those public discussions long enough, with sufficient human feeling, to form webs of personal relationships in cyberspace' (6). In particular we will focus on the key importance of 'webs of personal relationships' to show how sharing stories of self and experiences of higher education and research within a virtual academic community centred around a Facebook group can be emancipatory and transformative for individual members, for others in the online group and, importantly, for the academe itself. In order to build this argument, we will touch on the growing phenomenon of the 'digital academic' (Lupton, Mewburn and Thomson 2018) and the increasingly significant role of an online digital community (specifically Facebook in this case) as a means to develop self and career and to create tangible change in academe. As Lupton, Mewburn and Thomson (2018) point out, the very notion of online engagement has proven somewhat controversial among academics: 'Scholarship and learning for their own sakes have arguably become progressively devalued, making way for a vision of the university not as a community of scholars, but as a corporate enterprise – an engine to power economic demands for growth' (2).

In the context of these broader developments, academics have shown resistance to the demands that the forging of online professional personas, online self-promotion and self-branding and the emotional labour entailed place on them. Considered alongside concerns over the vulnerability that comes from exposure to the general public on platforms such as Facebook and Twitter, as well as personal blogs, it is understandable that pressures to engage online have at times been seen as a manifestation of what feminist scholar Rosalind Gill (2010) refers to as the 'hidden injuries of academia'. The argument she developed further with Ngaire Donaghue (2016) is that these online practices and the new demands attached to them are instances of 'technologies of the self in the neoliberal academy' which are the product of 'a work culture that requires that one is "always on"' (91). They also argue that these damaging additional pressures to overwork are more likely to impact women negatively, who are more likely to be in underpaid, precarious employment; on temporary or teaching-only contracts and expected to shoulder a heavier load of 'emotional labour' within their departments.

While it is important to bear in mind the valid concerns raised by feminist scholarship in relation to the added pressure that being active online as academic professionals brings for women, we want to offer here a different perspective. We want to focus on how online activity can become not one more extra task within an exploitative set of working conditions but, on the contrary, an avenue to creating forms of mutual support, advice, mentoring, signposting of training and job opportunities that actually go some way towards making academic life more tolerable. These might indeed go some way towards addressing the isolation and disadvantage that is so often part and parcel of being a woman in academia, especially when other facets of identity contribute to further marginalization within higher education. Through this new form of organizing, resistance become possible – through the development of online communities: 'Online groups are significant contemporary organizations that can generate impact and provide their members with a strong sense of community and belonging, despite not operating in physical space' (TheGovLab 2021: para. 1).

A meta-review of Facebook groups – how they operate, manage and grow their communities – conducted by TheGovLab (2021) concluded that despite the lack of physical proximity, members of these groups experienced a strong sense of community and connection. By interviewing the leaders of fifty different Facebook groups based on different interests and originating across the world, they looked at the groups' structures, their ways of functioning and the efforts put into them by community management teams within them. Despite the differences within the groups sampled, it is clear that *support* featured as a key common characteristic, which allowed groups to 'in many cases attract members and leaders who are marginalized in the physical societies they inhabit' (TheGovLab 2021: para. 2).

The concept of 'community' is a fraught and contested one, largely because of the uncritical and nostalgia-infused way that communities are often seen as inherently 'good' and cohesive, welcoming and offering individuals a sense of belonging, when in fact contemporary society offers plenty of examples of communities that operate in precisely the opposite way. It is impossible here to do justice to the academic debates that have developed around definitions of 'community', although it is important to acknowledge the contested and ambiguous connotation that the concept carries. To complicate things further, as Parks (2011) observes, 'debates about whether people can find community or community-like experiences online continue to reverberate in academic discourse'. Matters are further confounded by tensions between descriptive and prescriptive approaches to defining what communities are (106–7). Despite the wide range of definitions provided within the literature, there seems to be one point of agreement among proponents of different definitions of communities, both virtual and not: the idea that 'the ability to engage in collective action is generally considered to be an essential test of the authenticity of any community, including virtual communities' (Parks 2011: 108).

The ease with which Facebook groups can be set up and interested members added, or the groups themselves publicized through existing networks, has allowed their popularity to grow in a variety of sectors. As a result, over the past decade or so, social networking platforms have become the home of several different types of virtual communities, including those that centre on communities of practice and shared professional interests. In the health sector, for example, Facebook groups have become central to the sharing of personal experiences on the part of patients and their families, which improves therapeutic outcomes (Chan and Leung 2020). More relevant to our discussion, Facebook groups have developed into important self-directed and curated tools that allow clinicians to come together to keep on top of new research and therapeutic developments. Indeed, a study of a Facebook group for female haematology/oncology physicians found that, while the most common uses of the group were education (65 to 89 per cent) and advice on complex cases (65 per cent), emotional support (65 per cent) and networking (55 per cent) were also significant benefits that users identified, showing the importance that personal relationships play in these professional virtual communities (Graff et al. 2018). Similar findings have been identified by studies conducted on other health-focused virtual communities (e.g. Jackson et al. 2018; Teoh 2021).

In a parallel development, Facebook groups for academics are increasingly becoming spaces where members can learn about their craft as academics, find sources of research information and develop new forms of activism to figure out new understandings of the purpose of higher education and new ways of being as academics. We move next to a discussion of the Facebook-based WIASN and argue that the ability to engage in collective action through the power of shared personal histories and experiences in a caring and supportive environment is how WIASN functions as both a virtual support community and an agent of progressive change in higher education.

Women in Academia Support Network: Digital activism and resistance

Returning to our genesis story – when a group of strangers digitally met on an academic Facebook group for early-career academics of all genders – our engagement in that space made obvious that there were very few inclusive (of trans women and non-binary people comfortable in a women-centred space) platforms for women academics to come together to network, learn and share experiences that are unique to them as women in a very hierarchical and still male-dominated sector like higher education (Gill and Donaghue 2016).

These strangers (now colleagues and best friends) started the Facebook community group Women in Academia Support Network or WIASN (pronounced Wise-un) with a vision that access to academia and research can be changed from a grassroots approach through an online community collective. In this vision, solidarity, mutual support and encouragement become a care-based route to activism as resistance to a male-dominated sector and a way to embolden women navigating male-defined workspaces into pushing for actual changes. These changes might be small and may operate at the individual level, but in this vision of collective and mutual activation, it is a collective of small changes happening in different academic fields, at different career levels and in different parts of the world that can open up the road towards progressive systemic change.

Online community activism has been enabled by social media such as Facebook, and the politicization of these spaces in order to push for social justice is only just beginning to be understood in research. As described by Pruchniewska (2019), 'Private Facebook groups provide bordered, online spaces for forming virtual communities' (1363). These communities can vary hugely in their size and scope – as can their missions – and they can range in spatial focus too, from local to international. In her work on private professional groups on Facebook, Pruchniewska looks in particular at how they can become incubators for feminist action and activism. This is not surprising, since activism comes in many forms and shapes. As Yang (2016) explains, activism is 'an ambiguous word. It can mean both radical, revolutionary action and nonrevolutionary, community action; action in the service of the nation-state and in opposition to it' (1).

Facebook groups, thus, are perfectly designed to allow individuals to come together under whatever umbrella the organizers wish, to connect and share experiences, and from those discussions to develop forms of action that they feel are appropriate and required to bring forth the desired change. In the case of WIASN, the Facebook group acts as a conduit for women to share experiences and develop *their own* courses of action or small acts of everyday activism, as opposed to group leaders dictating how members should be organized and act in any given situation. The community managers are there to ensure that group guidelines are respected but take a very low-key approach to moderation and intervention (which is limited to situations of acute conflict and rule infraction), in the belief that the community runs more smoothly when members regulate themselves and their conduct. In this respect, the WIASN admin team is an example of 'connective leadership', which rejects the traditional dichotomy between the leaders and the led in favour of a function closer to that of 'broker' between different groups of people (Azer, Harindranath and Zheng 2019). As Azer, Harindranath and Zheng (2019) explain, 'connective leaders develop relationships between movements and the world, connecting people and information, and forming links between various online and offline social networks' (1142).

Indeed, precisely because of this flat structure, the group's activity falls into the category of 'connective action' as outlined by George and Leidner (2019) in their comprehensive literature study of different forms of digital activism. They define 'connective action' as a form of 'collective action that exploits the personalized connectivity afforded by digital social networks' and which is, therefore, especially successful at 'promoting messages and inciting action' (100,249).

Connective action is similar to collective action in that it involves individuals coming together, but connective action purposefully utilizes IS (information systems) to organize and communicate and often includes the use of social media. The international membership of WIASN falls neatly into this description of connective action as digitally mediated social activism, as the digital space allows the members to share interests, goals, opportunities, mobilization and participation.

Examples of the network being utilized by its members to engage others and draw on the wide variety of experiences in the group are varied. They are illustrated, for example, by a series of members' personal blog posts chronicling the experiences of academics living and working through the initial months of the COVID-19 pandemic. Blog posts on a variety of topics from March 2020 and December 2020 were initially drawn from a post on the group and are archived at 'The COVID-19 Chroniclers' (Carr 2021). Posts within the network have also inspired individual reflection from other members – with notable themes of isolation and the lack of representation within academia within various fields. For instance, in her blog, Angela Martin (2018) talks about how posts on WIASN inspired her to start 'taking notice of the ratios of men to women and white people to non-white people on the international stage'. Her field is marine biology, but the interdisciplinary nature of WIASN helped her to build on her own experiences and look beyond her field to recognize systemic issues of under-representation of women in particular fields.

The topic of representation in specific fields, or in academia in general, runs through another blog, in which Alana Harris (2019) reflects on the work she did alongside Abigail Woods to get accreditation for her institution's Athena SWAN. In reflecting on this official framework for the institutional promotion of gender equity and its application in UK universities, she mentions WIASN as a resource for 'external support scaffolding', which allows women to support other academics, especially those with less experience or in junior roles. The importance of this kind of support from more experienced colleagues for those who are still training or in the earlier phases of an academic career is highlighted by Vasudha Chaudhari (2017), then a second-year PhD student, in her blog post. Her piece talks about the role that WIASN has as part of her personal online support network or, as she puts it, as part of 'her village'. The supportive nature of the group is mentioned also in a blog post by researcher Liiri Oja (n.d.) reflecting on her PhD journey.

The wide range of experiences, backgrounds and career levels represented among the members of the group, and the wealth of past experience, knowledge, wisdom and advice that they unlock, is another recurring theme in writings that have covered the benefits that WIASN brings to its members. In an article poignantly entitled 'Reflecting on the Meaning of Academic Life', Ali Black (2018), pondering on a career that spans over two decades, mentions WIASN and the wide range of questions being asked on a daily basis by the members as a reflection of the persisting challenges of navigating the academy as a woman: 'They ask and answer every day, practical questions and hard questions too, questions which showcase the dilemmas of being a woman in academia.' In their blog post on 'learning communities', Hannah Busing (2020) reflects on WIASN as 'a community of practice that has helped me to understand and navigate the academic world as an early-career researcher and a Latina woman'. Busing's personal account is especially interesting as they outline the way in which, through enabling connection, exchange of personal experiences and advice, WIASN becomes a way to *do* academia differently and in a more nurturing, supportive way:

The group, with over 10,000 members, has become a safe space for finding support to navigate tricky job-academic related situations, and for receiving well intentioned advise [*sic*]. It is also a learning space where I find myself reading and learning from other women's questions ad experiences, interacting and exchanging opinions and debating topics related with being a woman in academia. (Busing 2020: para. 2)

The final example we will mention here is of a member who made a long post on WIASN to voice and face up to her academic anxieties over being able to turn her PhD thesis into a monograph, following a publisher's rejection. Brianna Robertson-Kirkland (2019) writes that the supportive comments to her heartfelt and vulnerable post about her experiences encouraged her to seek out further guidance and help in order to pursue her goal of an academic contract for her first monograph, which she achieved within six months of the original post. These are just a few members' publicly shared experiences and, while they are just a fraction of the career-changing, affirming and encouraging interactions on the group page, there is something powerful, humbling and significant in these women's experiences, which we believe is the essence of what WIASN has to offer to contemporary women academics.

In an effort to capture the importance of WIASN to the members beyond individuals' stories, one of the moderators collected information directly from the members by asking them to describe, in three words, the influence that WIASN has had on them, and then presented the responses in the form of a word cloud (see Figure 11.1). The informal data gathering exercise was posted as a link in the group: 212 respondents anonymously provided up to 3 answers to the question 'Which 3 nouns would you use to describe how WIASN has influenced you as

@ When poll is active, respond at **pollev.com/panagiotasot036**

The WIASN Effect: Which 3 nouns would you use to describe how WIASN has infuenced you as a member?

Total Results: 338

Figure 11.1 WIASN word cloud, 2021.

a member?'. The word cloud generated shows the most commonly occurring responses in the largest fonts. It's clear from this exercise that the members see the group mainly as a place of 'support', 'community' and 'solidarity', although these are by no means the only benefits identified.

WIASN is certainly not the only academic Facebook group out there. A quick search will throw up groups such as Teaching with a Sociological Lens, PhD Parents, Working Class Studies Association and Innovative Social Research Methods. Hundreds, possibly thousands, of online groups exist, each one managed by an administrator or team of administrators and moderators or, using the term Facebook uses, 'Community Managers'. Community managers give their time voluntarily and must learn to navigate the complexities, sensitivities and nuances of real communities, because while they might be virtual, these are nonetheless real communities.

Another aspect that makes running this kind of virtual community especially challenging is that the very nature of WIASN as a support network means that a lot of the group's activities focus on vulnerability and on offering a caring and supportive response to members who are willing (and brave enough) to expose themselves and their struggles honestly and trustingly to their peers and colleagues (among whom might well be future line managers). Ensuring that this process remains at all times as caring, safe and supportive as possible is not an insignificant effort and requires consistent and persistent emotional labour: a personal or professional crisis does not stick to a 9.00 am–5.00 pm, Monday to Friday timetable, and many a WIASN 'emergency collective support operation' has taken place late at night, at weekends or during holiday periods.

However, this kind of academic care and community caregiving and caretaking is only a small part of a new digital voluntary sector, which includes community activism. Throughout the COVID-19 pandemic, digital communities have really come into their own, taking on the brunt of community care and often providing a lifeline in terms of practical advice and emotional support where institutions have failed to do so. During the COVID-19 crisis these spaces of mutual support have experienced a huge surge in demand (Bolisani et al. 2020; Cabiati 2021). Insights data on the group offered by Facebook show that comments on WIASN more than doubled from the start of the pandemic onwards, and the group registered a member engagement rate of 90 per cent, meaning that most of the 12,000 members were actively contributing to the group, resulting in over half a million interactions on the group between March 2020 and March 2021. Spikes in engagement and activity during lockdowns, such as the UK January 2021 lockdown, saw commenting increase by approximately 30 per cent, with 25,000 comments posted during this period.

However, while academics are rapidly populating Facebook, curating their own digital personas, becoming members of different digital communities and demonstrating leadership and care, there remains a distinct lack of engagement from higher education institutions, or even awareness that these communities do indeed exist – that their academic staff are digital community leaders. There is little understanding of the types of work undertaken in these communities or how vital they are for challenging toxic ways of working, for developing global connections and for developing a positive sense of identity and belonging. In many ways, online mutual support communities are picking up the pieces of poor employment practices and failures to care for staff that mar the higher education sector worldwide. While higher education renders these spaces invisible, however, the social media industries are readily stepping up and into education territory to fill an obvious gap. For example, Facebook now offers a suite of qualifications through Blueprint, one of which is Digital Community Management, as well as PhD placements and research opportunities. This is 'proper' research and an intellectually substantive endeavour – definitely not 'messing about on the internet' for the purpose of purely private escapism.

WIASN's goal is that through large-scale digital collectives, or digital activism, a critical mass of support for women on the fringes should develop so that they can take up their place and space in higher education and research. We want the labour that so many put into keeping academia survivable for the most vulnerable, precarious and less experienced academics to be recognized, and for the extent to which this labour effectively patches over poor institutional support provision to be acknowledged and, most crucially, addressed. So, while WIASN may be relatively unknown to senior members within the community managers' and the members' own academic institutions, they make big waves externally and drive resistance to male-dominated academia – from the bottom up and from the inside out. Higher education needs to take note of their digital community managers and to recognize them as leaders because they are often leading communities much larger than the institution for whom they work and thus have the capacity to influence higher education on a global scale. Virtual communities like WIASN are not 'just a Facebook group'.

Conclusion

Facebook has enabled a new global village where voices can be heard, legitimized and seized upon in a form of digital activism, where members in the global, digital village can join in these small acts of rebellion and resistance. These small acts of resistance and rebellion grown through the digital Facebook phenomenon have global reach, yet foster trust and intimacy as part of communities with shared experiences. What WIASN has become since its inception as an impulsive act of rebellion is a mature, intellectually sophisticated, politically astute and expertise-rich community with real power to influence discourse and behaviour from an individual level to a global scale for the betterment of gender equity – one small act of everyday kindness and activism at a time. What we suggest is that there are ways to mobilize against patriarchy, to carve out new ways of being in academia through mutual support and understanding. Through them, women can be mobilized by subverting a technology that was originally made for the subjugation and objectification of women in higher education – where all the Soup Boys who profess feminist ideals, and the Harvard scholars rating women hot or not, not only can be held to account but can also have the power of their oppressive narratives stripped away and replaced with women's own narratives in acts of digital activism and resistance.

Authors' Note: With special thanks to Dr Maxine Horne and Catherine Beard for their contribution as directors of Women in Academia Support Network, and to Dr Nia Wearn and Dr Peny Sotiropoulou for their contribution to the chapter data and as WIASN moderators.

References

Azer, E., G. Harindranath and Y. Zheng (2019), 'Revisiting Leadership in Information and Communication Technology (ICT)-enabled Activism: A Study of Egypt's Grassroots Human Rights Groups', *New Media & Society*, 21 (5): 1141–69.

Black, A. L. (2018), 'Reflecting on the Meaning of Academic Life on Education', *Journal for Research and Debate*, 1 (3). Available online: https://doi.org/10.17899/on_ed.2018.3.4 (accessed 30 October 2021).

Bolisani, E., M. Fedeli, L. Bierema and V. De Marchi (2020), 'United We Adapt: Communities of Practice to Face the Corona Virus Crisis in Higher Education', *Knowledge Management Research & Practice*, 19 (4): 454–8.

Busing, H. (2020), 'Learning Communities and WIASN', ONL202 Reflections blog. Available online: https://onl202reflectionsdianamorales.blogspot.com/2020/11/by -hannah-busing-on-unsplash-discussion.html (accessed 30 October 2021).

Cabiati, E. (2021), 'Social Workers Helping Each Other During the COVID-19 Pandemic: Online Mutual Support Groups', *International Social Work*, 64 (5): 676–88.

Carr, G. (2021), 'About', *The COVID 19 Chroniclers*, March 2020. Available online: https:// covidchroniclers.com/about/ (accessed 30 October 2021).

Chan, W. S. and A. Y. Leung (2020), 'Facebook as a Novel Tool for Continuous Professional Education on Dementia: Pilot Randomized Controlled Trial', *Journal of Medical Internet Research*, 22 (6): e16772.

Chaudhari, V. (2017), 'Student Stories: Introducing Vasudha Chaudhari', *STRIDE: Social Transition Research into International Doctoral Experiences*, 14 December. Available online: https://strideresearch.wordpress.com/2017/12/14/student-stories-introducing -vasudha-chaudhari/ (accessed 30 October 2021).

George, J. J. and D. E. Leidner (2019), 'From Clicktivism to Hacktivism: Understanding Digital Activism', *Information and Organization*, 29 (3): 100, 249–100, 339.

Gill, R. (2010), 'Breaking the Silence: The Hidden Injuries of the Neoliberal University', in R. Flood and R. Gill (eds), *Secrecy and Silence in the Research Process: Feminist Reflections*, 228–44, London: Routledge.

Gill, R. and N. Donaghue (2016), 'Resilience, Apps and Reluctant Individualism: Technologies of Self in the Neoliberal Academy', *Women's Studies International Forum*, 54 (January–February): 91–9.

Graff, S. L., J. Close, S. Cole, L. Matt-Amaral, R. Beg and M. J. Markham (2018), 'Impact of Closed Facebook Group Participation on Female Hematology/Oncology Physicians', *Journal of Oncology Practice*, 14 (12): e758–7e69.

Harris, A. (2019), 'Gender Equity in Academia with Dr Alana Harris', *itellyouarise*, 24 May. Available online: https://itellyouarise.com/2019/05/24/gender-equity-in-academia-dr -alana-harris/ (accessed 30 October 2021).

Jackson, H. T., M. T. Young, H. A. Rodriguez and A. S. Wright (2018), 'SAGES Foregut Surgery Masters Program: A Surgeon's Social Media Resource for Collaboration, Education, and Professional Development', *Surgical Endoscopy*, 32 (6): 2,800–2,807.

Lupton, D., I. Mewburn and P. Thomson, eds (2018), *The Digital Academic: Critical Perspectives on Digital Technologies in Higher Education*, London: Routledge.

Martin, A. (2018), 'International Exclusion – Let's Do Better', *Women4Oceans*, 31 March. Available online: https://www.women4oceans.org/news/archives/03-2018 (accessed 30 October 2021).

Oja, L. (n.d.), 'Finding Relevant Information and Support: Online Community & Social Media'. Available online: https://www.liirioja.com/phd-reflections (accessed 30 October 2021).

Parks, M. R. (2011), 'Social Networks Sites as Virtual Communities', in Z. Paparissi (ed.), *A Networked Self: Identity, Community, and Culture on Social Network Sites*, 105–328, London: Routledge.

Pruchniewska, U. (2019), '"A Group That's Just Women for Women": Feminist Affordances of Private Facebook Groups for Professionals', *New Media & Society*, 21 (6): 1362–79.

Rheingold, H. (1993), *The Virtual Community: Homesteading on the Electronic Frontier*, Cambridge, MA: MIT press.

Robertson-Kirkland, B. (2019), 'Facing Fears Leads to an Academic Win!', *Research Adventures*. Available online: https://researchadventuresblog.wordpress.com/2019/09/18/fears-faced/ (accessed 30 October 2021).

Teoh, J. Y. (2021), 'How Occupational Therapy Practitioners Use Virtual Communities on the Facebook Social Media Platform for Professional Learning: A Critical Incident Study', *Scandinavian Journal of Occupational Therapy*, 29 (1): 58–68.

TheGovLab (2021), *The Power of Virtual Communities*. Available online: http://virtual-communities.thegovlab.org/index.html (accessed 10 January 2022).

Yang, G. (2016), 'Activism', in B. Peters (ed.), *Digital Keywords: A Vocabulary of Information Society and Culture*, 1–17, Princeton, NJ: Princeton University Press.

Chapter 12

Three Female Academics Discuss Gender Issues and Sustainability

A Water Engineer, a Consumer Psychologist and a Science Educator Walk into a Bar . . .

Alison Sammel, Lisa Watson and Dena McMartin

Introduction to the chapter

This chapter documents a conversation between three colleagues, from three very different disciplines, reflecting on the ongoing presence and pressure of ecological unsustainability in academia and what it means at a practical level for our research. With nearly sixty years of academic service between us, we have been writing the literature exploring and resisting the neoliberal agenda for at least two decades. As an act of defiance against neoliberalism, our chapter will be structured differently from usual academic convention. Instead, three long-term colleagues and friends got together informally and shared experiences at a virtual bar where we could relax and discuss things that might normally go unsaid.

The informal virtual bar conversation was influenced by Gadamer's (1989) concept of fusing horizons and the importance of informal dialogue. 'Horizons' refer to conscious and subconscious perceptions, beliefs and biases brought into any discussion. Horizons are twofold: historical (defined by the past and resulting traditions) and present (encompassing what is believed and understood by a person at this moment in their current situation). The explorations of these horizons result in their fusing. In fusion we are continually 'testing our prejudices' (Gadamer 1989: 306). Gadamer proposes that developing a rich understanding requires people to lay open their experiences and horizons to the possibility of change and growth. Besides, the three of us are known to make great points over a pint or two of beer!

Introduction to the authors

Ali: I am a European descendant Australian-Canadian living and working on the Yugumbeh/Kombumerri traditional lands, now known as the Gold Coast, in Queensland, Australia. I specialize in the teaching, learning and communication of Science, Sustainable Development Goals, climate change and freshwater. I am Head of Innovative and Disruptive Learning for the Climate Action Beacon at Griffith University, where I encourage questioning and unlearning of unsustainable mindsets. I seek to promote a transition towards sustainable ways of thinking and being from each person's unique perspective.

Dena: Oki. Welcome and greetings from traditional Blackfoot Confederacy territory comprising the Kainai, Piikani, Amskapiipikani and Siksika First Nations in southern Alberta, Canada. The University of Lethbridge has been honoured with a Blackfoot name Iniskim, meaning Sacred Buffalo Stone. And we, as people living and benefiting from Blackfoot Confederacy traditional territory, honour the traditions of people who have cared for this land since time immemorial. As vice president (Research) at the University of Lethbridge and a settler to this territory, I serve to facilitate, motivate and support the research, scholarship and creative activities and aspirations of faculty, students and communities. I am an advocate for diversity in STEM. My research focuses on environmental engineering approaches to water quality and quantity management in semi-arid and arid climates.

Lisa: I am a settler currently living on Treaty 4 lands, the territories of the nêhiyawak, Anihšināpēk, Dakota, Lakota and Nakoda, and the homeland of the Métis/Michif Nation. I am Dean, Faculty of Business at Athabasca University, Canada's Open and Online University, dedicated to removing barriers and increasing equality of access to post-secondary education serving adult learners who live and work on Indigenous lands across what is now known as Canada. Equity, diversity, inclusion are an inextricable part of sustainability. As a consumer psychologist, I seek to understand what drives unsustainable behaviour at an individual level and apply those micro-level insights towards achieving macro-level change.

First p[o]int: Power

Question: What is your experience of 'power' within the university systems you have worked within – the good, bad and even the ugly?

Ali: For me, is a sticky thing: it can keep us in one place or can work to restrict our movement in the directions we want to take. I now see myself more like a spider (and sometimes the fly victim) and power as the web. I see myself as entrapped and restricted while spinning the same web of power that reinforces and supports me. I now see how these webs of power trap us all in academia. I understand one of my goals is to pay attention to the conscious weaving of our individual and collective webs. The webs we weave (what we think, say, do, and the processes we support or challenge) make visible the movements we engage in when we maintain, destroy or create new webs with our connections to people, places, ideas or actions. It takes courage, resolution and creativity to weave a different thread within the existing web. The conscious, sustained movement along, within or extending outside of those threads are one essential part to progressing our unique and shared future visions.

I have found that over the years, my conscious witnessing of how power influences me is just as important as reaching an end point of 'change'. The process of spinning, weaving and making careful, chosen connections within the web is key. Therefore, my involvement in, not detachment from this web, is important.

Dena: I really like the imagery of webs and the creation of complex, yet beautiful and strong, connections that you're using, Ali. It's both illustrative and illuminating. If we take those ideas and apply them to our various research initiatives and goals relating to sustainability and climate change/climate action, the web analogy is similarly illustrative and illuminating. An essential element of the strength – and dare I say, power – of our work is the interdisciplinarity of language, knowledge, expertise and experience that we bring to a complex challenge and a necessary discussion.

The power of womxn in academia continues to confront patriarchal and 'traditional' obstacles to our ability and capacity to take space and add voice to the work we're doing. For instance, we know that research conducted and disseminated by womxn tends to receive lesser attention and fewer citations, to be funded at lower levels (both in terms of dollar value and success rate) and receive more muted recognition or celebration as models of excellence. These obstacles are even more devastating for women of colour, Indigenous women and LGBTQ2S+ womxn.

Lisa: I think being situated in a business faculty gives me a bit of a different perspective on neoliberalism as power in university systems. From where I sit, beyond the guise of a bicameral system, universities are not really any different than other large Western organizations, be they public or private. In my experience, most business schools espouse a capitalist approach and are therefore expected to be neoliberal. Neoliberalism as a philosophy is heavily tied to capitalism and the way the private sector does business in terms of supporting a free-market economy and competition. In short, money is power. Rather than focusing on our social mission, universities devote a lot of energy to institutional-level finances, the bottom line and growth as a key indicator of success. We think in terms of competing with other universities to grow our student (customer) base instead of looking at ways we can work together to shape civil society. I do think that this is a very masculine approach to business that has crept in from the private sector and is the predominant philosophy that is rewarded in Western society. And I do think it is because we still have so many white men at the helm who, consciously or unconsciously, have come to define success in terms of dollars and cents based on what is rewarded among their peers in the private sector – profit maximization.

I think we get so wrapped up in the business of higher education that we lose sight of the purpose and impact of higher education. Yes, we need to keep our eye on the bottom line – not-for-profit doesn't mean for loss – but the disconnect between budget and mission seems to be growing. Even when I try to use business terminology such as triple bottom line (where businesses measure success on the three pillars of social, economic and environmental impacts instead of just profit) to demonstrated that sustainability need not be contrary to neoliberal ideology to redirect emphasis back towards social mission, I am poo pooed. Taking a sustainable approach to how we operate is seen as a naive (feminine) notion by many of our (white male) leaders. It's a bit of a cliché, really. Upper administration sits on high making the tough monetary decisions while faculty members sit in their ivory towers sheltered from the complex financial struggles that universities face.

Ali: Academics in ivory towers is an interesting point.

I guess what I am hearing you say is that there seems to be at least two ideological agendas about the role or purpose of a public university. One would be a neoliberal agenda that is so pervasive that it is often invisible and thought of as a 'natural force'. Based on competition, it consciously reshapes beliefs, philosophies and actions by punishing inefficiencies and rewarding productivity (as it defines) and profit.

Somewhere along the line I started to understand this reality, to see the web, which was part of the reason I spent so much time being a graduate student: I wanted to be part of the 'resistance'. I wanted to serve my local community and collaboratively promote and act for social and environmental change. From this standpoint, I view the university's mission as in service of the local, regional, national and professional communities with an underlying agenda of moving towards a more socially and environmentally equitable society. As this agenda is most often counter to a neoliberal agenda, it usually necessitates critiquing neoliberal power structures. Hence, my assumption that neoliberal power is 'bad' and needs to be resisted. Moreover, the agenda of promoting continual economic growth has equated to environmental destruction. A new system is required, and I wanted to be part of this change. Change that ensures social and environmental factors are equally considered as economic ones (the triple bottom line that you spoke of Lisa). As an academic who does not encounter the administration side of the university (and probably has a them vs us mentality – not that I would admit it), it is easier to see the neoliberal web of power as worthy of resisting. As university leaders, help me to understand neoliberalism from a leadership perspective.

Dena: It's an interesting and important perspective to consider universities as centres of and for neoliberalism. Both as entities within a community, region and culture and entities apart from societal relationships or place-based considerations. If we think about the elements of what people often consider to be 'neoliberal', it does not imply the absence of rules or regulation, but it does imply the presence and imposition of externalities (markets, economic drivers and performance metrics) and increased corporatization and government intrusion into publicly funded post-secondary institutions. Unfortunately, there isn't one single or agreed-upon definition of neoliberalism, and so the term is often tossed into any debate that derides how universities in Western societies are structured and administered, as well as how faculty members – and our contributions – are evaluated and managed.

In my experiences as both faculty colleague and academic administrator at three Canadian universities, the internal impetus for shifts in faculty performance criteria most often arises at the urging of colleagues who feel vulnerable to those criteria instead of leading from the perspective of equity and inclusion – or as an approach to combat neoliberal constructs. The way faculty are evaluated for teaching, research and service most commonly adheres to the 40-40-20 rule in Canada and the flexibility in those ratios of how we spend our time and energy is often lacking. For instance, a colleague may be appointed to several high-profile and important service roles, leading to reduced activities and achievements in teaching and research. During a peer review of performance, there are many who will discount service as 'fluff' or not of equal or greater value to teaching and research. This is particularly true for efforts made towards improving diversity, equity and inclusion (DEI) and Indigenization, where contributions of womxn, people of colour and Indigenous colleagues carry the bulk of the workload. It is rather disappointing (and endlessly frustrating) when the discourse diverges from how to best use those discussions and paradigm-shifting opportunities to recruit, retain and support peers who bring diverse viewpoints, methods and impacts to the discipline or academic community.

To be truly sustainable in diversifying the academy, whether by ethnicity, culture and/or experience, we must ourselves confront the need to restructure towards inclusive and welcoming environments that respect and value equity and inclusion. And that restructuring requires that we confront and call out current cultures of behaviour and traditions of male whiteness.

Ali: That's an important perspective for me to understand. What I am hearing is that you feel a bit like the spider, or maybe even the fly, within the web of neoliberal power. Government structures, mandates and funding seem to expect a 'do better with less' mentality. What do you both see as a way forward in this infrastructural tug-of-war?

Dena: As academics, we are not particularly talented in doing less or stopping activities. We seem to always be seeking more without necessarily checking our physical and emotional capacity to do so.

This approach has certainly been true of my own career and determination to continue to be research active as a productive colleague and collaborator, as well as mentor for students striving to achieve their research goals. Take this chapter as an example if you will. Ali, did I have time to work on this chapter? No. So why did I say yes, other than I just can't say no to you and I love working with you? It's because I made myself a promise at the start of my career that I would always do my best to support, promote and advocate for women in academia (focusing on engineering, at that time). I'm doing differently with less. Choosing what is most important to me and learning to say no to the things that aren't. Leadership – whether as a faculty member who sets an example and mentor or as someone with a formal title – must include setting priorities, supporting others in achieving their goals and serving as a positive role model for those who come after us. There is a common refrain that conveys a shared wisdom each year during International Women's Day, and is often attributed to Maria Shriver and Annie Lennox, that *we stand on the shoulders of the strong women who came before us and we are the shoulders that the next generations will stand on.* To do that, we have to take care of ourselves. Sometimes saying no to others is saying yes to ourselves.

Lisa: Wow, Dena. I love everything you just said. I always talk in terms of doing different and better, but the reality is that we are being given the same or less to do it with. So, I listen to what my faculty want to achieve, and problem solve to help all of us as a collective to try to get there.

I hear the need to prioritize and love that you tied it, in a way, to a personal strategy. I also see it connecting to Ali's identifying as a disruptor. While your focus, Dena, has been on enabling womxn in STEM, mine has been about respect more broadly and treating people the way I would want to be treated. It typically manifests through improving the student experience on one side and leading by example on the other. I think the marketing academic in me equates customer service to creating the best possible student experience without sacrificing academic rigour. As a leader more generally, though, I want to lead by example in terms of creating positive spaces through culture and values. I want to demonstrate that work-life balance is important. (Yes, Dena, I am looking at you.)

Dena: (Hey, I resemble that remark!) I try to avoid using the phrase 'I'm busy' as some sort of badge of honour. I congratulate staff and students alike for seeking balance, asking for reduced loads when needed and taking real vacations where they don't have to check in or worry about what will be waiting for them when they get back. I've chosen to turn down or reassign projects that I see as incremental improvements in exchange for ones that make bigger, bolder changes. They usually involve upending process and culture. That is what gives me energy and keeps me going. Why did I take the time to write this chapter, besides really wanting to chat with my besties and feed my craving to deep-fried food? It's because I wanted my (new) faculty (I have been in this position for a month) to see that I both make time for and value research and publication in a range of forms, and more importantly, I wanted to give other academics a glimpse behind the curtain of my experience (insert Wizard of Oz meme here). If even one of my contributions to this 'trialogue' gets one person thinking or inspires one person, it will be a win. And trust me, one month into a new Deanship – we all need the hope of a quick win.

Second p[o]int: Gender

Dena: As much as we might wish it weren't the case, gender is always a factor. It's omnipresent. Whether from how some people say they must be careful about their language and behaviour (and frankly, yes, they should be; it should go without saying but it doesn't), or from some who would say that we are in our positions as a function of our gender rather than because of our expertise and skill. And as a woman in engineering, those same issues arise on the regular.

I think, too, that many people (of all gender identities) may not view or accept womxn as powerful leaders. We routinely hear that womxn are emotional leaders as a negative comment, without recognizing the value of emotional intelligence or acknowledging that men are emotional beings, too. We may feel that we must constantly defend and demonstrate our expertise, value and ability to conduct the research we do, teach the content we develop and work with and lead the initiatives, programmes and staff we support.

When you think about how your gender is seen or has affected your career progression and choices, Lisa, what rises to the top of mind for you?

Lisa: People have often asked if I've ever felt discriminated against at work because I'm a woman. Interestingly, for the longest time I used to say, 'only by students'. I don't know if you've seen that widget that graphs words and phrases from Rate my Professor (a website that lets students from all over the world leave reviews of their professors) against academic discipline and gender. Female business professors were most likely across all fields, and twice as likely as their male counterparts, to be called hard markers. I didn't necessarily give lower grades than the male professors, but students expected that I would be easier on them – more motherly. So, I started setting expectations at the start of term. I would outright tell them that if I wanted to, I'd have had kids of my own, and I'm not your mom. Never have I felt the need to walk into a university council meeting and remind people that I'm not their mom.

Now that I think about it, none of us has kids. Lots of brilliant womxn leaders do, but I am just noticing that we don't for whatever reasons, and I suspect it makes it easier for us to do these jobs.

Dena: While I think that womxn can have children and be strong, capable leaders I have also observed that many of those womxn either have at-home spouses or partners. The more common situation is that many womxn in leadership do not have children. I'm not sure which is the chicken, and which is the egg, though. Do more womxn without children advance in leadership roles because they haven't been penalized for taking parental leaves or not being as available to take on service work or certain types of research that require more time away from the home? Or is it that womxn who do not have children (by choice or not) tend to demonstrate behavioural norms and engagement that raise profile in our current academic (and societal) constructs that otherwise favour men? Because it doesn't follow that men with children are equally penalized. Indeed, our male colleagues traditionally tend towards fewer childcare expectations *or* are celebrated and promoted (figuratively or literally) for taking active roles in parenting.

Ali: In my generation of womxn, the understanding was that having children was our purpose, in a biological sense. If you liked men, and children, then it was assumed you would have at least one child of your own, more if you were financially successful. But it is now more about choice, opportunity and desire. This gives me hope when I see that the next generation of women understand that they have a choice to have children or not.

Lisa: I have the utmost admiration for my female counterparts who have had children and still managed to navigate the demands of academe. I can't even fathom how they juggle their home and work responsibilities. I was chatting with a male colleague recently who couldn't even tell me how old his kids were now, what grades they were in or what activities they were involved with.

Second, I have found that having to discipline men for bullying is quite an experience. Most don't even understand that they are in a position of power or what bullying is. They are so used to being in positions of power and being flippant in how they wield that power that discipline becomes an exasperating educational exercise. And even then, there is often a clear disdain for my being so 'soft' (read – respectful of other human beings). I often worry that lack of re-offence has more to do with knowing they are now being watched than because they truly understand what they did wrong.

Finally, I think womxn tend to take on more service than male counterparts, and it doesn't occur to anybody that it might be inappropriate or a gendered expectation. It is, however, my extensive service that allowed me to achieve the Dean's position I hold today, so not necessarily a bad thing.

Dena: I suspect that each of us could point to negative experiences and outright harassment or bullying that we would say helped us to become stronger leaders, more dedicated academics, or whatever. But honestly, how awesome would it be to just be treated as a valuable colleague with an equal voice?! I dream of the day when women in academia and academic leadership do not have to point to how adversity made us stronger. Oh, how I dream . . .

Lisa: I think this question links well with how I view power structures in universities and the idea of neoliberal and capitalist views as being an asset that is rewarded, for better or worse. I feel like womxn business academics continue to be enigmatic in many ways. Business professors are expected to be heartless capitalists. Womxn academics are expected to be agreeable teachers who take disproportionate levels of service. I think that puts me in a unique position to play to my strengths. A 'male, pale, and stale' neoliberal upper administrator is far more likely to listen to a business professor than a woman academic.

Ali, I love your earlier metaphor of working within a web of power. I spend a lot of time strategizing how to best navigate my current political web to achieve my desired outcomes. How do I use my perceived sameness as a businessperson to craft narratives that will be heard by the (white male) powers that be? How can I leverage my earned power of voice to advance a social sustainable agenda? For example, when I was trying to introduce new protections for vulnerable graduate students facing exploitative and harassing supervisor behaviour, I referred to the costs of inaction in terms of losses in future research funding, future students and possible legal action. In short, I understand the power structures and lean into them using my business background and all its associated stereotypes to my best advantage.

Dena: When we add the context of how neoliberalism is often seen and experienced by womxn in academia, and particularly womxn in academic leadership (how we are spoken to and about), we routinely experience white heterosexual cis-gendered men waving the neoliberal flag as an excuse for not responding to or respecting womxn's opinions, expertise, voice and leadership. It becomes less about structures and more about personal responsibility, accountability and vulnerability.

In adding the (perhaps) competing or opposing lenses of neoliberalism and sustainability to the experiences of womxn in academia, we can see the impact of external influences on how we approach our work and what we may feel hindered to take on. And that is truly terrifying for holding academic freedom paramount. In many ways, neoliberal forces can seemingly negate the ability to successfully conduct and disseminate research about sustainability because it confronts the status quo and systems of corporatization. Interestingly, as economic drivers of these confrontations take shape, there's more acceptance and support for research into sustainability and impacts of changing climate. However, the support continues to be primarily in the realm of providing evidence to achieve corporate goals and economic benefit. For instance, as research results inform actuarial sciences, the insurance industry re-evaluates the costs of not addressing climate change and not implementing sustainability principles to our actions, infrastructures and resources management plans, the world takes note. Suddenly sustainability and climate action matter.

When we consider this shift in the discourse, it says a lot about the synergies between economies and cultures. But it dismisses or avoids intersections with gender. Seeing how the research discourse around these topics is increasingly valuable as an economic good dismisses the important lenses of moral rights and criticality. Lenses that womxn scholars are more likely to embed in our work. Sustainability and climate action discourse remain in the context of brazen and emotional acts rather than the rational, evidence-based arguments of womxn who are invested in facilitating a strong and healthy shared future.

Ali, in my limited time in Australia, there is a more obvious and odious white maleness than we see in Canada. What is your experience?

Ali: I experience a lot of 'mansplaining' both at work and in social setting. I find men like to explain an overarching concept to me, even though my question was targeted and clear. For example, if I ask a targeted science question, specifically those involving physics or chemistry, rather than receiving a targeted answer, more likely, I will have the broader concept explained to me. The concept that I would have needed to inherently understand to develop the questions that I did. This is particularly the case when asking males these questions. So that leaves me in a predicament: do I remain silent like I was taught to as a child, or do I call the person on the mansplaining? Doing this in a 'nice' way, will still leave the person feeling discomfort and stimulate a conversation where they communicate their intention was to 'help' me. Rarely will the man take responsibility for their extra explanation. As an aside, sometimes I think that I am 'too sensitive' or that it is just a process the person needs to go through. For example, they need to talk to themselves about the broader concept before focusing on my question. However, I listen to how these same men answer their male colleagues and they do not start with an overarching explanation of the concept, but rather do assume this knowledge is understood and just answer the targeted question. To call people on this put me in a situation where I can only be perceived as a 'b*tch'. This entanglement represents a key point for me around being a womxn working with science.

Dena: B*tch, please. Aren't we saying 'correctile dysfunction' instead of mansplaining these days?

[Lisa high-fives Dena and screams YESSSS! as other patrons turn and stare at the old ladies causing a ruckus. When people turn back to their food Dena continues.]

Dena: I cannot tell you the number of times I have purposely downplayed my knowledge, understanding or expertise to 'keep the peace' with a male colleague. I am ashamed of it. But it was a successful coping mechanism for a very long time in an academic environment that did not welcome womxn's expertise. While it might have been easier in the moment, it made for a lot of sleepless nights and self-doubt. No more, buddy. No more.

Ali: Good for you!

Lisa: I hear you. My most used phrase is 'I'm sorry' because it opens the floor to listening. I am entirely willing to set ego aside to achieve my goals. I think there are process-oriented people and outcome-oriented people, and I long ago decided I am willing to sacrifice the process of being treated equitably to getting sh*t done.

Ali: I too think 'sorry' is my go-to word. How we abdicate our own ego when we play in the male sandpit! Yet if we don't, we are often not seen as collegial. Because I see the flickering light of retirement in my future, I am becoming bolder. I recently applied for a new job. Like most jobs of this era, it had the criteria of 'strong interpersonal and leadership skills and ability to mentor junior researchers'. I replied to this statement saying that I am not taking on the role of leadership to make friends across the university. In fact, if people don't groan when they see me in a meeting around climate action, then I am probably not doing my job (I asked for it to have the word 'disruption' in my job title). Hard questions need to be asked. I advised that strong interpersonal skills necessitate that we all must become comfortable with discomfort. And playing nice and abdicating my ego should not be my go-to response. It will be interesting how this plays out for me over the coming years. I think it is a good thing that we have each other to keep us on this quest and provide support and guidance as we grow into ourselves and our places within academia.

Third p[o]int: Promoting sustainability within an unsustainable system

[As Lisa and Dena grab snacks and another pint – Ali has her vegan hot chips (pub favourite)].

Ali: [munching on hot chips] I believe that we need to build the capacities of our students to deconstruct and reflect on the underlying agendas and goals of our social systems (including education) and have different, socially critical conversations than we have had before, in this Anthropocene area. Neoliberal's continued ecological violence and unjust environmental philosophies and actions are having a global impact. Universities need to teach and act in ways that acknowledge anthropogenic climate change is undeniable. However, the curriculum that I am mandated to teach in my university courses do not directly advocate social or environmental issues associated with science be discussed.

I found that student resistance to climate action is high. Victims of the same web of power, many students want the skills that will help them to be successful in a consumeristic, capitalistic society. This push back can be viewed in my course evaluations where they ask me to 'just teach the core information directly'. I have been called into the Deputy Dean of Teaching and Learning Office to encourage me to stick to the main aspects of the professional curriculum. He believed that I was being too 'airy fairy' when I included social or environmental issues associated with science. It's hard for some people to see sustainability or climate action as an important concept, rather than some agenda that a female teacher is 'promoting'. Although, I think this is changing.

The climate anxiety of this next generation is causing a crack in the assumption that 'the environment is important, and we will get to it *after* we learn the important stuff'. I am finding that increasingly, my students and colleagues are distressed about what is happening to the natural environment and believe that the government is not doing enough. Studies have shown that young people concerned with climate change feel ignored or dismissed when they talk about it (see Thompson 2021). There is an overall sense of being 'othered' or feeling ostracized or threatened by the dominant neoliberal narrative. I feel that I have lived with this professionally my whole life. I know this has held me back at work. Due to not feeling supported, I did not apply for promotion for fifteen years. With a ground swell of movement towards sustainability and climate action, my voice is finally being heard by people in the university. The neoliberal agenda has now picked up sustainability and climate action, and universities are being asked to be accountable. Even if the outcomes from this uptake are based more around mitigation rather than ideological change, at least these issues are now formally on the table.

Dena: [savouring my locally grown beef and potatoes] Sustainability of structures in a rapidly evolving environment – universities are slow to change and respond to externalities, even in the face of critical analyses, research evidence and awareness of the need to do so. Womxn are often thought to have more natural tendencies towards being lateral thinkers and problem solvers, which means that we may present information and challenge norms and assumptions in ways that differ from our male counterparts and from what our students are most comfortable and familiar with. Ali, does the fact that you're a woman teaching these ideas play any role in the students' reactions do you think?

Ali: The fact that I am a woman makes this more complex, yes. I am perceived as being more emotional, more nurturing of and more caring of nature – and less logical or rational. And nature, as culturally embodied as a female, is viewed as less than the 'hard' sciences that I usually teach [now that's a masculine term for you!]. I wonder what the response from the students would be to Thor teaching students about the Sustainable Development Goals and climate action (in keeping with the Australian celebrities Lisa started)?

Lisa: I think you would find a different reaction! [Sipping a local microbrew made with all locally sourced ingredients while reaching for a deep-fried zucchini stick]. Come on. Tony Stark was the one who was the green energy magnate. If you're really going to meet an Avenger in the name of science, it should be Robert Downey Jr., not your dreamy Australian neighbour.

Dena and **Ali** together: Nerd!

Lisa: Seriously, though, getting back to pushback on sustainability in a neoliberal university environment, business schools are still preaching profit at all costs. I had to fight for well over a decade to be able to offer a social enterprise class. My fight spanned two associate deans who just didn't see how it could possibly be more than a niche fad . . . for over a decade. I started my fight when the triple bottom line was already common vernacular, ESG was becoming an accepted accounting practice, and being acknowledged a B Corporation was already a highly recognized sustainable business certification. What I will say, though, is that the course was a huge success once I was allowed to offer it. It talked about dollars and cents and all the things you expect from a business class, but it did it through a sustainable lens and showed how sustainable businesses can outperform their capitalist counterparts. In that case, I think being a woman may have been of benefit because it helped me to balance talking about 'hard' numbers with more philosophical conversations that required a safe space and a bit of vulnerability.

Ali: What about in your research? How does sustainability vs capitalism play out for you?

Lisa: I get frustrated on several fronts. I find that research can take a back seat to teaching because tuition is our most obvious and visible source of revenue. Attracting grant money often gets more accolades than what gets done with it. We also tend to put more emphasis on quantitative academic measures of research impact than its societal impact. And in the face of COVID we have seen the extreme drop in publication that women academics have experienced in the face of changes in work-life than men. I find that approach to be extremely short sighted on several fronts that Dena can probably speak to better than I can.

Dena: Admittedly grant money is often trotted out as a key metric of success in any university setting. I certainly know that to be the case in the type of reporting I do as a vice president (Research). This is in part because of government and other external performance metrics, which are most certainly well defined as being part of a neoliberal agenda, but also because the information is readily consumable and available, and comparable year-over-year. Furthermore, in Canada, a healthy financial allocation is made to universities based on grant-getting performance. Those funds have become essential resources to pay for research staff, facilities and infrastructure. They also form the basis for national rankings. Please don't get me started on rankings. All I will say is that the quality of education and faculty contributions across Canada is so consistent and uniform, that national rankings say more about how data is reported than the so-called 'quality' of a university and its faculty.

    If I may return to externalities – and neoliberal agendas – there continues to be a challenge in defining and communicating universal impact metrics that go beyond the money. There are some good examples globally about how faculty and leaders can better share the importance of research impact, but none that pass muster with anti-performance colleagues who seem to believe that they should not be subject to nor required to explain the value, importance and impact of their research. Those same colleagues are often the quickest off the start to express (loudly) that their research has the best and highest impact in their field. And so goeth the mixed messages that imply a strong desire to be seen and recognized if not celebrated for doing important work but not if 'the administration' says so.

For sustainability and climate change/climate action research, there has been a longstanding dearth of recognition for the contributions made and impacts achieved to shifting common understandings as well as challenging the status quo of the business-as-usual model. For many years, sustainability research has been a difficult place to centre engineering research, but the dominant agenda is beginning to change towards understanding the need to quantify and adapt to changing climate and other environmental conditions. As we experience more climate extremes and the negative impacts to public infrastructure and systems, witness the rise of climate refugees across the globe, confront the loss of habitat and ecological integrity in sensitive climatic zones and encounter growing animosity from those unwilling to understand these changes, the impact of our work becomes increasingly powerful and visible.

A fascinating example from southern Alberta is related to water management and conservation. It's the one issue, environmental, economic or, otherwise, that most everyone in the region agrees on. Regardless of political views, religious leanings, education, experience or anything else. We know that water is a precious and limited resource, and we are resolute and in solidarity almost uniformly that water must be protected for community, infrastructure and economic resilience. Where the viewpoints diverge is on environmental sustainability. But, hey, we're getting there. Any agreement on the value of a precious natural resource is better than none. And change, never mind the paradigm shift we need, takes time (and sometimes a disaster). What about how sustainability plays out in your discipline area, Lisa?

Lisa: I think that conducting sustainability related research is a bit more of a struggle for me than for the two of you who work in hard sciences. In my experience, sustainable business research is still not very well respected and is most often relegated to niche journals. And don't get me started on the type of highly interdisciplinary work we do. The world of academia doesn't quite know what to do with the likes of us, on so many levels (bites off the end of a zucchini as she winks and grins). We all recognize that it's necessary to address wicked problems, but the publishing system is just not designed to handle it. Most journals have very narrow topical scopes and enough submissions that they don't need to think outside the box to fill issues. Publishing pressures on academics is higher than ever, so most can't risk the additional time it takes to find a home for that type of work. The system is fighting against the very thing it claims to want to support. Our most recent paper on extreme freshwater events (EFWE) is a great example of that. It uses scientific data, a content analysis of school curricula and a survey of preservice teachers to demonstrate how a lack of understanding of EFWE becomes perpetuated in society. It's *because* it uses a range of disciplines that it can demonstrate an important issue. It wasn't strictly educational enough for the education journals, it wasn't cultural enough for the more social scientific journals and it wasn't purely scientific enough for the scientific journals. As an industry where academic publication is the key currency, our reward structure discourages us from doing more of this work.

Dena: In engineering, anything 'environmental' is often seen as 'soft' or as being less technical or intellectually rigorous. It's the field of study that attracts and retains the highest number of women, so there's probably a thread there that hasn't been pulled too hard. It also requires that we include and understand elements of human behaviour and the social good, which have not traditionally played significant roles in engineering education or work. As we know, caring for the natural environment has strong connotations of being 'women's work' and the sentiment holds true in engineering.

When we add the layer of interdisciplinarity to that work, there is yet another downgrading in how it is seen and valued in the academic setting. Outside academia, however, engineering firms are increasingly more interdisciplinary and are seeking advice from non-engineers to make better decisions, improve designs for environment and society and to optimize community engagement in project development. This will drive sustainability in engineering education and research, as well as the integration of social sciences and humanities expertise to our work.

Lisa: As you noted much earlier in this chapter, Dena, change is inordinately slow in academia.

Dena: I love that we can have these chats, chaotic and rambling though they sometimes may be, about the big topics. That we can each bring our own perspectives and disciplinary languages to the table and toss around ideas and questions. And that we can each enjoy our favourite snacks – and Aussie celebrities – without judgement.

Ali: Just like the structure and ideas communicated throughout this chapter, we are all becoming more aware of what is expected of us by the dominant systems (the web), and we are choosing other ways of moving forward, through collaboration rather than competition. The conscious acknowledgement of the web, and the desire and process of spinning new strands of knowledge brings the intersection between power, gender and climate action together. And together, these new strands may be an example of hope for others who perceive themselves caught with this web.

I can't thank you enough for your time and your thoughts, wonderful womxn. As always, you are both an inspiration to me.

References

Gadamer, H. (1989), *Truth and Method*, 2nd edn, Trans. J. Weinsheimer and D. G. Marshall. New York: The Crossroad Publishing Company.

Thompson, T. (2021), 'Young People's Climate Anxiety Revealed in Landmark Survey', *Nature*, 22 September. Available online: https://www.nature.com/articles/d41586-021-02582-8 (accessed 5 May 2022).

Chapter 13

Cogent Themes from Women's Gendered Experiences in Academia

Michelle Ronksley-Pavia, Kelly Pickard-Smith,
Michelle M. Neumann and Jane F. Manakil

Introduction

In this final concluding chapter, we draw together recurrent themes from across the chapters to discuss understandings and implications from the sharing of women's narratives of gendered experiences in and through academia. It is essential to understand that these experiences are always raced, classed, gendered, abled and so forth, because of intersectional identities and experiences that take place in and across a varied assortment of global academic environments. Through the experience narratives shared in this book, chapter authors have provided nuanced understandings of how gendered experiences are shaped by different academic structures, systems and practices in their institutions and through different life-world global contexts. In this conclusion we also question why the onus seems to come back almost always to women in the academy devising answers to gendered issues, when meaningful responses require systemic changes that speak to (and from) the kinds of individual and collective experience narratives espoused in this edited volume.

Recurrent themes

In the opening words to this book presented in the Foreword by Professor Kelly Coate we are reminded that:

> Sometimes the experience [of women in academia] verges on being devastating, but to list here the snippets of narratives and statistics that most shockingly reveal misogyny, racism and inequalities would detract from the overall sense of optimism that is needed if women are to survive in academia. Optimism in these chapters often stems from the supportive communities and networks that women create. Whilst mentoring, networking and finding other feminist support groups can help women get ahead, it has to be acknowledged that academia remains a hyper-individualistic culture that more often rewards competition rather than collaboration.

The cogent themes across this book are echoed in Professor Coate's words, where academia is characterized by traditional hierarchies that are founded on colonialist, imperial, patriarchal and misogynistic *values* that maintain the status quo of gendered roles which clearly work to disadvantage women. Yet, there is also a consistent theme of optimism woven throughout the book's chapters. This optimism is in spite of evidence that discrimination against women, sexism, racism, ableism and objectification of women continue across the experiences of women in academia.

In Chapter 1, Ronksley-Pavia et al. drew our attention to some startling, yet unsurprising statistics about the roles women are able (or permitted) to take up in higher education across the world. Despite decades of women dominating as the majority of graduates from higher education, and the tripling of women's educational attainment across the world (1995–2018), fewer women obtain doctoral degrees and move into senior academic positions compared to men (UNESCO 2021). In different areas of the world, the picture is even more dire, where men dominate across almost all aspects of academic contexts (UNESCO 2021). This is despite the professed *female advantage (i.e. promising statistics suggesting women are accessing higher education at increased rates)*, and UNESCO's (2021) question: *Has the female advantage put an end to gender inequalities?* The short answer is 'No!'. As Ms Stefania Giannini, assistant director general for education – UNESCO elucidates:

> It would seem intuitive that women's leadership and their full and effective participation in public life and decision-making should correlate closely with their attainment in higher education. But this is not the case, revealing the paradoxes and pitfalls of achieving gender equality just over 25 years after the adoption of the transformational Beijing Declaration and Platform for Action ... inequalities run deep and glass ceilings are high. Women are under-represented at senior faculty level and in higher education decision-making bodies in many countries, with persistent wage gaps. They are heavily under-represented in STEM. ... Nor is the high proportion of women in tertiary education translating into a greater presence in research. Gender differences in academic publication rates remain and are most pronounced in top journals. (UNESCO 2021: 5–6)

Høg Utoft and Kongerslev presented in Chapter 2, autoethnographic vignettes of two cisgendered women working in separate academic fields, illustrating clear evidence of epistemic injustice, where they were frequently silenced, excluded and oppressed, evidence of wider systemic problems in Danish academia. Through the caring coven Høg Utoft and Kongerslev attempted to provide hope because of collective voices of care, using humour as resistance through the 'rebellious witch figure' and endeavours for female solidarity. The collective hopes conveyed in this chapter, in spite of the systemic injustices that need addressing, offered hope that within the walls of academia more spaces to care can be created.

Crimmins et al. in Chapter 3 remind us of the ever-present sexism that we encounter as academics, and collective strategies of resistance to slay the 'seven-headed dragon of sexism' (van den Brink and Benschop 2012), and to be ever vigilant in eliminating its multiple 'heads'. One of the most threatening dragon heads of sexism identified by Crimmins et al. is gender-based violence. Their overview of shocking events and statistics of violence from 2014 to 2020 reveals the impacts of sexism evident as gender-based violence, while exploring the higher education contexts and beliefs systems that are recognized as foundational to gendered violence. The chapter authors each shared with readers personal narratives of how they engaged with critical pedagogies in higher education to work towards exposing sexism to attempt to support gender equity, and in so doing slay the 'seven-headed dragon of sexism' in academia.

Traditional roles assigned to women as 'cherished and protected daughters, wives and mothers' were highlighted by Hossain in Chapter 4, where she explored the often-problematic return home experiences for Bangladeshi women academics. Their experiences reflect a common experience for many women in academia, the pull between family and career. For these women academics their empowering experiences of academia outside Bangladesh contrasted starkly with the gendered expectations on their return to their families, where societal pressures and expectations about traditional gendered roles for females, of marriage and family were often felt and enforced. Despite being well educated the futures of these women became dependent on their male partner and/or family's gendered-decisions. Hossain offers up some suggestions of ways forward for academic women feeling these stereotyped pressures on returning home, such as targeted support and social awareness programmes.

Johnson, Schwabenland and Maylor in Chapter 5 keep to front of mind that 'Black women remain the most marginalized and socially disadvantaged group' working in academia in universities in England. Although the ethnic composition of universities in England likely mirrors that of many other countries around the globe, Black women academics continue to be in the minority. The authors highlight that Black women academics tend to be working mostly in teaching-intensive roles, rather than research intensive ones, due to the fact that is where most higher education institutions (HEIs) continue to hire staff – from Black and minority ethnic backgrounds. Through using critical race theory approach Johnson, Schwabenland and Maylor provide insights into how Black women academics are positioned through power and politics in English HEIs; through storytelling the authors explored the intersectionality of Black women academics, and entrenched racism. Moreover, Johnson, Schwabenland and Maylor contend that to eradicate racism and to ensure that Black women academics can thrive in their roles, then *everything* must change at *once* so that HEIs do not absorb smaller advances, yet there is still no substantive overall change to entrenched racism and gendered practices. Furthermore, the chapter authors found that existing equality, diversity and inclusion policies do little to actually support Black female academics, the need for substantive systemic change is obvious, but little if anything seems to be being undertaken in this regard.

We were led through the discriminatory institutionalized practices of student evaluations of teaching by Ronksley-Pavia in Chapter 6, where she provided an extensive unpacking of the issues of the ingrained institutional practice of student evaluations that perpetuate student bias, prejudice and discrimination against women academics. Women who also possess other intersecting identities, such as having an accent, being a woman of colour, coming from a different cultural background to the majority of students and academics, having disability and so forth, are particularly impacted by these so-called measures of teaching effectiveness. Despite it being well recognized by researchers for almost fifty years that gender bias is endemic in teaching evaluations (Mengel, Sauermann and Zolitz 2019), these biased methods are *STILL* being used by institutions, with little if any recognition of the inherently flawed nature of these surveys. Moreover, the impacts of these flawed evaluations are weaponized against women when it comes to applying for advancement and promotion in the higher education sector. How can a fundamentally defective tool continue to be used? Ronksley-Pavia suggests that extensive reform is required.

The complex challenges faced by international Chinese women doctoral students in the United States are exposed by Liu in Chapter 7, calling these challenges the new invisible foot-binding cloth impeding the career development of these women. In the United States undertaking doctoral studies, Liu contends that these women face many challenges due to differences in cultures, backgrounds, educational aspirations and microaggressions from an often-alien culture, with overtones of anti-Asian sentiments and discriminatory practices. Liu suggests that discrimination against females in the United States is much more indirect than in China, but the intersection of the patriarchal natures of both cultures is doubly discriminating for these women.

Limited representation of women in academia in terms of occupying positions of power (e.g. leadership positions) is explored in Chapter 8 by Bray and Shaffer. The authors' mixed-methods study explored experiences of women working in a university in the North-western United States. An exploration of the seemingly endless barriers to women being able to occupy leadership positions in higher education was concluded with suggestions of some strategies that study participants used to gain advancement and promotion. The study uncovered that the majority of women academics did not believe that they had been victims of gender discrimination, but in spite of this they identified some impeding factors evident in the limitations to women being in leadership roles. Among the findings, Bray and Shaffer identified: male-focused leadership, lack of progressive ideologies, stereotypes about outspoken women and the necessity for more education about gender bias and sexual harassment. These findings exemplify the continuing presence and dominance of misogynistic and patriarchal institutionalized practices.

Imposter syndrome and women academics' lived experience of this phenomenon were explored through a joint autoethnographic approach by C. Wilkinson and S. Wilkinson in Chapter 9. Through the intersectional lens of age and gender the authors provided excerpts from their private research diaries of how they overcame feelings of being imposters in their roles in UK higher education institutions. Two key themes were identified by the authors in relation to imposter syndrome: 'practical and purposeful solutions' and 'changing life circumstances'. Reflecting on these themes C. Wilkinson and S. Wilkinson not only shared intentional strategies that they adopted but also reflected on how changing life circumstances (e.g. marriage, pregnancy) also contributed to address their feelings of imposter syndrome. Further, that 'putting things into perspective because of their changing life circumstances assisted in creating a sense of detachment where they did not care as much about how others' perceived them.

Seeking to address the absence of women's voices and voices of other marginalized genders in STEM (science, technology, engineering and mathematics), Leigh et al. in Chapter 10 focused on their experiences through an international online network of Women in Supramolecular Chemistry (WISC). The authors shared their narrative experiences of finding and creating 'intersectional kinship', and support for women in the group to 'step outside disciplinary norms' associated with STEM. Leigh et al. unpacked some of the historical barriers faced by women in science, that although seemingly small when looked at individually, when seen together represented a 'series of microaggressions'. Often, work is produced about women in STEM but not by these women, Leigh et al. attempted to redress this somewhat by providing voice for WISC network members by communicating some of their own experiences and sharing ownership to be able to feel less isolated, thorough providing kinship and sources of information and solutions to common challenges faced by WISC members.

Chapter 11 saw Pickard-Smith, Belfiore and Bonsall discuss shared experiences of another global online network of women through the Women in Academia Support Network (WIASN), where they collectively practise what can be described as a form of online activism. Through the sharing of personal experiences, as well as professional expertise, this extensive network seeks to not only keep women in academia but to equip each member with the tools to succeed into senior positions. The chapter authors described how, through activism, they are collectively challenging the structures of oppression, one member at a time, where a collective force can improve gender equity from within the system through collegiality, rather than through competition. In doing so, the chapter authors call out the ways in which women are increasingly told to minimize their academic care work in order to progress 'professionally' and, instead, the authors argue the opposite, that collegiality and care should be repositioned as integral and crucial components of academic life, which should contribute equally to promotion criteria and renumeration. After all, if everyone stopped caring what kind (pun intended) of academia would we be left with?

Sammel, Watson and McMartin in Chapter 12 took a dialogic route to explore gender issues and sustainability through an interdisciplinary approach from the perspectives of each author: a water engineer, a consumer psychologist and a science educator. What began as a discussion centred around ideas about sustainability and teaching in higher education, very quickly materialized into a rich, deep discussion on the sustainability of women's careers in academia. The informal 'pub' discussion was a jarring juxtaposition to the intense discussion where a spider and web metaphor captured how neoliberal and capitalist ideas (sometimes in opposition to sustainable goals), were also in juxtaposition to women's career sustainability – women caught in a web of complexity in trying to overcome gender inequity. As the authors stated, 'to be truly sustainable in diversifying the academy, whether by ethnicity, culture, and/or experience, we must ourselves confront the need to restructure toward inclusive and welcoming environments.' The argument proposed by the authors being that in teaching sustainability we also need to look closer to home and explain what we think sustainability is and apply the same understandings to university structures as a means to break the web of patriarchal power that entraps us.

Conclusion

As the chapters throughout this edited volume have exemplified, women academics' experiences are always intersectional (raced, classed, gendered, abled etc.). It is impossible and objectionable to be asked (forced) to tease apart these identities and life-world happenings (which take place in and across these varied assortments of global academic contexts), just to satisfy policy or reporting obligations. Through the experience narratives shared in this book, chapter authors have provided nuanced understandings of how gendered experiences are shaped by different academic structures, systems and practices in institutions and through different life-world global academic contexts.

Collectively, as academic women, we have voiced our gendered experiences to identify misogynistic, patriarchal and gendered-institutional practices that continue to impact on the work and lives of women in academia. Despite the advent of many policies and practices that have purportedly been developed by institutions to address these very issues, they are *still* happening! Some of our voices have identified and suggested approaches that may support women to thrive in their academic careers. But should this be the sole domain of those who are oppressed to come up with solutions to addressing historically gendered-institutional practices?

Throughout the process of conceptualizing and editing this book, we continued to be confronted by views from well-meaning people, about problematizing conceptions of women's experiences in academia, where we were advised, counselled, opined and repeatedly made aware that the focus should be on women being in many ways, responsible for *fixing* issues for the future. Discourse about our edited collection frequently reverted at some point to questions of 'Yes, but what can be done to *fix* these issues?', 'What advice do you propose?'. This is not a self-help book; it is not a book about what to do if . . . when . . . in response to . . . Putting the onus onto women in academia to attend to fixing, repairing, mending, correcting, resolving, renewing, addressing, overhauling and *putting right* all of the inherent, historically entrenched gendered practices and processes in academia, some of which we have collectively narrated throughout this book, is especially perturbing.

As such, we respond with our narratives of collective resistance to the expectations for women needing to be the *fixers*. Women should not be solely responsible for the work needed to attend to the foundations, practices and continuing impacts of gender inequality in higher education (or societies in general). Women do not need to change themselves. Meaningful responses to address gendered experiences of women in academia require deep systemic changes that speak to (and from) the kinds of individual and collective narratives espoused in this edited volume.

References

Mengel, F., J. Sauermann and U. Zolitz (2019), 'Gender Bias in Teaching Evaluations', *Journal of the European Economic Association*, 17 (2): 535–66. Available online: https://doi.org/10.1093/JEEA (accessed 21 June 2021).

United Nations Educational, Scientific and Cultural Organization (2021), 'Women in Higher Education: Has the Female Advantage Put an End to Gender Inequalities?', *IESALC Report*. Available online: https://unesdoc.unesco.org/ark:/48223/pf0000377182 (accessed 1 December 2021).

van den Brink, M. and Y. Benschop (2012), 'Slaying the Seven-headed Dragon: The Quest for Gender Change in Academia', *Gender, Work & Organization*, 19 (1): 71–92. Available online: https://doi.org/10.1111/j.1468-0432.2011.00566.xVan (accessed 20 April 2020).

INDEX

Note: Pages in Italics and Bold refer to figures and tables

9 781350 274273